'Ritual has been an overlooked asset to the healing of trauma and to restoring broken connections. The diverse contributors to this volume make this a widespread and accessible work for all those interested in ritual and social trauma.'

– Peter A. Levine, *author of* Waking the Tiger: Healing Trauma *and* Trauma and Memory

'A delightful exploration of meaning-making beyond the frontal cortex. This fascinating book describes secular ritual as "multi-media packages" of "human technology" for making meaning through sound, touch, smell, taste, color, shape and motion. A sensual map for times of transition.'

– Lisa Schirch, PhD, *author of* Ritual and Symbol in Peacebuilding *and Research Professor at Eastern Mennonite University, Virginia, USA*

"This book is indeed a transdisciplinary conversation on how ritual supports society in its primary role. The writers remind us that throughout the history of civilization we have used ritual to deal with potentially traumatic events. As a therapist I particularly appreciate how Robert C. Scaer relates ritual to the neurophysiology of trauma. In trauma therapy our first challenge is helping people feel safe so they can self-regulate. Matthieu Smyth considers ritual a privileged means for group self-regulation through attachment and emotional attunement. Michael Picucci contributes outstanding resources for the use of ritual in clinical practice as well as in intimate relationships. The case studies and research demonstrate the importance of respecting ritual timing, interpersonal resonance and our own biological rhythms. Integrating all of these aspects in one book was a stroke of genius!'

– Sonia Gomes, *PhD in Clinical Psychology, International SE Advanced Faculty of the Somatic Experiencing Trauma Institute, USA, creator of SOMA (Embodiment – Touch & Movement in Somatic Experiencing) in Brazil and USA*

'Why do citizens of secular societies continue to ritualize? Contributors to this provocative volume answer with a focus on how we are actually doing it, documenting the immense creativity with which people craft and enact new rituals to celebrate unions, mark life transitions, say goodbye, heal, reconcile and remember, but also to experience the world afresh.'

– Jane K. Cowan, *PhD, Professor of Anthropology, University of Sussex, UK*

'*Emerging Ritual in Secular Societies* is a rich collection of essays, case studies and interviews that help us understand how people make meaning, mark life transitions and construct spiritual journeys without benefit of religious institutions. It contributes not only to our knowledge of ritual practices and secularization, but also to our appreciation of the multiple ways people employ their imaginations to connect with the mystery of grace and the power of human community.'
– *The Rev Dr Deborah Kapp, Edward F. and Phyllis K. Campbell Professor of Urban Ministry, McCormick Theological Seminary, USA*

'Based on instructive case studies, this book contributes very valuable insights on the importance and functions of non-religious rituals within secularized pluralistic societies in order to create individual meaning in life and establish social cohesion in heterogeneous contexts.'
– *Professor Dr René Gründer, sociologist, Germany*

'As an artist I'm drawn to secular ritual – those events where we "make meaning" with each other outside of (though perhaps borrowing from) traditions. We dearly need guidance in this moment, as traditions harden into entrenched divisions. This book on contemporary ritual encourages us to rethink what it is that unites us, what deserves to be celebrated and how to reinvent rituals to bridge our differences.'
– *Suzanne Lacy, PhD, artist, Professor, Roski School of Art and Design, University of Southern California, USA*

'Through ritual we can experience stability and safety. As we "do something" to mark an occasion, we connect with other people and something beyond ourselves. Those with complex trauma suffer greatly from loss of equilibrium and connection with others. Emerging Ritual in Secular Societies opens the way to treating emotional responses to trauma by ritualizing transitions and celebrating life. This is effective when, as Jeltje Gordon-Lennox writes, ritual is a body-based, rather than a cognitive experience.'
– *Dagmar Härle, Master of Psychotraumatology (University of Zurich); practitioner of Somatic Experience, TCTSY-Facilitator (Traumacenter Traumasensitive Yoga)*

'*Emerging Ritual in Secular Societies* constitutes an important contribution to the burgeoning field of Ritual Studies. The essays featured in this edited volume, written by leading anthropologists, psychologists and sociologists as well as ritual professionals, present a unique vantage point that combines both academic and practical concerns. Focusing on contemporary secular rituals, Emerging Ritual in Secular Societies successfully navigates between ritual theory and practice, offering answers to such issues as the role of ritual in modern life and the mechanisms involved in constructing new rituals to celebrate life events in a non-religious context. For far too long, modern scholars of ritual have ignored the perspectives of living ritualists in favour of developing theoretical frameworks that analysed ritual from a supposed perspective of scientific cognitive distance. Following in the footsteps of contemporary ritologists such as Ronald L. Grimes, this volume aims to rectify this situation by offering a transdisciplinary exploration of ritual presented by experienced professionals involved in the creation and practice of new forms of ritual activity. This well-written and informative work will be of strong interest to scholars and students of ritual alike.'

– *Ori Tavor, Lecturer in Chinese Studies, Department of East Asian Languages and Civilizations, University of Pennsylvania, USA*

'This fine volume shines a much-needed light on the growing field of secular ritual, and its breadth and depth offer rich insights for scholars and practitioners alike. It's a wonderful contribution to the important conversation about finding meaning and connection in an ever more complex world.'

– *Sarah Kerr, PhD, Death Doula and Ritual Practitioner, Soul Passages, Canada*

'A well-researched book with engaging dialogue on emerging ritual through the human sciences, art and life experiences, which leaves the door open for intelligent discussion. This is more than an academic book, it's a well-intended and clear-sighted discussion. I believe this book will benefit any reader and is an absolute must for many years to come.'

– *Cécile Wesolowski, www.cecilewesolowski.com*

'This creative, enlightening book is rich in perspectives. It conveys a deep understanding of the value and meaning of rituals and incorporates many moving and powerful examples. It will appeal to anthropologists and psychotherapists, celebrants and faith leaders and individuals looking to express themselves at significant moments in their lives. It has the potential to spark ideas and give depth to people's experience.'
– *Dr Sharon Pettle, Consultant Clinical Psychologist and Systemic Psychotherapist, UK*

'Demonstrating the need for a more inclusive ritual grammar, *Emerging Ritual in Secular Societies* meets the demands of a changing world. The variety of discussions in this book contributes generously to the bricolage that is the secular ritualist's toolbox. It is a highly useful methodology for practitioners.'
– *Nina Faartoft, Head of Ceremonies, Danish Humanist Society, anthropologist and funeral celebrant*

'*Emerging Ritual in Secular Societies* is a timely addition to the scholarship of sociology and culture, and indeed, to sociology of religion as well. Often overlooked by those who equate ritual with religion, the authors of this book provide rich descriptions of how secular rituals bind communities together and create meaning for groups and individuals.'
– *Sharon L. Miller, PhD, Director of Research, Auburn Theological Seminary, USA*

EMERGING RITUAL
IN SECULAR SOCIETIES

of related interest

**Crafting Secular Ritual
A Practical Guide**
*Jeltje Gordon-Lennox
Foreword by Isabel Russo*
ISBN 978 1 78592 088 2
eISBN 978 1 78450 350 5

EMERGING RITUAL IN SECULAR SOCIETIES
A Transdisciplinary Conversation

EDITED BY JELTJE GORDON-LENNOX

Jessica Kingsley *Publishers*
London and Philadelphia

First published in 2017
by Jessica Kingsley Publishers
73 Collier Street
London N1 9BE, UK
and
400 Market Street, Suite 400
Philadelphia, PA 19106, USA

www.jkp.com

Copyright © Jessica Kingsley Publishers 2017

Front cover image source: Shutterstock®

All rights reserved. No part of this publication may be reproduced in any material form (including photocopying, storing in any medium by electronic means or transmitting) without the written permission of the copyright owner except in accordance with the provisions of the law or under terms of a licence issued in the UK by the Copyright Licensing Agency Ltd. www.cla.co.uk or in overseas territories by the relevant reproduction rights organisation, for details see www.ifrro.org. Applications for the copyright owner's written permission to reproduce any part of this publication should be addressed to the publisher.

Warning: The doing of an unauthorised act in relation to a copyright work may result in both a civil claim for damages and criminal prosecution.

Library of Congress Cataloging in Publication Data
A CIP catalog record for this book is available from the Library of Congress

British Library Cataloguing in Publication Data
A CIP catalogue record for this book is available from the British Library

ISBN 978 1 78592 083 7
eISBN 978 1 78450 344 4

Printed and bound in Great Britain

CONTENTS

Acknowledgements		9
Introduction: Opening the Conversation *Jeltje Gordon-Lennox*		11

Part I: The Origins of Ritual

1. The Art of Ritual and the Ritual of Art   22
   Ellen Dissanayake
2. Human Rituals and Ethology: A Scholar's Journey   40
   Matthieu Smyth
3. The Neurophysiology of Ritual and Trauma: Cultural Implications   55
   Robert C. Scaer

Part II: Sensemaking in Life Events

4. The Rhyme and Reason of Ritualmaking   70
   Jeltje Gordon-Lennox
5. Case Study: A Nordic Rite of Passage Comes of Age   87
   Jeltje Gordon-Lennox in collaboration with Lene Mürer (Norwegian Humanist Association), Marie Louise Petersen (Danish Humanist Society), and Bjarni Jonsson (Icelandic Ethical Humanist Association)
6. Multicultural Wedding Ceremonies: Venturing into the World of Diversity   104
   Andrés Allemand Smaller
7. Case Study: A Funeral Ceremony for a Violinist   119
   Christine Behrend
8. Case Study: A Memorial and a Wedding Rolled into One Humanist Ceremony   127
   Isabel Russo

Part III: Ritualizing in Intimate Spaces

9   Ritual as Resource: Health and Transformation in the Twenty-First Century   140
Michael Picucci

10 Sensing the Dead: The Role of Embodiment, the Senses and Material Objects in the Ritualization of Mourning   158
Joanna Wojtkowiak

11 Food and Ritual   172
Lindy Mechefske

Part IV: Ritualizing in Public Places

12 Commemorative Ritual and the Power of Place   188
Irene Stengs

13 New Ritual Society: Consumerist Revolution and the Rediscovery of Ritual   203
Gianpiero Vincenzo

14 Ritual and Contemporary Art   217
Jacqueline Millner

15 Interview with Ritual Artist Ida van der Lee   232
Christine Behrend

    Conclusion: Conversation to Be Continued   246
Jeltje Gordon-Lennox

    Notes on Contributors   248

    Index   251

LIST OF FIGURES

Figure 1.1. In all times and places artists work to make even the simplest things special. Copyright © Robin Dreyer, courtesy of Penland School of Crafts 23

Figure 1.2. Ritual performance and art can meet our need for emotional concord and publicly manifest matters of vital concern. Copyright © Robin Dreyer, courtesy of Penland School of Crafts 25

Figure 1.3. Craftworkers today, just like their predecessors, need artfulness to function. Copyright © Robin Dreyer, courtesy of Penland School of Crafts 34

Figure 1.4. Craft is ineluctably grounded in the body, the physicality of material and material objects. Copyright © Robin Dreyer, courtesy of Penland School of Crafts 35

Figure 1.5. A bespoke object implies not only hands, but the human being who fashioned that object. Copyright © Robin Dreyer, courtesy of Penland School of Crafts 37

Figure 1.6. Craft practitioners generally learn their work within the guild-like process where the tradition is transmitted from master to apprentice. Copyright © Robin Dreyer, courtesy of Penland School of Crafts 38

Figure 3.1. The human brain. Copyright © J. Gordon-Lennox 60

Figure 4.1. Ritual as strategy in context. Copyright © J. Gordon-Lennox 72

Figure 4.2. Creative process of ritualmaking. Copyright © J. Gordon-Lennox 79

Figure 5.1. The first humanist confirmation in Norway (Oslo, 1956). Copyright © Human Etisk-Forbund (Norwegian Humanist Association) 91

Figure 5.2. Youth number 250,000 in a humanist confirmation in Norway (Arendal, 2016). Copyright © Human Etisk-Forbund (Norwegian Humanist Association) 92

Figure 5.3. A course in humanist confirmation in Norway (2010). Copyright © Human Etisk-Forbund (Norwegian Humanist Association) 93

Figure 5.4. The humanist confirmation ceremony in Oslo in 2002 took place at the town hall. Copyright © Human Etisk-Forbund (Norwegian Humanist Association) 94

Figure 5.5. A confirmand in traditional Norwegian dress has her photo taken with her family after the humanist confirmation ceremony in Oslo, Norway (2014). Copyright © Human Etisk-Forbund (Norwegian Humanist Association) 95

Figure 5.6. Humanist confirmation ceremony in Reykjavik, 24 April 2016. Copyright © Sidemennt (Icelandic Ethical Humanist Association) 98

Figure 5.7. Humanist confirmation ceremony in Copenhagen, 30 May 2015. Copyright © Willi Prochnow Sletten, Humanistisk Samfund (Danish Humanist Society) 98

Figure 9.1. Source energy. Copyright © Michael Picucci 143
Figure 12.1. The *Maas Tunnel Monument for Traffic Victims* (Rotterdam). Copyright © Irene Stengs 192
Figure 12.2. The plateau of the monument frames one-half of the granite memorial stone in remembrance of Raymond Stevens and John Goossens (Rotterdam). Copyright © Irene Stengs 192
Figure 12.3. The switchboard box is ornamented with brass plates that are engraved with newspaper articles relating to the accident (Rotterdam). Copyright © Irene Stengs 193
Figure 12.4. At the tunnel exit below, the other half of the granite stone is inset in the pavement, marking the exact spot of the accident (Rotterdam). Copyright © Irene Stengs 193
Figure 12.5. At the unveiling ceremony of the *National Monument for Railway Accident Victims*, employees of the Dutch Railway honour the victims with roses, 16 April 2004 (Utrecht). Copyright © Irene Stengs 198
Figure 12.6. Victims of all rail accidents are remembered at the unveiling ceremony, 16 April 2004 (Utrecht). Copyright © Irene Stengs 198
Figure 12.7. The *National Monument for Railway Accident Victims* (Utrecht). Copyright © Irene Stengs 199
Figure 14.1. *Sonic Alterations of Constructed Space, with Metal Objects* – 1, 2011–. Copyright © Laure Stephen, courtesy of Bianca Hester and Sarah Scout Presents 228
Figure 14.2. *Sonic Alterations of Constructed Space, with Metal Objects* – 2, 2011–. Copyright © Mark Schroder, courtesy of Bianca Hester and Sarah Scout Presents 228
Figure 14.3. *Solar Objects: Various Objects Held toward Evening's Diminishing Westerly Light* – 1. Copyright © Sam Nightingale, courtesy of Bianca Hester and Sarah Scout Presents 229
Figure 14.4. *Solar Objects: Various Objects Held toward Evening's Diminishing Westerly Light* – 2. Copyright © Sam Nightingale, courtesy of Bianca Hester and Sarah Scout Presents 229
Figure 15.1. *Moving Goods*. Copyright © Kick Smeets 238
Figure 15.2. *Zaandam Treasure Box* – 1. Copyright © Bart Homburg 238
Figure 15.3. *Zaandam Treasure Box* – 2. Copyright © Jeroen Breeuwer 239
Figure 15.4. *All Souls' Day Everywhere*. Copyright © Ida van der Lee 240
Figure 15.5. *Names and Numbers* (Amsterdam). Copyright © Ida van der Lee 241
Figure 15.6. *Irritation Game*. Copyright © Ida van der Lee 243
Figure 15.7. *Oracle Game*. Copyright © Bill Wei 244

ACKNOWLEDGEMENTS

As far as we know, the first academic exploration of the role of secular ritual in society took place in 1972–3 during a seminar at the University of Southern California. A year later, at the end of the summer of 1974, Max Gluckman, Victor Turner and Sally F. Moore held a conference entitled 'Secular Rituals Considered: Prolegomena toward a Theory of Ritual, Ceremony and Formality' at Burg Wartenstein, Austria. The purpose of the conference, described as a feast of ideas, was to explore the nature of non-religious ritual, ceremony and formality in social life. Subsequently, Sally F. Moore and Barbara G. Myerhoff gathered the conference papers into book form.

While this volume claims no direct descendance from *Secular Ritual* (1977)[1] it is indebted to the book's overture to debate on the subject. The fact that our collection appears on the 40th anniversary of Moore and Myerhoff's landmark publication indicates ongoing concern about the role of secular ritual in contemporary society. This book is not intended as an epilogue but as a continuation of the discussion. I am grateful to each one of the authors for their contribution to this current feast of ideas. They expand on what is known about how ritual functions on many levels including neurological and social; they explain and influence how we practise secular ritual in the world today. The freshness of the writers' exploration of the nature of non-religious ritual and ceremony demonstrates the extent to which secular ritual has become the new mainstream of our ultramodern society.

I would also like to thank the team at Jessica Kingsley Publishers for taking up the challenge of publishing this new collection on secular ritual. In particular, I am grateful to commissioning editor Natalie K. Watson for her enthusiastic support of the project, to production editor Alexandra Holmes for her relentless attention to detail and to Hannah Snetsinger for her patience and organizational abilities.

---

1 Published by van Gorcum in Assen/Amsterdam, The Netherlands.

Writing that takes place outside traditional academic contexts requires non-traditional means of support. I am grateful to my sister Anastasia Aukeman for her advice and encouragement, to Joanna Wojtkowiak at the Humanistic Studies University in Utrecht (NL) for her timely invitation to the Expert's Meeting in 2015 where this collection of articles germinated in my mind and to Philip and Junko Gordon-Lennox for the use of their place in Llafranc, Spain where, warmed by the winter sun, the project put forth buds. I am aware of the compromises, adjustments and even sacrifices required of those who live with an author and editor. Love and thanks to my children, Sushila and Jefferson, for giving me the physical space I needed to write in our home and for distracting me regularly with silly jokes, K-dramas and photos of their meals and adventures on WhatsApp. I would also like to acknowledge my husband, a busy professional musician, who has always supported me in the pursuit of my own artistic projects. Ian is also a talented cook who insists on ritualizing meals by eating at the table and on time; his creations literally fed me throughout the duration of this project.

Introduction

OPENING THE CONVERSATION

Jeltje Gordon-Lennox

About a year ago, I went to great lengths to obtain two recent collections of essays on ritual, performance, emotions and the senses. These attractively packaged volumes promised new insights from diverse areas of study by focusing on the body and the experiential nature of ritual as well as on the role of ritual in the creation and communication of emotion; yet they both let me down on two counts.

First of all, they reflect a general tendency among scholars to consider traditional ritual as 'aristocrats' while treating emerging ritual as 'poor cousins'. The post-war Beat culture that began in the late 1950s and became the hippie movement in the mid-1960s rejected Western rituals but was attracted to Eastern religions.[1] Both 'beatniks' and hippies invented ritual performances where 'improvisation, direct experience, immediacy, and spontaneity were priorities' (Aukeman 2016, p.107). Non-traditional ritual has evolved since then. Many of us create and practise secular ritual with respect and rigour.

Second, both volumes – in spite of their promising titles – deal almost exclusively with religious contexts and rites. Exactly 40 years ago Sally Falk Moore and Barbara G. Myerhoff published a collection of essays entitled *Secular Ritual* (1977), yet little has been written on secular ritual

---

[1] Alan Watts: '[W]hen somebody comes in from the Orient with a new religion which hasn't got any [horrible] associations in our minds, all the words are new, all the rites are new, and yet, somehow it has feeling in it, and we can get with that, you see, and we can dig that!' (quoted in Cohen 1991, n.p.).

in its wake. Ritologist Catherine Bell allowed for empirical difference between religious and secular ritual (1997, p.139), but even today few scholars see the need to open a separate category for non-religious ritual. Criteria for distinguishing between the two allegedly hinge on definitions of religion: presumably, a substantive, rather than a functional, definition of religion leaves space for secular rituals as a meaningful subset of ritual (Warburg 2016, p.141). Despite my strict theological training – or perhaps because of it – I see no reason to yoke ritual to any definition of religion, functional or substantive.[2] Our ideas of religion are inextricably tied to modern European history and to our experience of Western monotheisms, which tend to partition life into the sacred or the profane. Over the last few decades, the conscious practice of non-religious ritual, associated with the concept of mindfulness, has generated discussion around habits versus ritual. Habit is now commonly associated with ritualized gestures or words performed unconsciously. While habit is seen as being toxic to relationships, ritual enhances them.

As a psychotherapist in an increasing secular society, I am acutely aware of a growing loneliness and anxiety, particularly among youth. My experience as a celebrant demonstrates that authentic secular forms of ritual can enhance life by making us feel happier, stronger and more connected to each other – without religious belief. Religion, more specifically institutional religion, may help people survive in the world, bind them together socially or support them psychologically and emotionally but it is simply one ritual context among many. Ritual identity and practice may be influenced by religious or philosophical content but they are not – and perhaps never were – strictly limited to formal belief systems. As a celebrant I have seen the power of authentic forms of secular ritual reveal people's profound values and enhance their lives, making them feel happier, stronger and more connected to each other.

Western society no longer functions as a customary society. Interactions with others are essentially virtual. Face-to-face encounters take place

---

2   My theological studies were followed by an intensive study of world religions that led to the AnamCara Project, the creation of a website (Anamcara.ch) and two free games: *Small Planet BIG Questions* and *Labyrinth Quest* (in English and French on the App Store and Google Play).

on Skype. One rarely hears people singing or whistling, as voices and music pour in through personal ear buds. Chemical plants produce (too) much of what we taste and smell. Touch is kept to a minimum for risk of being misinterpreted as sexual. Shopping[3] in malls or online far surpasses jogging, yoga and museum-going as a popular pastime. People are 'connected' 24/7 but they feel isolated and unhappy. Many are poly-addicted not only to shopping, sex, video games, alcohol and drugs, but also to other destructive pursuits: dysfunctional relationships, and acquiring money and power. We have devolved into consumers. Our holidays are commercial occasions; eCommerce dictates our rituals.

Consumer values contribute to a social, cultural and intellectual void, but also to political, economic, spiritual and even biological fragmentation. Addiction – a mechanism that helps people cope with the loss of personal integration to society – represents a considerable risk to people who actively seek happiness (Alexander 2008). How people feel about happiness and how they go about being happy plays a profound role in whether or not they *are* happy.

I am inspired by stories about people like Nelson Mandela, Aung San Suu Kyi and Liu Xiaobo,[4] who, having lost all – including their freedom – manage to find peace and even joy in daily life. Happiness does not come from stuff, and it is certainly not an end in itself. Sustainable happiness, says writer Sarah van Gelder, is 'built on a healthy natural world and a vibrant and fair society...[it] endures through good times and bad because

---

3 Shortly after the end of the Second World War, market researcher Victor Lebow remarked: 'Our enormously productive economy demands that we make consumption our way of life, that we convert the buying and use of goods into rituals, that we seek our spiritual satisfactions, our ego satisfactions, in consumption. The very meaning and significance of our lives is today expressed in consumptive terms... [The consumer articulates] his aspirations and individuality in terms of what he wears, drives, eats...' (Lebow 1955, p.7).

4 Liu Xiaobo was awarded the Nobel Peace Prize in 2010, but was not allowed to attend the ceremony. In his absence, Norwegian actress Liv Ullmann read a statement Liu had written as a defence in a Chinese court the previous year. It read, in part, 'I have no enemies and no hatred. Hatred can rot away at a person's intelligence and conscience. Enemy mentality will poison the spirit of a nation, incite cruel mortal struggles, destroy a society's tolerance and humanity, and hinder a nation's progress toward freedom and democracy' (quoted in Encyclopædia Britannica 2015).

it starts with the fundamental requirements and aspirations of being human' (2014, p.1). We all have a vested interest in sustainable happiness, not least of all because achieving sustainability will enable Earth to continue supporting human life.

Being fully human means existing – creatively meeting our basic needs for food, drink, clothing and shelter – but also making even ordinary days special through play, art and ritual pursuits with others. The hands on the cover of this volume remind us that our hands, complete with opposable thumbs, are our principal tools for play, feeling and caring for each other, as well as for creating art and ritual.

My disappointment with the two volumes on ritual mentioned above led to the compilation of this collection of essays, case studies and an interview about contemporary secular ritual. The 15 chapters navigate between ritual theory and practice. They take the reader beyond academic acknowledgement of the absence of meaningful ritual to focus on the different ways people are responding today to our innate need to ritualize life events and public occasions.

What is ritual for? What does it do? What is the nature of its effects? It may surprise many of us to discover how much our modern notion of ritual is reliant upon ideas about art, beauty, performance and play, and entangled with those of individualization, commerce and the hegemony of hierarchical institutions. Why do non-religious people seek to ritualize life events? How do they go about creating ritual in secular societies? Understanding the function of non-religious ceremonial behaviour in society is central to effective ritualizing.[5] Small egalitarian band societies practised rituals, indicating that then, as now, ritual is an essential

---

5   More than half of the world's population now live in urban areas. Saskia Sassen says of the city: '[H]istory has given us glimpses of a very different kind of space, one that is less ritualized and with few if any embedded codes... [I] have called it "the global street" (Sassen 2011). This is a space with few, if any, of the ritualized practices or codes that the larger society might recognize. It is rough, easily seen as "uncivilized"...a space where the powerless can make history in ways they cannot in rural areas... Ours is a time when stabilized meanings have become unstable. The large complex city with all its diversities is a new frontier zone. This is especially true if it is a global city, defined by its partial shaping within a network of other cities across borders.' (Sassen 2013, pp.213, 219).

emotional and social component of human life. It is my hope that this collection on the rediscovery of ritual in secular societies will stimulate people to be ritually creative in order to support society in its primary role.

The contributors to this volume are experienced professionals who constitute an international group from North America, Europe and Australia. Their distinctive writing styles reflect their transdisciplinary, but complementary fields. Part I examines the origins of ritual from three different perspectives: ethological, anthropological and neurological. Part II addresses the emergence of secular life event rituals; it is completed by case studies of secular ritualmaking for coming of age, marriage and death. How we ritualize in private settings is dealt with in Part III, where particular attention is paid to the use of ritual in intimate relationships, mourning and with food. Part IV explores secular ritualizing in public places; it includes discussions of public monuments for the dead, consumerism and performance as well as an interview with a ritual artist who creates public rituals designed to foster social cohesion.

CHAPTER SUMMARIES
Part I: The Origins of Ritual

Ellen Dissanayake opens the volume with her observations on the origins of play, art and ritual. She sees them in evolutionary terms as universal cultural and social behaviours that have been adaptive for human survival. Our very first relationships, those of parent and child, prime us for self-regulation and social interaction. By defining play, art and ritual as activities for 'making special' Dissanayake neatly skirts the pitfalls of ethnocentrism and opens the way to looking at contemporary secular ritualizing as an adaptive human activity informed by biology, environment, culture and society.

Matthieu Smyth maintains that rituals have been part of human experience for a very long time, possibly since the origins of humankind. Quite a number of other higher mammals also benefit from some form of ritual practice. Since we tend to apprehend ritual mainly within a religious framework, it is important to put contemporary ritualizing into a broader anthropological context. When thinking anew about ritual it is necessary to go back to anthropology, prehistory and even ethology.

Robert C. Scaer brings his medical experience to the fore in his chapter about the neurophysiological features and power of ritual. Scaer's work with trauma led him to look at the function of ritual, which – like many somatic therapeutic techniques – has its roots in the rewarding and healing functions of the brain. Rites of passage, governance, celebration and virtually all social functions depend on the implicit brain rewards that are associated with these practices. In the case of the resolution and healing of life trauma, ritual may actually be an essential ingredient. The commonality of a ritual and its acceptance by the group give it special neurophysiological features and powers that promote healing from trauma.

Part II: Sensemaking in Life Events

Jeltje Gordon-Lennox holds that the effectiveness of ritualizing depends more on the senses and sensemaking than on thinking or dogma. Ritualizing must touch the body's felt sense and effect a felt shift. Coherence with the values and culture of the person at the centre of the ritual ensure that the ritual is right because it feels right. Over the last 17 years, Gordon-Lennox developed, tested and refined a naturalistic approach to the creation of secular ceremonies for the major passages of life. Her training as a psychotherapist, in particular for the treatment of trauma, and her expertise in world religions enriches the approach she summarizes with three watchwords: accompaniment, authenticity and affect.

A case study explores how a humanist movement rehabilitated the coming-of-age tradition in Nordic countries by adding a secular twist that gives young people a choice between a religious or a non-religious confirmation ceremony. Confirmation has deep roots in traditional popular Nordic culture. For hundreds of years Nordic state churches held the key to adulthood. Until 1849 in Norway and Denmark, young people could not legally marry, wear adult clothing or hold adult jobs until they had been approved by their parson and confirmed by the Church in a public ceremony. The confirmation tradition still represents a proud moment for confirmands and their families. For well over half a century now, humanist organizations have been conducting humanist preparation classes and confirmation ceremonies. Each year over ten thousand of Nordic youth celebrate their coming of age in a secular confirmation ceremony.

Andrés Allemand Smaller argues that a wedding always represents the union of two different individuals; it does not matter whether those differences are in their personalities, origins or cultures. Andrés was born in Buenos Aires, grew up in New York and then moved to Geneva. Life taught him to value diversity. His loved ones are Christian, Jewish, Muslim, Buddhist, Hindu, agnostic and atheist. He believes that everyone is searching, each in their own way, for the meaning of their existence. He is interested in what union means to a couple. As a trained journalist and wedding celebrant, he is passionate about social ritualizing and in helping fiancés create a wedding ceremony that reflects who they really are as a couple.

Christine Behrend presents a funeral ceremony that she crafted for a violinist. The ceremony used the deceased's violin as a symbol for the musician himself, first, during the ceremony, as a symbol of his life, and then, at the time of committal, as a symbol of his death. The symbolic silencing of the violin visually expressed the fact that the musician was dead. At the same time, it shifted the focus to the immaterial legacy the violinist had created in terms of music, emotions and humanitarian values, and the way this legacy will live on in future generations.

Isabel Russo reflects on an unusual request she received as Head of Ceremonies that called for a memorial and a wedding to be performed in the same ceremony. Humanist Ceremonies™ is the growing network of 300 celebrants trained and accredited by the British Humanist Association (BHA). What the BHA does isn't *new*, observes Russo. The Association is proud of its history: BHA members were conducting humanist funerals as long ago as the 1890s. Humanist ceremonies are not *unusual* either – BHA celebrants do thousands each year, but perhaps this isn't surprising since half of Britain's population say they are not religious, and indeed, only a third of marriages in England are held in a church. Although humanist ceremonies are not unusual, every situation is unique, so BHA celebrants are prepared to take on atypical requests.

Part III: Ritualizing in Intimate Spaces

Michael Picucci argues that ritual is much more than just an artefact of religion and diplomacy. Removed from narrow settings, it remains a powerful tool for our time. This chapter proposes re-envisioning ritual as an innate human technology, one that is highly adaptable to almost any situation, and uniquely suited for personal transformation and balance. By rediscovering grounding, tuning, focusing, amplifying and directing as socio-personal tools, individuals can call up energetic resources that are capable of fuelling a variety of transformative experiences in personal or collective settings.

Joanna Wojtkowiak maintains that in a post-secular society, where traditional belief systems are questioned, the individual is the authority figure when it comes to finding meaning in life. Meaning-making is not just a mental process, but is also experienced in an embodied, sensory and material way. Mourners often keep objects that belonged to their deceased loved ones, such as jewellery, clothing or cremated ashes, and engage with them in a ritual manner. In this chapter, Wojtkowiak uses insights from embodiment theory and research on the role of the senses to focus on the material connections the living preserve with the dead.

Lindy Mechefske examines food rituals the world over. Food and the rituals surrounding food are integral to every aspect of our human experience. From the time we first latch onto our mothers' breasts, to the birthday cakes of our childhoods, to our last suppers, our entire lives are woven around food. With 7.3 billion people around the globe all aspiring to eat, often three times a day, food is both about sustenance and also the world's largest single industry. From hunter to gatherer; from farmer to chef; from chopsticks to cutlery; from corn to guinea pigs; from takeaway to gourmet; from solitary dining to gala banquets; from farmers' markets to supermarkets; from manners to mayhem; from weddings to funerals; and from Italy to India to Iqaluit – food and food rituals permeate every aspect of life. It is not a question, then, of whether or not food rituals are a profound human need, but rather, given the importance of food to life and mortality, how could we not ritualize our relationship with others through food?

Part IV: Ritualizing in Public Places

Irene Stengs addresses the increasing need to commemorate violent deaths (traffic deaths, killings, work-related tragedies) in the public domain. Whether an accident occurs on the railways or in traffic, each event represents an intense personal drama for the people whose world is torn apart by the sudden incursion of death into their lives. For many of the bereaved, the radical and irreversible nature of such a loss attaches itself where it can, in many cases to a place. A new culture of public mourning finds material expression in the ritualized spaces of informal roadside memorials as well as in officially sanctioned monuments. Ethnographically, this contribution focuses on the need felt by Dutch authorities to channel or even prevent unruly ritualization in public space by establishing general monuments for specific categories of victims.

Gianpiero Vincenzo explores the emergence of a society based on consumer rituals. The transition from traditional rites to modern ritualizing has meant profound changes in views and perspectives. In the pre-modern age, 'community' – with its rites and symbols – took centre stage and played a main role in the structure of human life. Today, the supermarket and, on a broader scale, the shopping mall, shapes public space in much the same way as the cathedral or the town hall did in the pre-modern age. Once people went to church or out of town on Sundays; now families go shopping and have lunch in the 'eternal spring' of shopping malls.

Jacqueline Millner argues that contemporary art is an important site of secular ritual today. Many contemporary artists, in particular those engaged in performance and social practice, invoke ritual to re-inscribe spaces and activate audiences using the same 'materials' as ritualmaking – people, participation and place. Millner traces the development of early performance art through to contemporary social practice by following the path of ritualmaking. By analysing the work of artists Yoko Ono, Gina Pane, Suzanne Lacy and Bianca Hester, Millner proposes that such practice can share the underlying aims of ritual: to bring people together for transformation or reintegration.

The collection closes with an interview by Christine Behrend of Dutch ritual artist Ida van der Lee, who relies on art for ritualizing in public spaces. With the abandonment of traditional rituals, van der Lee's work on the design of emerging rituals is much appreciated. As van der Lee talks about the public rituals she has designed, she exposes some of the ideas, principles and childhood memories behind her work. Working with a team composed of people concerned about a particular situation and a group of artists, van der Lee creates beautiful ephemeral art forms that tap into the capacity of public places to foster social cohesion and harmony.

REFERENCES

Alexander, B.K. (2008) *Globalization of Addiction: A Study in Poverty of the Spirit*. New York: Oxford University Press.

Aukeman, A. (2016) *Welcome to Painterland: Bruce Conner and the Rat Bastard Protective Association*. Oakland, CA: University of California Press.

Bell, C. (1997) *Ritual: Perspectives and Dimensions*. New York: Oxford University Press.

Cohen, A. (ed.) (1991) *The San Francisco Oracle. The Psychedelic Newspaper of the Haight-Ashbury (1966–1968)*. Berkeley, CA: Regent Press.

Encyclopædia Britannica (2016) 'Liu-Xiaobo.' Available at www.britannica.com/biography/Liu-Xiaobo, accessed on 15 August 2016.

Lebow, V. (1955) 'Price competition in 1955.' *Journal of Retailing* Spring 5–10, 42, 44.

Moore, S.F. and Myerhoff, B.G. (eds) (1977) *Secular Ritual*. Assen, Netherlands: Van Gorcum.

Sassen, S. (2011) 'The global street: Making the political.' *Globalizations* 5(8), 565–571.

Sassen, S. (2013) 'Does the City Have Speech?' In T. Haas and K. Olsson (eds) *Emergent Urbanism: Urban Planning and Design in Times of Structural and Systemic Change*. Burlington, VT and Farnham, Surrey: Ashgate Publishing.

van Gelder, S. (2014) *Sustainable Happiness: Live Simply, Live Well, Make a Difference*. Oakland, CA: Berrett-Koehler Publishers.

Warburg, M. (2016) 'Secular Rituals.' In P.J. Stewart and A.J. Strathern (eds) *Ashgate Research Companion to Anthropology*. London and New York: Routledge.

PART I

THE ORIGINS OF RITUAL

1

THE ART OF RITUAL AND THE RITUAL OF ART[1]

Ellen Dissanayake

All artists and writers know that inspiration may come suddenly and from a surprising source. My work was given an unexpected and powerful new direction in the autumn of 1983 when I taught a class called 'Ritual, Play, and Art' at the New School for Social Research in New York. At the time, I was formulating my hypothesis that what artists do in all times and places is to 'make special' (see Figure 1.1). The class was a way of exploring other behaviours – play and ritual – which also make special, to see what else art, ritual, and play had in common.

A colleague at the New School told me about the playful ritual between mothers and their infants described in a book called *The First Relationship* by Daniel Stern (1977). As I read about the affectionate sounds, gestures and facial expressions that adults (not only mothers) use when they talk to babies, I realized that 'play' and 'ritual' were not the only way to describe what was happening. Stern's descriptions reminded me so much of what *artists* do. I began to wonder: Could it be that artistic making and aesthetic responsiveness originate at the very beginning of life?

---

[1] This chapter appears as Chapter Four (pp.66–72) in *The Nature of Craft and the Penland Experience*, published in 2004 by Lark Books as part of the celebration of Penland's 75th anniversary. The book contains nine essays on craft by scholars and writers from a variety of fields including poetry, anthropology, chemistry, folklore, and material culture as well as a short history of Penland. Ellen Dissanayake's chapter is reprinted here with permission of Penland School of Crafts.

The Art of Ritual and the Ritual of Art   23

Figure 1.1. In all times and places artists work to make even the simplest things special

At first, this was only an indefinite question, one that I wasn't really sure how to approach. But, as with the germ of any fruitful idea, my rudimentary insight gradually unfolded, inspiring further ideas which themselves have become intriguing paths to explore. During the 20 years between my first exposure to Stern's book and today, I have continued to find truths about art and life in this 'first relationship'.

Eventually I would be led to learn about such unexpected subjects as hominid evolution, the anatomy and function of the brain, and 'ritualized' displays in birds. I would study the behaviour of humans in other cultures with their young and of primates with theirs. Such subjects do not noticeably seem to have anything to do with art, or, for that matter, much to do with ritual or play. But, like the unpromising and recalcitrant mud or metal, planks or fibres with which artists make their creations, my findings from biology, anthropology, and psychology have become, after careful consideration and handling, something worth working with, something to share with others, and something to enrich our understanding.

The elements of the mother–infant playful ritual really *are*, I believe, the origin of later aesthetic behaviour – although not in the simple, nurturant way ('good mothering produces artists') that might be expected. What I will describe in this chapter is the importance of the innate psychobiological mechanisms that create emotional intersubjectivity (that is, the ways in which emotions between two or more people are coordinated and exchanged), which is at the core of making and experiencing art. My studies show that the techniques of making special as manifested in art and ritual turn out to be elaborations of the standard human equipment for creating and maintaining intimate and affiliative relationships (Dissanayake 2000).

What does this mean for us as makers and experiencers of the arts?

Today, ritual is often dismissed as empty and conventional, while art may be thought of as a self-indulgent pastime or a sham. However, describing the components and commonalities between ritual and art makes clear how important they are to our species and, by extension, to us as individuals. In their origin, ritual performance and artistic making were like two overlapped lenses trained on the same needs, arising and developing as ways to achieve and demonstrate emotional concord, and to publicly manifest matters of vital concern (see Figure 1.2). The psychobiological vestiges of these origins remain and remind us of the continuing importance of art as ritual and ritual as art to full human lives today. It is in rare communities such as the Penland School of Crafts that these values flourish and persist, even though they may not be explicitly articulated.

Penland School of Crafts

A remarkable woman named Lucy Morgan – always known as Miss Lucy – started Penland School of Crafts in Penland, North Carolina, in 1929 as an outgrowth of a craft-based economic development project she had initiated several years earlier. She based the School on a few simple values that have guided Penland throughout its history. She once described these as, 'the joy of creative occupation and a certain togetherness – working with one another in creating the good and the beautiful'.

Today, Penland encompasses about 420 acres and 57 buildings, and more than 1400 people come each year seeking instruction. The School also offers artist residencies and a gallery. Students come to Penland from all walks of life. Some see it as a productive retreat, some as a source of inspiration for their creative lives, and others as a network for the exchange of information. Nearly 90 years after it was founded, the School still attracts people who share a love of materials and making, and a desire to experience working alongside others in a supportive community atmosphere.

The photographs that accompany this chapter show activities at Penland School of Crafts.

Figure 1.2. Ritual performance and art can meet our need for emotional concord and publicly manifest matters of vital concern

THE ART OF RITUAL

My studies reveal that mother–infant play can be justifiably described as a dyadic (that is, two-person) ritual in which innate aesthetic or protoaesthetic elements first appear and are developed (Dissanayake 2000, p.214). Although the following description may seem at first to be far removed from the making (or the 'ritual') of art, it is good, I think, to be aware of the deep-rootedness of our aesthetic nature as it appears even in infants.

MOTHER-INFANT PLAYFUL RITUAL

Babies come into the world prepared and eager for human company. They prefer human faces to any other sight (be it sharply contrasting or brightly coloured shapes, or cute stuffed animals) and human voices to any other sound (be it tinkling bells, soft music or Alvin and the Chipmunks). They can estimate and anticipate intervals of time – that is, form expectations of when the next beat will come, based on a pulse or rhythm that has been set up, say, by gently patting, rocking, or singing rhythmically to them.

These inborn abilities allow normal infants to interact with the people around them, and unobtrusively to persuade these people to talk, make funny faces, and move their heads in ways they would never do with anyone except a baby. It is a mistake to think that we speak in high-pitched voices to babies, or make abrupt head-bobs, nods, and open mouths just to attract their immature attention. On the contrary, babies train *us* to do these things because such sounds and expressions are what they most like and need; they are born wanting others to act like this. For our efforts, they reward us with their smiles and kicks and reachings-out, persuading us to do it even more. For them and for us, this is *play*.

Adult behaviour to babies seems natural, because it is. People in cultures everywhere spontaneously (that is, without deliberate practice or intention) talk to babies in short rhythmic, repetitive utterances, at a high pitch and with exaggerated vocal contours. They exaggerate and sustain certain facial expressions: wide eyes, open mouth, or pursed lips; they move their head forward toward the baby's face and back again; they look deeply and intimately into its eyes. They pat or stroke or rub babies steadily and rhythmically.

Although these behaviours are 'natural', they are nevertheless quite unusual. At least they would be noteworthy – or even alarming – if we adults did them to each other. What is unusual is that these vocal, facial, and gestural expressions are extreme or 'special' forms of the ordinary, daily ways we show friendliness to, interest in, and accord with other people. When used with infants, our everyday and unremarkable smiles of pleasure and affection, nods of agreement, looks of interest, or sounds and pats of support or sympathy become stereotyped or simplified (formalized), exaggerated in time and space, and elaborated through repetition (sometimes with variation). What is more, these vocalizations, facial expressions, and body movements are temporally coordinated, with adult and infant responding to the other as if in reference to a common pulse. It is possible to accelerate or decelerate gradually, but a sudden change of tempo disrupts the smooth flow. The behavioural coordination echoes or reinforces emotional conjoinment, where both partners are feeling and acting not alone, but with reference to each other.

Until films revealed the intricacies and exquisite attunement of these interactions, no one suspected that infants of only six weeks of age – before they can even hold their heads up reliably, or reach for and grasp an object – could be so receptive to these special signals and their presentation in time. Although the adult leads the performance, the baby is essential to it, for with its own sounds, facial expressions, and body movements it influences the pace, intensity, and variety of signals that are improvised. Indeed, one can think of adult–infant interaction as an impromptu multimedia duet, in which each partner responds with supreme sensitivity to the other's moods and actions.

Film analyses of this interaction show that it is also a multi*modal* duet. Each partner will respond pretty much the same to a signal whether it is aural, visual, or gestural. That is, a baby's sudden arm movement might be answered with the mother's voice becoming suddenly, sharply loud; as her remarks become faster, the baby might kick faster. A blind baby in a film I saw raised her arm and spread her fingers as her mother's singing swelled.

In a later book, Stern (1985) introduced the concept of 'vitality affects' to describe the emotional valence of qualities of such multimodal behaviours and responses – qualities related to intensity, shape, contour, direction, duration, and movement. In *Art and Intimacy* (2000, pp.6–7, 130), I called these qualities 'rhythms and modes'. They are not exactly emotions, but kinds of abstract 'forms of feeling' that are common to many sensory experiences, whether from sight, hearing, touch, or movement. Although difficult to describe, the words used to try to describe these are often drawn from music or movement – such as 'accelerando', 'crescendo', 'steady' or 'jerky'. But these and other descriptive words – such as fleeting, surging, fading away, tentative, smooth – also apply to vision and touch. Visual artists who read this will easily think of lines, shapes, forms and colours with these and other 'multimodal' qualities.

Most parents are unconcerned about the 'purpose' (or the silliness) of their interactive play – like babies, the important thing is to have fun together. But a biologist or psychologist has to wonder about what is accomplished by such a complex, closely attuned behaviour. A number of intellectual, emotional and social benefits have been identified. For example, mother and baby can adjust to each other's individual tempo or personality, gradually coming into 'sync', as the level of arousal is mutually modulated up or down. The baby discovers that its behaviour has effects on others – an important social lesson. The interaction contributes to eventual learning of language, both words and grammar, and the non-verbal indications of a partner's age, sex, mood and intention. The interaction helps a baby 'self-regulate' its feelings, that is, to become familiar with them, calibrate them with those of another and eventually deal with them.

A scientist might also wonder how such an interaction came about. It is possible to infer that as humans evolved over several million years, the mother–infant ritual arose as a behavioural adaptation that contributed to the ancestral baby's very survival. Because of upright posture, the birth canal in humans is smaller than in a four-legged creature. Obviously, as brain size was increasing over evolutionary time childbirth became a serious predicament for both mother and baby. A number of anatomical changes are known to have taken place to permit easier births of large-brained infants: their skulls can be compressed at birth, much brain growth takes place outside the womb and the female's pelvic symphysis can separate slightly at parturition. But in addition to these changes, it is clear that mothers of babies who were born at a less-developed, smaller stage had a better chance of a successful birth, and those smaller, less-developed babies would themselves later tend to produce smaller, less-developed babies. (For a human infant to be as mature at birth as a newborn chimpanzee would require a 21-month gestation period, and the baby would weigh 25 pounds.)

By simplifying, repeating, exaggerating, and elaborating the already existent signals that communicate good will to other adults, an ancestral mother expressed intense love and abiding interest to her baby. Additionally, she unwittingly reinforced affiliative neural circuits in her own brain, thereby helping to ensure that she felt such positive emotion toward her infant that she would be willing to devote the necessary effort and time required to care for such a helpless and demanding being. Infants who called forth these sorts of behaviours by coordinating with maternal rhythms and showing other appealing responses (like smiling) helped to assure that their mothers felt this way. Gradually, over generations, infants and mothers who became affectively attuned survived and reproduced better than those who did not.

ADULT RITUAL

The word 'ritual' typically refers to prescribed performances required by a religious or other solemn occasion, such as an inauguration, graduation, baptism, wedding or funeral. Although the term can be broadened to refer to almost any activity that has a conventional kind of progression – a meal, sports event, class, church service, even the pattern of an ordinary working day – typical usage presumes that a ritual is characterized not only by repeatability or conventionality but by unusual behaviour that sets it off from the ordinary or everyday. Time, space, activity, dress, paraphernalia are made special or extraordinary, and so we can speak of ritual time, ritual space, ritual activity, ritual dress, ritual paraphernalia and so forth.

What is the purpose of unusual, special, *extra*ordinary behaviour? In our remote past, tens of thousands of years ago, our ancestors, at some point and for some reason, began to invent the multimedia packages that we today recognize as ceremonial rituals. These exist in every society that has ever been known, and enormous amounts of time, physical effort, and material resources are often devoted to them. Ceremonies obviously contribute something important to the people who perform them.

My suggestion is that ceremonies began as the behavioural expression of people's feelings about what they desired and needed most. They were a society's way of exhibiting in the most vivid, compelling ways how much they cared about the vital subject of the ceremony, whether it be procuring food, protecting from harm, ensuring prosperity or healing the sick. At first, perhaps people simply moved and moaned together at a time of anxiety. Finding that it made them feel better, they were inclined to do it again at a later anxious time. Perhaps they imitated for each other the animal they wished to kill, were successful in the hunt, and decided to imitate again. Over time the movements and sounds became more elaborated to what we recognize as dance and song, with visual decor added to attract even greater attention to what was done and said. When dress, implements, and surroundings were made more considered, sumptuous, and dramatic, they became more expressive of the underlying need or wish.

Because these early humans had of course all been babies, they had an innate susceptibility to emphasis and extravagance in visual, vocal and kinesic[2] modalities; they were already responsive to the emotional effects of formalization, repetition, exaggeration and elaboration. Without consciously setting out to build upon these protoaesthetic sensitivities, they discovered that it was exactly these 'operations' on sounds, words, movements, sites, objects and bodies that gave form and expression to

---

2   The term 'kinesic' refers to non-verbal communication through gesture or other body movement.

their deepest concerns and made them feel emotionally united with each other. As in maternal messages to babies, these operations communicated: 'Look at [pay attention to] this message [matter, outcome]!' or 'I care about this, and I care that you know that I care. I want you to care too.'

In this way, components of 'the first relationship' – between mother and infant – became transmuted into the first arts, developed in ritual ceremonies as what we now call dance, song, poetic language, dramatic performance and visual display. As with mothers and infants, ceremonial arts generally occur all together as 'multimedia' and have multimodal, interpenetrating effects.

In adopting the protoaesthetic operations of formalization, repetition, exaggeration and elaboration, ritual ceremonies became the cradle of the arts. The 'art of ritual' is not only a metaphor, but also an accurate description of what makes ceremonies emotionally affecting. They are troves of arts.

THE RITUAL OF ART

In a similar way, the 'ritual of art' is not only a metaphor for, say, the way an individual artist sets to work every day, or for the customary routines of an institutionalized art world. In this section, I want to make the case that the arts today still contain important components from their origin in ritual – deriving from both the playful ritual of mother–infant interaction and ritual ceremony itself.

It may sound simplistic to say that fundamentally what artists do with their materials, images, and ideas is – like mothers (as well as practitioners of ancestral rituals) with their sounds and facial-bodily movements – to shape or formalize, repeat, exaggerate and elaborate them. Yet to realize this is also to realize how the arts are embedded in our biology. These aesthetic operations attract and hold attention, and make us recognize that the material or image or theme has been made special and that someone wants us to notice and heed. Drawing a frame around something, making it or part of it larger or smaller than one might expect, emphasizing one place rather than another, adding colour or a repeated design – these are the sorts of practices and decisions that artists deal with, unlike, say, makers of ordinary tools or dwellings, hunters or fishers, and food preparers or herb gatherers in early societies or the industrial designers, engineers, cooks, and pharmacists who do such work today. Insofar as these occupations do emphasize or elaborate (and so forth), they are adding ritual or art, but in the simplest sense, aesthetic operations are not strictly necessary to achieving the practical goal. This use of aesthetic operations is what I described in the previous section as the 'art' of ritual, and these same operations are used, and further elaborated, in the arts today. If ceremonies are troves of arts, the arts are suffused with the physical and emotional components of ritual behaviour.

CRAFT AND RITUAL

So far in this chapter I have used the word 'art' pretty much as a generic category that refers as much to 'craft' as to 'art'. That is, I have not tried to distinguish between craft and art in my examination of what makers or practitioners do when they make their behaviour, materials, or ideas special. In this concluding section, however, I am going to be more direct and claim that it is in craft, and craft communities like Penland, that the 'ritual of art' (or the ritual in art) is most evident and contiguous with ancestral forms.

Bruce Metcalf, a metalsmith and craft historian, points out that the ideas comprised by today's term 'craft' are, like those of 'art', of relatively recent origin – even though, of course, the roots of craft are in pre-industrial technology (2003, pp.13–23). Both are post-Enlightenment concepts that come out of a cultural world that is heavily influenced by the marketplace, with its concomitants of buying, selling, advertising and competition. In this recent usage, craft has typically been considered the stepsibling of art – although, as Metcalf notes, there are degrees of both and they may meet in the middle (for example, the 'artist-craftsperson').

Metcalf, however, chooses to consider the two categories separately. Among his criteria for craft are (1) hand work, (2) knowledge and use of traditional craft media, techniques, formats, and history, and (3) a sense of the primacy of the object and its function. Although he recognizes that contemporary craft includes 'hybrids', many of which may be interesting and worthwhile, his notion of craft generally would exclude activities such as installations or performances, techniques like computerization or electroforming, materials like plastic, and useless or found objects or the 'anything at all' that has come to characterize visual art of the past several decades.

I like Metcalf's analysis of craft history and his insistence on the differences between craft and art today, based on historical knowledge and acquaintance with the contemporary art scene. The view that I have presented in this chapter – which might be called prehistorical – supports Metcalf's criteria of craft, although I speak here of craft and art when they were the same activity, when all art (including music and dance) was craft, in Metcalf's sense. That is, in its origins and in subsistence societies, 'art' was – and had to be – functional, material and communal.

Function

As I have described, the aesthetic elements (or artful 'operations') of mother–infant playful interaction arose to aid the survival of helpless babies; in ritual ceremonies, they were co-opted and developed in order to make the ceremony work – to better achieve its purpose. Presumably, an ailment could be healed simply by applying a poultice or drinking a potion. But in healing rituals around the world, these remedies alone are usually perceived as insufficient. Special (that is, formalized, repeated, exaggerated, elaborated) words, movements, designs, costumes and behaviour are required, not optional. They demonstrate that their makers have taken the trouble to show how much they care.

This notion of function allied with specialness or artfulness remains inherent in craft. Although any hollowed-out piece of wood can serve as a container, or a cured animal skin be worn as clothing, craftworkers of today, like their predecessors, include artfulness as necessary to function (see Figure 1.3). In this they are aware that humans evolved to care about their lives, and to show this care by making special what is most important to them.

Figure 1.3. Craftworkers today, just like their predecessors, need artfulness to function

Materiality

Our ancestors evolved in a material, physical world to which they had to adapt. Their bodily attributes and abilities, their psychological needs and desires were developed with reference to that world in which they had to make a living. Craft is ineluctably grounded in the life of the body, the physicality of material and material objects – their feel, their weight, their resistance, their fragility or durability (see Figure 1.4). Humans are familiar with the products of craft in a way that they may not be with 'works of art' that are meant to fool the eye or mind, that disguise the marks of the hand that made them, and which suggest a transhuman world. We focus not only on the subject or theme of a craft work, if there is one, but also on its *thereness*, its substantiality, its *madeness*.

Figure 1.4. Craft is ineluctably grounded in the body, the physicality of material and material objects

Makeness implies a hand or hands. Hands are one of our most distinctive human characteristics, one of the bodily attributes that evolved so that we could make tools and construct from natural materials the necessities of our lives. Humans possess *joie de faire*, the pleasure of making things with their hands (Dissanayake 1995).

Apart from appreciating how it is to make things, we have other associations with hands. We know how things feel to the hand and we know the varied touches of others' hands. The sense of touch and being touched (like the senses of vision, hearing and movement, which also evolved in relation to materiality) provides us with rich, interpenetrating, multimodal associations – the 'vitality affects' described earlier – with the natural world and the products made from it, as well as with our earliest interactive experiences with other people.

If hands communicate directly by touch, they do so indirectly, too, with gestures. (Even infants make hand gestures that are communicative, different from their attempts to grasp and manipulate.) And in what we make, our gestures take on permanent form so that, whether intended or not, making is a sort of presentation. Something made implies the age-old, open-handed gesture – 'here, take this from my hands' – which offers not only a handmade object but evidence, as in one's handwriting, from which other humans can sense what underlies the maker's action and experience.

For the perceiver, a made object implies not only a hand, but also a *person* with hands – someone mortal like ourselves who fashioned this object, brought it to being (see Figure 1.5). The knowledge that 'someone made this' can become an integral part of our experience of the object. In some cases of strong emotional connection, it can even lead to something very like 'affect attunement' with the work/maker, an ardent, moving certainty of shared human feeling and the quality of that feeling.

Figure 1.5. A bespoke object implies not only hands, but the human being who fashioned that object

Communality

At the core of ritual and art as I have described them is the emotional intersubjectivity developed and practised in mother–infant interaction. Making and making special are inseparable from the innate human impulse to share feelings and from the need and ability to express ourselves in relationship with others. And as just described, we also experience the works of others intersubjectively. The gestural traces in handmade objects, like the bodily signatures in dance and song, contribute directly to another's reception or appreciation of them.

Yet in contemporary art theory and practice, works, their makers and their perceivers are typically treated as lone individuals. Works are decontextualized and displayed as isolated, unique entities. Makers are said to be exploring their unique subjectivity and its preoccupations. Perceivers typically view works silently and alone, from a unique personal sensibility.

Although contemporary craft partakes of the modern art world's insistence on museum-like display and its requirement of originality – these being necessities of the marketplace – I believe that insofar as hand and material presence are maintained, the transaction between maker/work and audience remains insistent and inescapable. Additionally and importantly, human relationship is manifested in craft not only horizontally, in the immediacy of close association, but also vertically through time.

Craft practitioners generally work within the communal, guild-like process of tradition transmitted from master to pupil (see Figure 1.6). This can be a powerful source of meaning. I remember feeling solemnly touched when my piano teacher told me that he had studied with Karl Schnabel, who had studied with his father, Artur Schnabel, who had studied with…back to Carl Czerny, who had studied with Beethoven. A poet friend, David Evans, tells me that he writes 'for or towards those writers whose works I can't get enough of – artists who have given me great pleasure and understanding of myself as well as other human beings and the physical world. I've always had a great driving need to be a part of what they do and are.'

Figure 1.6. Craft practitioners generally learn their work within the guild-like process where the tradition is transmitted from master to apprentice

At Penland School of Crafts, the vertical and horizontal of communality intersect. Members of the immediate community live and work together, but even when working alone after leaving Penland, the community is implicit. Creative artists sometimes feel that they are conduits for messages from something or somewhere else. Such a feeling takes on a natural, as opposed to supernatural, relevance when one becomes aware that at Penland, one belongs not only to the accidental community of everyone who happens to be there at the time, but additionally of all who have been there over the past 75 years, and the company of handworkers from the Pleistocene to today.

REFERENCES

Dissanayake, E. (1995) 'The pleasure and meaning of making.' *American Craft* 55(2), 40–45.

Dissanayake, E. (2000) *Art and Intimacy: How the Arts Began*. Seattle, WA: University of Washington Press.

Metcalf, B. (2003) 'Contemporary Craft: A Brief Overview.' In J. Johnson (ed.) *Exploring Contemporary Craft: History, Theory, and Critical Writing*. Toronto: Coach House Books with The Craft Studio at Harbourfront Centre.

Stern, D. (1977) *The First Relationship: Infant and Mother*. Cambridge, MA: Harvard University Press.

Stern, D. (1985) *The Interpersonal World of the Infant*. New York: Basic Books.

2

HUMAN RITUALS AND ETHOLOGY

A SCHOLAR'S JOURNEY

Matthieu Smyth

Since the beginning of my university studies the ritual aspect of religion has captured my attention. My interest has been personal as well as academic. My intuition told me that rituals were a profound resource for human wellbeing. Moreover, they struck me as an essential part of how human societies function. Emile Durkheim, the founder of French sociology, wrote: 'Religious force is only the sentiment inspired by the group in its members, but projected outside the consciousnesses that experience it, and objectified. To be objectified, it is fixed upon some object which thus becomes sacred' (Durkheim 1995 [1912], p.327).

Today I would take Durkheim's understanding of religion with a pinch of salt: in his view all religions depend on external 'sacred' principles, but this does not seem to be corroborated by facts. Nonetheless, Durkheim reflects my own view about the vital importance of collective rituals to human society. To a large extent rituals are historically related to the formal structures of organized religion, though not necessarily dependent on particular religious beliefs. Moreover, I gradually came to the conclusion that our understanding of 'religion' is very heavily determined by our modern European historical experience, and Christian monotheism in particular, which is, in turn, determined by the rigorous distinction between the sacred and the profane, as well as by the belief in transcendental metaphysics, or, from a different angle, by the underlining of individual conscience. Unconsciously, we project this point of view on the various forms of human culture, each of which have a different experience of what we call religion. Should Christianity, for example, be discussed within the same conceptual category as polytheism and animism?

My academic background is mostly centred on the history and anthropology of religion within Mediterranean or European cultures, where most rituals do take place within the context of religion in the modern sense. Therefore, my scholarly work concentrates on the study of rituals in their religious context, in the sense by which this term is usually understood. I studied in detail celebrations of baptism and sacred meals within different religious contexts, Jewish, Christian or some ancient other religious groups belonging to late Mediterranean antiquity. My particular passions were the nearly timeless carnival rituals from rural Europe. They were, I confess, a welcome exception to the study of organized religious bodies, which is obligatory for any academic doing research in religious history and anthropology. A vast number of the recorded rituals only appear within a religious context, so they must be apprehended from this angle. Nonetheless, it is interesting to note that, while many religions practise rituals that are essentially similar, the beliefs that underpin them vary considerably. It is quite likely that this observation first led me to examine rituals beyond their strictly religious contexts, although it has never been my intention to sever rituals either from their broader social framework or their phenomenological expression.

RITUAL AS HUMAN BEHAVIOUR

There is one approach where religious context is of little use in the study of rituals, that is, when they are considered from the angle of ethology. Rituals are first and foremost a biological reality specific to higher social animals. We have known for some time that socially higher mammals have developed their own rituals when faced with certain kinds of events. Dolphins, for instance, have funerary rituals. The same is true of wolves, foxes, elephants, chimpanzees and others. A wolf pack howls together to establish internal structure, territorial limits as well as simply to experience the pleasure of harmonizing together as a group to strengthen their social bonds. Most of these mammals have greeting rituals – very elaborate ones in the case of apes. It would even appear that chimpanzees enjoy complex rituals around sacred trees, including stone throwing and associated stone tumuli (Kühl *et al.* 2016). Regardless of their precise purpose, it is clear that these animals adopted such behaviours because they are beneficial for them from an evolutionary point of view. These animals' instincts drive them to concentrate their energies on activities advantageous for survival. In this regard, we identify three aspects of animal ritualization: their rituals are collective, experienced as something good, and serve diverse purposes, all of which are relevant for the survival of the species. Undoubtedly, the same holds for the origins of human rituals.

Since we inherited ritualizing from our primate ancestors and share the practice with many other higher social mammals, at first glance it might appear that ritual represents a form of non-verbal or pragmatic language. However, in the case of humans, who developed a form of verbal language that delivers a story, the non-verbal language conveyed by rituals is intrinsically coupled with storytelling and meaning, to the point where these two aspects cannot be separated. Even in the simplest rituals, such as non-formal greetings rites, verbal communication underlies the gestures.

RITUAL AND WAYS OF BEING-IN-THE WORLD

It is easy to regard ritual as a religious or political phenomenon without considering its roots within the animal world and its non-verbal communication. We might say that religions and elaborate political structures eventually emerged (among other things) in the wake of the conjunction between rituals, their social shaping and their functional stories (that is to say, myths). As we will see below, animism is not a religion in the usual sense of the term, but a way of 'being-in-the-world' that is no more religious than our own modern relation to our surroundings. These two ways of being-in-the-world are in many ways very different indeed, if only because animism lays no claim to have any control over our world.

From the ethological viewpoint (and even the biological sense), rituals are a privileged means for group self-regulation through attachment and consequent emotional attunement. When a mother takes her baby in her arms to soothe her, the mother helps the child regulate her emotions. When an animal pack or a human tribe performs a ritual (all those in attendance participate in one way or another), they attain analogous emotional regulation. That is, the group attains a state of homeostasis that is controlled by the parasympathetic vagal ventral branch of the autonomic nervous system, as described in Stephen Porges' groundbreaking polyvagal theory (2011). Among humans, this kind of ritualization may be very down to earth: what is known as good manners and signs of politeness include simple greeting rituals that serve to regulate society. When strangers meet, they naturally refrain from spontaneously expressing reciprocal fear and hostility. Instead, they make an effort to give a good first impression. What passes for ordinary politeness has a deep and powerful effect on regulating emotions and thus on society at large. A society that loses such rites is likely to be more at risk of falling into chaos.

While the study of human rituals as a biological reality should justifiably be considered outside the context of 'religion' in the modern sense, this does not hold true for the study of the archaic rituals that can be found among hunter-gatherers, nor for the remains of rituals that survived across the centuries within some isolated rural societies, notably in mountainous areas. As we will see, what matters here is our understanding of the place of narrative in these rituals, while the narrative content itself remains secondary. The narrative content is based on myth, yet it is, in fact, the narrative's function that allows it to be considered as a myth. What some may call 'religion' among extremely archaic societies is no more and no less than the expression of how the tribe's members experience the world, individually and collectively. The relationship of these ancient societies with their world can be compared to the way modern societies perceive the cosmos through technology and the experimental sciences. Although this relationship with the world is deprived of ritual expression, and differs from that of ancient societies in other aspects as well, neither the ancient nor the modern relationship with the world can be considered religious in the traditional sense of the term. Both relationships constitute an experience of reality that is perceived as a totality present within the whole universe. Humans belong to an experience of this reality that is deprived of a radically alien (or 'transcendent') principle. It is difficult to speak here of 'religion' as it is understood now since the triumph of the two universal monotheisms. There is no continuity between the two contexts: monotheism seems to address the same fundamental questions as do other forms of religions, but the latter never respond in a dualistic way (Augé 2008). The cosmos is not an external principle for the society that celebrates rituals that give the world meaning.

THE ELEMENT OF TIMELESSNESS IN RITUAL

Through rituals, humans participate collectively in a cyclical dynamic that is, so to speak, timeless. This particular human experience of reality, that of being-in-and-of-the-world, is perceived as occurring in a privileged way during ritual. But it is experienced in a particular place and time: here and now. The perception of the world then is experienced as something that is shared with the community and with each person individually. This is true on the rational level as well as on the emotional and somatic levels; the empowering and healing dynamic of being immersed in one's own 'here and now' should be noted. Although reality is then perceived in a peculiar manner, the focus of this perception is no less real than what may be apprehended daily in the ordinary human experience of the real world. This hidden reality is not radically different from visible reality. Contrary to what monotheisms describe as a transcendent reality, the reality hidden behind the animistic world does not go beyond sensorial experience. Nor does it coincide with the unknown, which is challenged by the modern scientific perception of the world. These two orientations are poles apart: while the modern scientific mind strives for a rational unveiling of its object (the observed), the animist seeks to transform the subject (the observer). To the animist, the hidden dimension of reality that is apprehended through ritual only becomes perceptible in these privileged moments. Thus, human experience then appears to be endowed with a unique and noteworthy quality. Through ritual, the dull veil of everyday life is rent. A human being perceives himself, existentially, as a member of a community and a universe that exceeds his cognitive capacities in many aspects, but to which he fully belongs. This privileged existential experience obtained through ritual is by its very nature deeply transforming.

THE HUMAN NEED FOR RITUAL

The incompatibility of these conflicting orientations has tempted many to look for the origins of ritual in what they believe to be an archaic mentality. In this respect, Freud's approach is emblematic (1959 [1907], pp.117–127). Rituals are akin to what he describes in his vocabulary as an obsessional neurosis. Freud saw the origins of ritual in what he believed to be the universal human need for shelter from *Angst* (which implies that he believed all humans are exposed by nature to anxiety disorders). According to Freudian mythology, collective rituals are linked to repression, through guilt and the fear of punishment, of sexual and murderous drives that supposedly threaten social cohesion. Ritual supposedly circumscribes *Angst*, thus inhibiting people's need to develop an individual neurosis. However, in as much as it appeases *Angst*, it also nourishes it. More recently, Jaak Panksepp and Lucy Biven, working from a mostly neurological perspective, hypothesized that religious rituals may be part of a codified expression of a stress response that is produced by a frustrated 'seeking' emotional system, called 'autoshaping' (2012, p.116). They suggest that primitive religious rituals might thus have been born out of a systematized emotional drive that pushes a person suffering from frustration stress to repeat the same gesture over and over in the hope that at one point a tangible positive outcome might ensue (or, we might add, simply to soothe the nervous system). Of course, according to these authors, religion cannot be reduced to this aspect. In agreement with Thandeka (2009), they believe that one driving force behind human religions is 'our affective nature, especially our desperate need for nurturance and understanding, to ward off grief through community' (Panksepp and Biven 2012, p.116). This seems to be a more promising path.

RITUALS BEFORE CIVILIZATION

It should be noted that these considerations about ritual are not based on a direct study of the history and of the practice of rituals. Regarding the conclusions drawn by Panksepp and Biven, one suspects that they may have confused archaic rituals and magic/sorcery, a much later phenomenon (Augé 1975). Sorcery and the claim to hold magical powers reveal an assertion of dominance by humans upon the cosmic forces from which they feel relatively independent. Through gestures and speech, sometimes performed individually, the participant believes that these forces may be bound, to some extent, to his will. It represents an inchoative technological assertion, proper to more 'advanced' societies, while archaic rituals, as opposed to magic, manifest humans' experience of the world and an individual's relationship to the communities to which he belongs.

In this respect, the advent of the 'religious' in the modern sense, that is to say, the experience of a somehow transcendent reality, unfolded while social structures were becoming more and more complex. The dawn of social stratifications and of chiefdoms was mirrored in a corresponding inflation of complex and inegalitarian rituals, such as the funeral of a chief (Hayden 2013). Later, with the advent of agriculture, humans developed a new relationship with nature, thus loosening the bond between humans and their ecosystem. This relationship, based more on power balance and control, was more alien to the universe upon which humans depend.

GESTURE AND WORD

The very transformation of human rituals that mirror the cultural changes of societies fits into an aggregate of mutations that radically sets the evolving human behaviour apart from that of other mammals. Furthermore, as mentioned above, most human rituals take place, in varying proportion, through both gestures and words. This conjunction also differentiates human rituals from those of other mammals. The richness of human speech is intrinsically correlated with conscious thinking and with the unique cognitive faculty of our neocortex. However, this human specificity remains relative, since gesture and word cannot be opposed. Word itself is a bodily action. Even if in this case conscious intentionality does not reach a comparable degree, other mammals also use signs to carry out ritual. Therefore, on the one hand, human rituals require non-verbal language that constitutes their backbone. On the other hand, they require a faculty of perceiving the world as exterior to themselves. The latter is brought forth from our consciousness of this world, as well as from our consciousness of another 'self' to whom we speak. As a result, community is built upon one's individual self and this other 'self', or these other 'selves'. This is why the philosopher of religions, Gerard van der Leeuw (1890–1950), in his masterpiece *Religion in Essence and Manifestation* (1938), could claim that ritual is nothing but an action driven by a word and that reflects the being-in-the-world of every human.

Rituals are indeed carried out through signs, and what they represent brings about meaning: we may use the term 'symbols' here. Actually, the force of rituals relies largely on the rightness of the symbol. The power that some symbols wield over human emotions is quite remarkable. In fact, rituals depend on powerful symbols, such as the assembly, the common meal, the greeting, dramaturgical staging... However, as far as their purpose is concerned, rituals operate first on the somatic and emotional level in order to restore and heighten the social bond with the same kind of positive outcome for everyone. Humans, like all social animals, but more than any other due to the unique length of their growth to maturity, cannot survive without this bond. In sum, human rituals make use of reason and meaning, but their aim goes deeper than that. The finality of ritual remains fundamentally emotional and communal; the benefit of the species is at stake.

STRENGTHENING SOCIAL BONDS

Even the actual topic of the verbal exchange of a conversation does not matter that much in this respect. The deepest purpose for talking among humans is to maintain and enhance their social bonds. Hunter-gatherers spend an enormous amount of time in chat... It is, in fact, the simplest human mechanism at our disposal of fostering a peaceful social bond.

Chimpanzees thrive under a hierarchical structure, and have a tendency to uphold social peace in a rather brutal fashion. Bonobos make the most of sexuality. Humans, on the other hand, resort to talking. The topic of the chat matters little. What matters is the all-important non-verbal exchange lying beneath the chat, but which is not supported without the friendly verbal exchange.

From this point of view, friendly small talk is already an inchoative form of ritual. When we go beyond the formal aspect of ritual, and consider its emotional purpose, both communal and individual, should we restrict ourselves to thinking of rituals only as the non-verbal language society uses for collective and individual communication? I was leaning in that direction when I exposed the biological roots of ritual shared by the other higher social mammals. However, it would seem that, within the human context, both sides must be considered: the non-verbal and the fully narrative language. Moreover, we cannot overlook the fact that human rituals come about within a collective narrative from which they are distinct but to which they are connected at the same time. The human emotions that are enhanced by ritual are not cut off from the narratives to which they somehow belong. These narratives bestow emotional meaning upon the collective destiny of the group and of its members. In other words, ritual provides an affective bond wrought through a common identity. Not only do rituals allow a human being to experience his own self within the 'here and now', and to experience the other with whom he shares his being – his collective identity – but, therefore, who he is himself.

It has been shown that being aware of one's affiliation to a particular collective history and being conscious of belonging to a common narrative are paramount to an individual's mental equilibrium. We have the example of the situation of disintegrating Canadian First Nations communities, where the suicide rate among young people is astonishingly high, not to mention other social issues, notably addiction – a mechanism that helps people cope with the loss of personal integration to society (Alexander 2008). In contrast, other indigenous communities where young people still feel part of the history of their nation do not suffer from these high rates of youth suicide. The youth in the latter group receive a sense of self through the traditional stories told by their elders and the rituals performed upon them. They feel part of a broader narrative, into which their own stories fit (Lewis 2015, pp.202-203). It appears obvious that integrating and assimilating a collective narrative takes place naturally through rituals.

Collective narrative is brought forth through ritual, and the latter is vivified by the narrative's dynamic. One need only be exposed to rituals deprived of their meaning to acknowledge that intimate link. This happens when discrepancy is too great between the extinct group that wrought the rituals long ago and its modern heirs who live in a totally different form of society. These rituals are dead gestures and dead words – unless, of course, the very simplicity of the symbols allows the ritual to retain some vestige of their former power, or unless the new society which received them endows the rituals with fresh, more suitable meanings.

Last but not least, another essential feature specific to human rituals is that they unfold across a wide range of configurations: from the simplest ritual to the most elaborate, from the most familiar to the most extraordinary. A ritual may be structured around a simple everyday gesture such as the sharing of a meal – one of the most essential acts of human sociability – as well as on a collective trance or the fury of a wild transgressive festival. Such rituals, as contrasting as they may seem, share a deep connection with the fundamental unity of human social activity that thrives on affective interactions and the sharing of signs.

COLLECTIVE DYNAMISM

This collective dynamism is universal. It is palpable in seasonal cycles, and, at the other end of the spectrum (although also part of the cycle of life and death), it vivifies the rites of passage that unfold along the more linear axis of human existence (birth, coming of age, marriage and mourning). It is no less present among the more discrete rituals designed to cope with wounds, diseases and potentially traumatic tragedies. As mentioned before, the somatic tools at our disposal are numerous.

They may be summed up under 'feast', whether joyful or not that joyful: gathering (a compulsory preamble to any kind of ritual and already a ritual in itself); the meal, drinking or fasting; dance; music; songs; the telling of a story; drawing; perambulation... Some of those tools by their very nature may seem uniquely connected to rituals, such is the case of bodily transformation, controlled intoxication, particular kinds of ritual transgression, dramatic staging, masques, ordeals (very often linked to competitive contests), risk-taking and physical feats...

It is precisely during these paroxysmal ritual events that the human being experiences more deeply and genuinely his membership in the group, his being-in-the-world, and the peculiar vital energy by which he is stimulated in those moments when he enters or brushes against a modified state of consciousness. Although there are not yet any exhaustive studies of the value of the dissociation induced by trance (or near to trance) states, we already know that it can be beneficial. These paroxysmal experiences are what early cultures describe as the intrusion of the vivifying chaos within the necessary, but ultimately deadly, order of the world. This chaos is the world of the spirits, whose cyclical coming and going in our world is staged by various symbolical representations of the savage spirits of the wilderness – both threatening and beneficial. A case in point is the European woodwose, a mythical wild man figure in medieval art and lore (Hell 1994).[1] These characters constitute one of the central figures in the universal phenomenon among archaic cultures known in the West since the Middle Ages as the 'carnival' (Gaignebet 1974). The essayist Roger Caillois was one of the first to understand this relationship (I translate): 'one returns [during festivities] to the creative Chaos, to the *rudis indigestaque moles* [raw and muddled mass], whence the organized universe has been born and would be born again' (Caillois 1939 [2008], p.287).[2]

---

[1] See also other works by Hell: Hell, B. (1999) *Possession et chamanisme, les maîtres du désordre.* Paris: Flammarion; and (2002) *Le Tourbillon des génies. Au Maroc avec les Gnawa.* Paris: Flammarion.

[2] See especially Chapter IV, reprinted in 2008 in *Œuvres.* Paris: Gallimard, pp.263–288.

CONCLUSION: RITUAL IN FRAGMENTED MODERN SOCIETIES

At this point in my journey, however, I face an obstacle. A significant number of human rituals were devised while societies were becoming stratified. Thus they convey elements that are definitely traumatic for those upon whom they are performed. Rites of initiation such as the various forms of female genital mutilation come to mind. Not to mention ritual rapes, such as the oral sex brutally enforced by their elders upon the young Papuasian Baruyas tribesmen during their warrior initiation ritual with the purpose of bestowing on them the elders' manly power (Godelier 1982). Recent widows are ritually raped in order to purify their bodies of evil spirits in central African cultures, notably in Kenya (Waard and Ernst 2006).[3]

Incomparably less brutal, but nevertheless meaningful here, are the humiliating 'ragging' rituals inflicted upon young pupils in boarding schools (Scaer 2005, pp.127–128). All these traumatic rituals induce pathological feelings of anxiety, anger, dissociation and lack of empathy. As such, they are quite remote from parasympathetic homeostasis – although efficient tightly structured societies somehow manage to reduce the emotional impact of these customs. In many cases, it seems that they are the result of deliberate techniques (albeit empirical, of course) designed to produce implacable warriors or submissive spouses… Thus, ever since the advent of the first warlike hierarchical societies, we have been living in a milieu that seems out of tune from our deeply collaborative human biology. Such an evolutionary twist encourages a handful of 'domineering' humans to treat people they have power over as if they were sub-human. This twist was formidably amplified during the Neolithic era. The ultimate stage of this evolutionary mutation until now, the industrial/mercantile consumerist societies, goes so far as to set up humans in competition against each other at the very heart of their own 'society' (if we may still call it such). The collaborative nature of the human species seems thus to be challenged head on. Such dysfunction within human communities creates a need for

---

3   See notably Chapter 12, 'Abuse of Older Women.'

social overcompensation, to the point where the less privileged members of these societies may be described as being overwhelmed by a continual state of 'stress dyshomeostasis'. That is to say, their nervous systems oscillate continually between parasympathetic dissociative freeze and excessive activation of the sympathetic system, instead of oscillating smoothly from one branch to the other of the autonomous nervous system.[4] Partly, at least, rituals mirror this evolution by becoming inegalitarian and cruel, or even both, that is, when they don't simply wither and die since they have become meaningless. In the wake of these ritual mutations, individual members of these non-collaborative 'societies' often assume behaviours that echo to some degree the inegalitarian paradigm. For this reason, they seem less or differently receptive to the efficacious power of rituals.

It may very well be that, within our consumerist and individualistic worlds, in the midst of a social body under threat of disaggregation, we are hence less receptive than ever to the dynamic of rituals. Since modern societies consider themselves to be by and large secular, we have no choice but to consider modern rituals as set apart from religion. However, there aren't many rituals left. And the tales that should come along with them have vanished. This might be one of the reasons why rituals are so difficult to envision outside their religious context. A ritual naturally belongs to the community. It has become hard to find a tightly knit community that is not pre-modern. Social cohesion is now only experienced within elective communities, such as sports communities, or indeed, religious bodies that are more or less counter-cultural. This experience is very peculiar, quite different from what we might experience within the harmonious communities among which our ancestral rituals were developed. As for the new rituals that have been crafted and still thrive nowadays in

---

4   To be precise, instead of gentle oscillations between the vagal ventral branch (corresponding to peaceful social interactions) of the parasympathetic system and suitable activations of the sympathetic, the state of continual disrupted homeostasis corresponds to extreme oscillations between the vagal dorsal branch ('freeze') of the parasympathetic system and a hyper-activated sympathetic system ('fight'/'flight'). Consequently, the hypothalamic–pituitary–adrenal axis is dysregulated, which comes along with a great many biological overcompensations. See Porges (2011) and Scaer (2005).

our consumerist, hedonistic and individualist (but gregarious) societies, such as the winter and summer sales, or the American 'Black Friday', it takes a huge intellectual effort to consider them somehow related to the rituals of rural or archaic societies. Maybe sporting events, such as competitive matches, are one of their last vestiges, since the collective, festive, meaningful and ordeal-like aspects persist to a great degree.

When I reflect on contemporary rituality, I see an internal contradiction. Within a society motivated by selfish drives, contained through a balance of power, and deprived of any strong affective bonds, rituals tend to convey the negation of their own finality. Present-day rituals reflect this ambiguous rapport to social bonding. We need to explore how rituals and their corresponding narratives unfold among the new 'tribes', for want of a better word, since the factions arising from our modern 'societies' do not really resemble the concept associated with the word 'tribe' – that manage to flourish at the heart of our own fragmented social body. On the next leg of my journey, it would be interesting to study how ad hoc rituals, such as non-religious weddings or funerals, survive today among the informal communities that benefit from them. In particular, I should like to examine how these rituals function to bring people together and might help provide a common narrative of the origins and destiny of humankind.

REFERENCES

Alexander, K.B. (2008) *The Globalization of Addiction: A Study in Poverty of the Spirit*. New York: Oxford University Press.

Augé, M. (1975) *Théories des pouvoirs et idéologie*. Paris: Gallimard.

Augé, M. (2008) *Génie du paganisme*. Repères. Paris: Gallimard.

Caillois, R. (1939 [2008]) *L'Homme et le sacré: Mythes et religions*. Paris: Gallimard.

Durkheim, E. (1995 [1912]) *The Elementary Forms of Religious Life*. Trans. K.E. Fields. New York: The Free Press. [Original published in French 1912.]

Freud, S. (1907) 'Obsessive actions and religious practices.' In J. Strachey (ed. and trans.) (1959) *The Standard Edition of the Complete Psychological Works of Sigmund Freud*. Vol. 9, p.115–127. London: The Hogarth Press.

Gaignebet, C. (1974) *Le Carnaval: Essai de mythologie populaire*. Paris: Payot.

Godelier, M. (1982) *La Production des grands hommes: Pouvoir et domination masculine chez les Baruyas de Nouvelle-Guinée.* Paris: Flammarion.

Hayden, B. (2013) *Naissance de l'inégalité. L'invention de la hiérarchie.* Paris: Éditions du CNRS.

Hell, B. (1994) *Le Sang noir: Chasse, forêt et mythe de l'homme sauvage en Europe.* Paris: Flammarion.

Kühl, H.S. *et al.* (2016) 'Chimpanzee accumulative stone throwing.' *Scientific Reports 6,* 22219, doi: 10.1038/srep22219

Lewis, M. (2015) *The Biology of Desire. Why Addiction is not a Disease.* New York: Public Affairs.

Panksepp, J. and Biven, L. (2012) *The Archaeology of Mind: Neuroevolutionary Origins of Human Emotion.* New York: Norton and Company.

Porges, S.W. (2011) *The Polyvagal Theory: Neurophysiological Foundations of Emotions, Attachment, Communication and Self-Regulation.* New York: W.W. Norton & Company.

Scaer, R.C. (2005) *The Trauma Spectrum: Hidden Wounds and Human Resiliency.* New York: Norton & Company.

Thandeka (2009) 'Future designs for American liberal theology.' *American Journal of Practical Theology 30,* 1, 72–100.

van der Leeuw, G. (1938) *Religion in Essence and Manifestation: A Study in Phenomenology.* London: Macmillan. [Originally published in German 1933.]

Waard, J. and Ernst, L. (2006) *Broken Bodies, Broken Dreams: Violence Against Women Exposed.* Nairobi: Office for the Coordination of Humanitarian Affairs (OCHA)/Integrated Regional Information Networks (IRIN).

3

THE NEUROPHYSIOLOGY OF RITUAL AND TRAUMA

CULTURAL IMPLICATIONS

Robert C. Scaer

Rituals exist in virtually all human societies. They occur in many forms and involve almost all of the elements and categories of human behaviour. Although primarily associated with religions and prescribed political and social events, such as marriage and funerals, schools and ceremonies, they are the substance of most human interactions. They define much of the content of how we relate to each other.

Ritualization represents a broad spectrum of human behaviour and encompasses a vast variety of specific and mutually accepted behaviours. These include singing, chanting, dancing, drumming, making certain gestures, wearing of specific costumes, partaking of certain foods, drinks, drugs and touching special objects. Some cultures practise the induction of trance states for healing and bonding purposes.

The complexity of rituals depends to a certain extent on whether they occur in a traditional or modern culture. Although in many complex urban cultures rituals appear to serve defined religious and celebratory events, in many indigenous cultures they are specifically aimed at tribal bonding, rites of passage and actual physical healing. Tribal shamanism is an example of the use of ritual to heal physical and emotional afflictions.

Although these practices have declined with the relentless assimilation of indigenous cultures into modern societies, shamanic practices remain a widely used form of healing in many parts of the world. These practices employ the manipulation of the sensory experiences of the individual as a means of actually inducing a state of physical healing. Through ritual, the visual, auditory, vestibular and tactile stimulation regulates, induces, promotes and establishes a state of what one might call autonomic homeostasis.

Unresolved life trauma leads to disruption of autonomic homeostasis when the motor and sensory experiences of the traumatic event are retained in procedural memory. When this happens, any external cues related to that event may provoke the emergence of conditioned motor patterns and sensations much as they were experienced during the traumatic event. This is the physical substrate for what we call trauma, or Post-traumatic Stress Disorder (PTSD). Recognition of the physical base for trauma has led to the emergence of what is often referred to now as somatic psychotherapy. Since the *Diagnostic and Statistical Manual of Mental Disorders* (3rd edition) (DSM-III) definition of PTSD came out, trauma therapies have basically relied on cognitive and exposure techniques. Controlled studies, based on cognitive-behaviouralism and on forms of intense exposure, have indeed shown improvement of the arousal and reminiscence symptoms of PTSD, but they have been much less effective for the avoidance criteria.[1]

In the 1990s, therapists specializing in trauma treatments began to recognize many symptoms that appeared later in the course of treatment that did not fit with the specific diagnosis of PTSD. Researchers, in particular Bessel van der Kolk and Judith Herman, introduced the concept of

---

[1] Definitions of PTSD in DSM-III and DSM-IV, the standard classification of mental disorders used by mental health professionals in the US, depend on conceptual definitions of events or stressors sufficient to produce three main criteria for traumatic symptoms: re-experiencing, arousal and avoidance. DSM-5 proposes four distinct diagnostic clusters instead of three: re-experiencing, avoidance, negative cognitions and mood, and arousal. It is unfortunate that PTSD remains classified as an event-triggered condition and that the DSM criteria still fail to take into account scientific data by Scaer, Levine, van der Kolk and others which demonstrates that 'the spectrum of responses...clearly varies widely between individuals' (Scaer 2001, p.134).

complex, or late, trauma, falling under a new designation of Disorders of Extreme Stress, Not Otherwise Specified (DESNOS). Many of the symptoms of DESNOS suggested personality traits, and particularly somatic symptoms, designated as Somatization Disorders. Although not universally recognized, these findings indicated that the body and its dysfunction played a substantial role in the perpetuation of symptoms in victims of trauma.

Another important discovery involves the observation that trauma as a syndrome involves a corruption of memory, not only under the DSM category of reminiscence, but also of procedural, or somatic, memory. Procedural memory is the means by which we learn skills or tasks involving body functions, such as athletics, musical performance, dance and the like. Just as flashbacks relate to the cue-induced emergence of explicit, emotional memory, a myriad of somatic symptoms, both visceral and skeletal, reflect implicit, procedural memory for what the body tried unsuccessfully to do or perform to protect the trauma victim. Researchers, in particular van der Kolk, realized that extinguishing these post-traumatic procedural memories was essential for the healing of trauma.

With the development of Francine Shapiro's Eye Movement Desensitization and Reprocessing (EMDR), the field of somatic psychotherapy was reinforced. Peter Levine's Somatic Experiencing (SE), Gary Craig's Emotional Freedom Techniques (EFT, or Energy Therapy), David Grand's Brainspotting (BSP) and David Berceli's Trauma Releasing Exercises (TRE) have also been developed in recent years. Each of these therapies was 'discovered', mostly by chance, when a physical process, experience or act suddenly resulted in a favourable therapeutic response in the client(s). These new treatments open up a whole new field of trauma therapy that involves and incorporates the body. Interest in this field is spreading rapidly among trauma therapists across the world. Many of these techniques are now under intense study and research to document their efficacy. At this point, only EMDR has built up a solid scientific basis in controlled research studies.

There are compelling reasons to pursue this emerging field of therapy, which includes frankly ritualistic elements. Many researchers acknowledge that PTSD or trauma has its basis in fear conditioning modelled primarily in animal studies. Pavlovian conditioning is a prime example of fear conditioning; all of the stimuli on which the conditioning works are based on procedural memory related to survival. Therefore, healing from trauma must include extinction techniques involving somatic procedural memory. The body is basically the primary reservoir for Criteria 1 of the DSM-IV.[2] The amygdala is the source of fear conditioning, the centre most susceptible to kindling,[3] the neuro-sensitization process that defined the evolution of PTSD over time. Stored procedural memories are the cue-based engine for propagating kindling and maintaining the symptom complex of PTSD and DESNOS. Under this model, trauma cannot be cured by words and cognitive processing alone. The sensory experiences of the body must be introduced in the ritualistic extinction of the brain/body traumatic connection.

INHIBITING THE SOURCE OF FEAR

A method needs to be incorporated that inhibits/down-regulates the amygdala while gently engaging explicit conscious and implicit procedural memories of the traumatic event. When analysed, all of the primary somatic trauma therapies possess these features: attunement, bi-hemispheric brain-alternating stimulation, ritual and empowerment.

---

2 Editor's note: Scaer criticizes the antiquated and inadequate definitions of trauma in the DSM-IV because it ignores the pervasive influence of life trauma (2005, p.2). While the DSM-IV was replaced in 2013 by the DSM-5, it is widely held that the definitions of trauma in the DSM-5 represent no improvement over the previous diagnostic system (van der Kolk 2014, p.165).

3 The kindling effect or syndrome was discovered in the 1960s by neuroscientists who noted that stimulation of certain neuronal centres could affect adjacent regions of the brain, in particular, in the amygdala. They referred to this neurosensitization as 'kindling', because it resembles the way in which wood kindling sets nearby logs afire (Scaer 2005, pp.62–64). People who have experienced life traumas are easily sensitized to virtually any sensory input known as a Sensory Processing Disorder (SPD). The most sensitive sense to kindling is smell. After repeated stimulation, the brain may register certain smells as a threat, engaging the process of sensory hypersensitivity in an effort to protect them (Scaer 2012, pp.119–121). This process may be considered a form of negative neuroplasticity.

The Neurophysiology of Ritual and Trauma

Attunement[4]

Somatic techniques involve intimate mutual participation in a process that incorporates physical acts/rituals/interaction. Touch per se is not the only source. Rather, the mutual performance and the physical response to guided actions are incorporated in the process. All of these techniques require attuned interaction – verbal (auditory), visual and tactile. All of these processes facilitate the social bond between therapist and patient, a state of attunement that is required in any therapeutic technique.

This is quite analogous to the eye-to-eye mutual attunement of the mother to the infant while feeding/nursing or play. This attunement promotes the development of the brain that regulates the autonomic nervous system and the limbic/emotional brain. These areas include the right orbito-frontal cortex (OFC), the anterior cingulate gyrus and the insula. These brain centres down-regulate the amygdala when the threat is not sufficient to elicit the fight/flight response.

This process also relates to the attunement of members of a family or tribe generated by the rituals of rites of passage, celebration or healing, potentiated by the presence of the tribal elder or shaman. Attunement is a neurophysiological process that actually enhances growth and function of portions of the brain's right frontal hemisphere – the OFC – which facilitates effective communication and emotional connection between mother and infant as well as between members of the family and tribe. The optimal development of this brain area is essential for sustained resilience in the face of trauma or negative life events.

Bi-hemispheric brain alternating stimulation

We know though brain-imaging techniques that specific areas of the brain 'light up' with specific activities. When a person perceives, remembers or addresses a traumatic event, the right limbic system – the part that deals with threatening experiences – 'lights up', and the left prefrontal cortex (thinking brain) and Broca's area (speech expression) 'shut down'.

---

4   In this context, 'attunement' refers to the process of being in tune with another human being or group. It implies an understanding of what is needed or wanted by that person or group.

60 Emerging Ritual in Secular Societies

Conversely, when we are meditating (left frontal cortex) or verbalizing non-traumatic information (Broca's area, left frontal lobe), the right limbic system (arousal) is relatively shut down. Alternating stimulation of the left-right cerebral hemispheres, counting (left) and humming (right) hemispheres, and following a visual stimulus from right-to-left, and in-and-out are all methods of inhibiting the right limbic area. These tasks inhibit and down-regulate the amygdala through the patient/therapist bond, and the activation of both hemispheres, much like the process of attunement (see Figure 3.1).

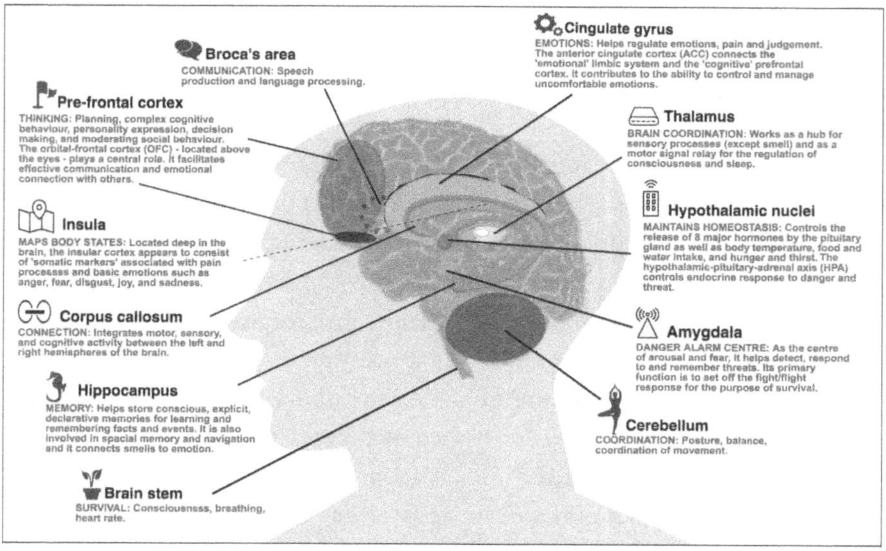

Figure 3.1. The human brain

Ritual

Ritual may be defined as a common practice, developed and approved by a group, congregation, tribe, culture or society, which has been given special meaning, often celebrates events, is used as a rite of passage or actually has healing implications. The commonality of the ritual and its acceptance by the group give it special neurophysiological features and powers, which promote healing from trauma. Indigenous tribes engage in rituals whose purpose is bonding between its members or healing the injured/sick member. Trance states accompany this process. Trance is not dissociation,[5] but a state that is closely allied with meditation, during which the left dorso-lateral prefrontal cortex is activated, while also inhibiting the amygdala. Trance is induced with hypnosis, a well-documented technique for healing trauma. Indigenous societies use a variety of techniques to achieve trance states. Drumming, chanting sacred songs, dancing in tightly proscribed patterns, even self-mutilation with proscribed penetration of the skin – all these activities promote a trance state, and therefore promote healing. In more 'advanced' societies, rituals are mostly practised in religious settings, but they have these same postural, vocal, consumption and environmental specificities. Rituals practised in many secular organizations in advanced cultures also reflect these specificities. All contexts profit from the mutual benefits of social bonding.

Empowerment

Freeze/dissociation in trauma is dependent on a state of helplessness. Helplessness, in turn, is the required state for the freeze state to occur. Many of these techniques involve repetitive statements of self-empowerment that also contribute to the ritual nature of the event. Empowerment, essential for the healing of trauma, extinguishes the post-traumatic procedural memories that perpetuate the trauma cycle. Empowerment can be achieved through a wide variety of techniques: imagery, mantras about one's own power and even physical replication of acts of self-defence. Many of these empowering acts are part of the rituals in indigenous tribes, as noted above.

A number of these techniques also address the issue of what might be called our 'perceptual surround'. Humans, as with all animals, possess an unconscious awareness of events within the entire 360 degrees of our sensory perception. This allows us to function in all matter of physical activity. This 'perceptual surround' will be disrupted by the sensory

---

5   In psychology, 'dissociation' refers to a mental defence mechanism that involves a process wherein certain thoughts or mental processes may be compartmentalized in an effort to avoid or reduce emotional stress caused by traumatic life experiences.

experience in a traumatic event, and result in demonstrable sensitivity to unresolved threat/trauma within that area of perception, a state that can be described as a 'boundary rupture'. Female victims of sexual abuse and soldiers involved in prolonged combat may exhibit arousal and anxiety to events occurring behind them, out of the range of their visual perception. Gradual, titrated[6] exposure to that sensitized region of perceptual arousal, provided in a measured, ritualistic manner, may 'extinguish' the sensitivity to this area of unconscious threat.

Trauma is often perceived as a primarily sympathetic nervous system state, an over-sensitive fight/flight response. Although the sympathetic nervous system is activated with exposure to threat or danger, the parasympathetic nervous system is brought into play if self-defence and flight are both impossible. The freeze, or immobility, response, a state of immobility and paralysis, ensues. The freeze state is characterized by the slowing down of pulse and blood pressure, and the activation of the gut and bladder, a parasympathetic state. Emptying of the gut or bladder reflects the profound parasympathetic state of the freeze. Soldiers in combat are prone to emptying their bowels and bladder when threatened in a state of relative helplessness. Analgesia from release of endorphins also occurs. In the wild, prey animals will enter a state of flaccid immobility and analgesia. In circumstances where the prey animal leaves the prey, it will emerge from its immobility, and tremble or move in a fashion replicating the act of flight. This 'freeze discharge' will extinguish the procedural memory for the entire traumatic event, and render the animal restored from the trauma of the attack.

If the 'freeze discharge' does not occur, procedural memory for all of the sensory experiences will be stored in the motor centres of the brain and will be triggered by any experiences that are cues to the traumatic event in day-to-day life. This exposure will be manifested in pain and

---

6   'Titration' is a term used in scientific studies to describe a process or method in which small amounts of reactive agents are added together in a test solution. In this context, the term refers to a therapeutic approach that involves exposing patients to emotional issues or situations slowly and in small doses. Peter Levine applies it in his therapy called Somatic Experiencing (SE).

spasm in the muscles used for self-defence, to panic and replication of the freeze. It will also produce unconscious repetitive movement patterns, such as 'tics' that replicate the failed movement patterns of self-defence in a traumatic event. Furthermore, it will be associated with activation of the heart and viscera, with palpitations and irritable bowel complaints. Trauma, therefore, is a profound activation of both sympathetic and parasympathetic nervous systems.

Homeostasis is the optimal state of the autonomic nervous system. Unresolved trauma represents a state of profound loss of homeostasis, the orderly sequential transition between optimal sympathetic/parasympathetic states. In trauma, both sympathetic and parasympathetic states and symptoms occur in excess. Sympathetic symptoms include anxiety and panic, palpitations, insomnia with nightmares, exaggerated startle responses and perspiration. Parasympathetic symptoms include irritable bowel, gastro-oesophageal reflux and chronic fatigue. All of these occur in exaggerated cycles – the antithesis of homeostasis and the orderly transition between sympathetic and parasympathetic states. Healing of trauma is therefore best achieved through therapeutic or cultural exercises that gently activate the conditioned procedural memories of the trauma and the autonomic dysregulation accompanying it in a state of complete safety and harmony, a state where extinction of these procedural memories may be achieved.

The use of ritual in all cultures has many purposes and effects, one of which is healing. In all cases, the function of ritual has its roots in the rewarding and healing functions of the brain. Rites of passage, worship, governance, celebration and virtually all social functions depend on the implicit brain rewards that are associated with these practices. In the case of the resolution and healing of life trauma, ritual may actually be the essential ingredient, although there will most likely be controversy over this within the behavioural science community. The burgeoning growth of 'somatic psychology' regarding trauma may well ensure this connection.

All of these measures of homeostasis are dependent on the interpersonal relationship between the client and the therapist in the therapeutic setting. They also relate to the interpersonal experience in any setting.

Stephen Porges defines the neurophysiology of the interaction of human beings in a social setting as the social engagement system. In his model, homeostasis is dependent on optimal communication between individuals in a fashion that promotes harmony and engagement, primarily through the sensory-motor functions of the organs of the head and neck. Components of several cranial nerves develop together to form the neural substrate of a social engagement system. The nerves that innervate the muscles of eyelid opening (looking), facial muscles (e.g., emotional expression), middle ear muscles (e.g., extracting human voices from background noise), muscles of mastication (e.g., ingestion), laryngeal and pharyngeal muscles (e.g., prosody of speech) and head turning (e.g., social gestures and orientation) are essential for non-verbal communication and attunement within the act of bonding throughout the human experience. These functions determine the character and effectiveness of human communication, and are a critical factor in the process of healing through ritual. They enhance the efficacy of communication, and are thus an essential contributor to the effectiveness of ritual within members of a society or tribe. They also promote the effectiveness of maternal/infant bonding, and if successful, the growth and effective function of the right OFC in the nursing infant, providing a powerful source of homeostatic resiliency throughout the lifetime. The purpose of rituals that are developed and used by cultures and societies depend to a significant degree on this neurophysiological process.

SOMATIC APPROACHES TO THE TREATMENT OF TRAUMA

The efficacy of somatic methods of treating trauma is also dependent on the effectiveness of the social engagement provided by the therapist. These techniques depend on the ritualistic application of attunement, bi-hemispherical sensory stimulation and empowerment.

EMDR (Eye Movement Desensitization and Reprocessing)

EMDR was the first prototypic technique of somatic psychotherapy. Francine Shapiro developed this technique in the 1980s and set up a network of training and certification programmes for its use. Since then, its use has spread nationally and internationally. It has been studied extensively. The technique involves the patient following a back and forth movement with his or her eyes; the stimulation may be a moving hand, a pointer or lights on a bar. The stimulus can also be provided with alternating bilateral sound or vibration. Statements of self-empowerment are also used. This technique clearly fulfils the criterion of using alternating bilateral cerebral stimulation to 'shut down' the amygdala, and extinguish traumatic memories.

Somatic Experiencing (SE)

Peter Levine developed this technique in the 1990s. He used the ethological theory of the freeze discharge in animals to devise a technique for eliciting this discharge in traumatized human beings. By guided following of the 'felt sense'[7] in the bonding presence of the therapist, the patient is able to access somatic sensations linked to the traumatic experience, a process that prompts the emergence of the self-defensive motor action that was aborted during the traumatic experience. This replication of the failed act of self-defence in a safe setting 'uncouples' or extinguishes the retained procedural memories of the trauma, and heals the patient. In a sense, the brain now perceives that the threat is gone. SE is clearly based on fear extinction. It is a widely accepted form of treatment across the world.

Emotional Freedom Techniques (EFT)

Gary Craig developed EFT, a rather arcane spin-off of Roger Callahan's Thought Field Therapy. The technique generally falls under the category of 'energy medicine', but has largely been applied to the field of trauma therapy. Although the esoteric nature of the technique has made it the subject of fierce criticism by the academic establishment, the methods it uses reflect many of the criteria that I feel are necessary for fear extinction. EFT involves having the patient repeatedly tap acupuncture meridian points on the face and chest with his/her forefinger and middle finger

---

7   The phrase 'felt sense' refers to a subtle or even vague internal bodily awareness.

while repeating a mantra-like phrase of self-empowerment. The patient then rotates the eyes to the right and to the left, hums a few verses of a song, counts from 1–5, and then repeats the humming. Although these admittedly peculiar actions would seem to defy logical function, they do indeed contain the elements that would inhibit the amygdala: empowerment, brain hemispheric crossing (alternating rotation of the eyes, humming to activate the right side, and counting to activate the left), and even ritual. EFT has become a popular adjunctive tool in community-based psychotherapeutic treatment of trauma. Outcome studies of its effectiveness have been quite positive, but controversy still exists in the academic community.

Brainspotting (BSP)

David Grand, one of Shapiro's early trainees, devised this technique. He discovered that by slowing down the alternating visual stimulation he could evoke subtle but reproducible 'somatic responses', usually an eye blink or facial or upper-body twitch. Postulating that these somatic responses represent a perceptual/sensory memory for a traumatic event, he then sets about extinguishing this 'brain spot' through subtle sequential exposure. He has refined the technique by gradually incorporating subtle nuances of arousal in horizontal, vertical and near/far representations of the 'brain spot'. The technique also uses alternating auditory stimuli through earphones during the process. It should be noted that intense attunement is required by the therapist to attain the 'brain spot', a potentially important element for its efficacy.

CONCLUSION

Human beings unwittingly strive to achieve homeostasis, our state of intrinsic emotional and physical wellbeing. We do so through the unconscious trial-and-error search for physical and emotional stability and pleasure. The perceptual rewards for this ideal state of being are profound. Balanced and imbalanced states of autonomic function are associated with positive and negative sensations or 'feelings' that prompt us to seek or avoid such perceptual states. Inevitably, through trial and error, we seek events and procedures that provide the physical and emotional rewards of homeostasis. The most prominent rewards are those that enhance affiliation within the family, group, neighbourhood, tribe, congregation or country. Through trial and error manipulation of rewarding behaviour, we establish rituals that perpetuate the physical and emotional rewards of homeostasis, heal the group's trauma and consolidate the bond that is necessary for perpetuation of homeostasis through affiliation.

REFERENCES

Scaer, R.C. (2001) *The Body Bears the Burden: Trauma, Dissociation and Disease.* New York: The Haworth Medical Press.

Scaer, R.C. (2005) *The Trauma Spectrum: Hidden Wounds and Human Resiliency.* New York: W.W. Norton & Company.

Scaer, R.C. (2012) *8 Keys to Body–Brain Balance.* New York: W.W. Norton & Company.

van der Kolk, B. (2014) *The Body Keeps the Score: Brain, Mind, and Body in the Healing of Trauma.* New York: Viking Books.

PART II

SENSEMAKING IN LIFE EVENTS

4

THE RHYME AND REASON OF RITUALMAKING

Jeltje Gordon-Lennox

Human beings are very resilient. During precarious periods of history, humankind's adaptive capacity is put to the test. As a species we have braved – and so far survived – wars, disasters (natural and human-made), violence and personal betrayals. In the face of uncertainty, ritual contributes to our sense of security by beating time to our natural rhythms, helping us make sense of our world and enhancing our social bonds. The dislocation[1] of modern Western society causes suffering on both public (political, economic, social, cultural, spiritual) and intimate (emotional, sensory, sexual, relational, neuronal) levels. Rarely, if ever, has humankind experienced fragmentation to such an extent. Rarely have people been shielded by so few meaningful social rituals.

This chapter explores how ritual and ritualmaking as social activity – remarkable for how it sustains wellbeing for individuals and society as a whole – meets the unprecedented challenges of multilevel dislocation. I came to ritology through the backdoor as a practitioner. This means that practical experience filters my exploration of ritual theory. As a psychotherapist, I am well placed to see the pain and damage caused by inadequate ritual as well as the sense of joy and rightness when milestones

---

1   In chemistry, the term 'dislocation' refers to irregularities in the fine structure lattice of an otherwise normal crystal. In this context, the word refers to subtle and not so subtle irregularities in the fine structure lattice of modern society.

are appropriately observed. After several years of presiding at religious rites, I left the religious institution to craft secular life event ceremonies. My move from religious to secular ritual was motivated primarily by a desire to meet the growing need for non-religious ceremonies. In the process, I realized that it corresponded to changes in my own experience and thinking. I also learned that ritualmaking has not always been the domain of specialists.

SECULAR RITUAL

While observing people go about their everyday lives, ethologist Ellen Dissanayake noticed that humans everywhere avidly engage in playful, artistic and ritual pursuits. She became convinced that these activities represent a biologically endowed need, and called this compelling and 'deliberately *nonordinary*' activity 'making special' (1992, pp.42–48). Rituals have been invented and reinvented ever since humankind first felt the need to connect events with thoughts and feelings, hopes and fears. Rituals 'are adaptive', affirms Dissanayake, 'not only because they join people together in common cause but because they also relieve anxiety. It is better to have something to do, with others, in times of uncertainty rather than try to cope by oneself or do nothing at all' (2016).

Over the last century, ritual experts led us to believe that all ritual is religious, or at least sacred. Yet religion, like secularism, is just one type of worldview (see Figure 4.1). Anthropologist Mary Douglas insists that secularism is 'an age-old cosmological type, a product of a definable social experience, which need have nothing to do with urban life or modern science [...or] transcendent explanations and powers'; it can turn up in any historical age and locale (cited by Bell 1997, p.200). Anthropologist Talal Asad[2] sees the secular as 'a concept that brings together certain behaviours, knowledges, and sensibilities in modern life' (2003, p.24). Ritual studies scholar 'Catherine M. Bell's profound insight', states her friend Diane Jonte-Pace, 'was that ritual, long thought of as thoughtless

---

2 'The secular is neither continuous with the religious [phase that supposedly preceded it (that is, it is not the latest phase of a sacred origin) nor a simple break from it (that is, it is not the opposite, an essence that excludes the sacred)' (Asad 2003, p.24).

action stripped of context, is more interestingly understood as strategy: a culturally strategic way of acting in the world. Ritual is a form of social activity' (Jonte-Pace 2009, p.vii). As such, ritual is neutral: it has been used to promote love, healing and social cohesion but also to foment war, hatred and racism. How it is used makes it a culturally strategic way of acting in the world.

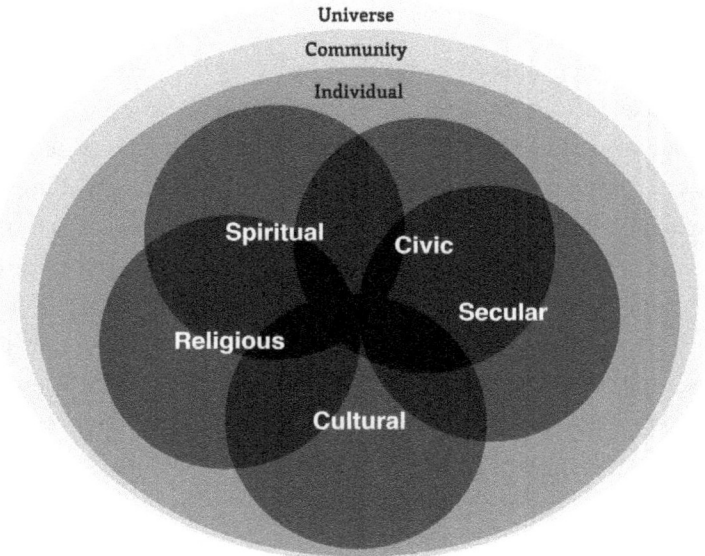

Figure 4.1. Ritual as strategy in context
Ritualizing is a culturally strategic way of acting in the world. Religious and secular rituals are different forms of social activity that can also be spiritual, cultural or even civic. Coherence between the occasion, the context and relationships is *sine qua non* for effective ritualizing.

RITUALIZING IN AN ULTRAMODERN ERA

Whether we live in a megacity or on a small remote island, we must all adapt to urban rhythms and an ever-increasing pace of change. Moreover, society barely functions today as a social entity. Globalization and individualization, the 'free market' and relentless competition have destroyed our sense of belonging to civilized, supportive groups.

French philosopher Frédéric Lenoir dubs our era 'ultramodern',[3] and puts the hazards of accelerated change into historical perspective:

> Humanity took a giant leap at the turn of Palaeolithic and Neolithic ages. These changes affected society, religion, value systems and the way of life; they also touched and transformed the human brain. I'm convinced that what we are living today will generate equally sweeping changes that concern our innermost being. We will not emerge unscathed from these tremendous upheavals... What our ancestors dealt with in a couple millennia, we have to grasp the significance of in a few decades. (2012, p.63)

Only 5000 years ago, spirituality was still inextricably tied to ancient hunter-gatherer traditions. Societal structures were small and for the most part, horizontal. Maintaining relationships within the community and assuming responsibility towards nature are recurrent themes in hunter-gatherer rituals, because they contribute to individual and group self-regulation. Today, too, we function best when our priorities focus on sustaining our relationships with others and nature. Yet this way of functioning is incompatible with complex hierarchical social structures.

Our need for landmarks

Over the last two to three millennia, traditional ties between spiritual and cultural ritual practices crumbled as religious institutions arose capable of absorbing adherents across cultural, political and geographical frontiers. With the verticalization of socio-political structures, participative ritualizing gave way to institutionalized rites. Centralized religions and governments alike placed people in leadership roles to oversee healing, spiritual practice and moral guidance. Recent crises within these hierarchical structures – many of which concern leadership – have contributed to the breakdown of their monopoly on traditional ritual. With the dawn of the ultramodern

---

3   Lenoir (2012) prefers the term 'ultramodern' to 'postmodern' because the latter gives the false impression that we are disenchanted with the myth of progress and the modern process when in fact we are in the midst of an unprecedented acceleration of modernity (critical reason, individualization, globalization).

era, our vertical and horizontal safety zones disappeared. 'We have killed the gods', remarks Lenoir, 'we have abolished or erased our borders. It is within ourselves that we must now find these "safety zones"' (2012, p.64).

Change itself is neither good nor bad: it can bring relief and renewal, but it inevitably implies loss and separation from the familiar. The young, old, sick and injured are most vulnerable. Low adaptive capacity means a high need for the familiar, protection and clear markers in relationships, time and space. The momentum of change today does not take into account our individual and collective need for consistent landmarks, our capacity to adapt, or even the health of our planet.

Technological advances, in particular the internet, fundamentally revolutionize how humankind functions on all levels: social, psychological, economic, cultural, intellectual, spiritual, academic and even neuronal. Young people in particular are bombarded by a host of information they must absorb and sort. This adaptation has a price: as communication with people from around the world is facilitated, warm-hearted face-to-face talk with those around us grows increasingly difficult.

Our need to feel safe

Biophysicist Peter A. Levine,[4] formerly a NASA stress consultant, states: 'Though we as a secular society are deluged with information (much of it stimulating and useful), at the same time, we suffer from a paucity of wisdom and have the desire for more personal warmth, connection and

---

4   Peter A. Levine developed Somatic Experiencing (SE), a naturalistic approach to the treatment of trauma based on the observation that wild prey animals, in spite of being repeatedly threatened, are rarely traumatized. According to Levine, the symptoms of trauma are not caused by the dangerous event itself, but by our reaction to it. The reaction may be a debilitating 'large-T' trauma or a seemingly inconsequential 'small-t' trauma. The symptoms of trauma may arise soon after the event or even much later. They are caused by the residual energy of the reaction when it is not discharged from the body. Levine describes traumatic memories as being implicit and stored in the body and the brain as automatic or 'procedural' sensations, emotions and behaviours. Trauma cannot be cured by advice, drugs or understanding, observes Levine, but it can be 'renegotiated' – rather than relived – by accessing procedural memories. 'Pendulation' is a fundamental SE concept used in resolving implicit traumatic memories. It involves touching on the inner sensations and then learning how to carefully access this 'felt sense' and to tolerate the feelings by noticing that one can survive them (Levine 2015, pp.xv, xvi, 38, 55).

engagement' (2005, p.xvii). Like Lenoir, Levine encourages the building of 'islands of safety' within ourselves to keep from being overwhelmed by the after-effects of highly charged life experiences. He observes that 'whether we are survivors of trauma or simply casualties of Western culture' (2010, p.256) we suffer from what he describes as 'an impairing disconnection from [our] inner sensate compass' (2010, p.355).

Severed contact with our inner sensate compass is experienced as fragmentation or disembodiment. Psychiatrist Bessel van der Kolk explains that when the connections within the brain as well as those between the mind and the body are disrupted through trauma, we become trapped in the emotions and feelings of the past (2014). As survivors of trauma and Western culture we expend inordinate amounts of energy just keeping these sensations under control – usually at the expense of concentration, the ability to memorize and simply pay attention to what is happening around us. Neurologist Robert Scaer describes this frightening experience as 'an aberration of memory' (2001, p.43).[5] The inability to live fully in the present impedes adequate preparation for the future, which in turn wreaks havoc on health and social relationships such as marriages, families and friendships (Scaer 2005, p.152; 2012, p.114).

> **The Book of Changes**
>
> A shock occurs, then there is a tremor caused by fear. This tremor is a good thing because it allows inner gladness and joy to follow. Even if rumbling thunder sows terror a hundred miles around, we remain so calm that we do not interrupt the ceremony by dropping the ritual spoon filled with spicy wine. (Hexagram 51, *I Ching*, late 9th century BCE)

---

5   In the case of trauma, memory imprints (known as 'engrams') are experienced – not as a recurring recollection of a terrible event that happened in the past, but as overwhelming life-threatening physical sensations in the immediate present (Levine 2015, p.7). These physical sensations are ever the more frightening in that they may be tied to events that we do not remember and then triggered without warning by anything, a sudden noise, a smell, a taste, a colour or a tone of voice, usually totally unattached to a conscious memory of an event.

RITUAL AS A SAFE FRAMEWORK FOR EMOTION

Ritualizing life events, in particular weddings and funerals, often evokes potentially destructive memories and feelings. When intense emotions are expressed and harnessed through ritual in a safe setting, they contribute to turning off what Scaer refers to as the 'fear generator' from the past. Ritual thus regularizes our perception of time and allows us to stay in the present to safely experience attuned relations with other people (Scaer 2012, pp.141–143). Psychophysiological researcher Stephen Porges insists that feeling safe is the decisive factor for both our wellbeing and creative activity (2012). When solving complex, deep-rooted conflicts that require lasting transformation of worldviews, identities and relationships, peacebuilder Lisa Schirch promotes the use of ritual because it can help people see each other as human beings rather than as enemies. 'Ritual is a powerful form of communication precisely because it involves people's bodies, senses, and emotions' (Schirch 2005, p.83).

While conducting secular funeral ceremonies I observe that mourners can experience and express powerful feelings while safely surrounded by friends, family and well-intentioned strangers. The grieving assembly's attention span is extremely short, but the senses are acute, particularly touch and smell. Mourners spontaneously oscillate between sadness and gladness. Tears and laughter may follow in rapid succession. The process flows in a fulfilling manner when the ritual context, the assembly and an attentive, skilled celebrant support the oscillation by gently keeping the mourners physically in the present time. There may be signs of release or discharge: yawning, moist eyes, trembling in the face or lips, a deep breath, a shiver in the torso, the stretching of shoulders, neck, hands or legs. At that point, mourners often feel growing gratitude for their dear one's life and the times they shared.

As the ceremony draws to a close, I see people glancing around. They appear to be waking up, reorienting themselves to the present moment, the room and the people around them. Later, some describe the funeral as a time of feeling supported in a 'time-out-of-time experience'. Others speak of having sensed their loved one's passing from the realm of the living to that of the deceased. With a gut-level calm that does not exclude deep grief, they move away from the casket, urn or grave and return home, physically anchored in a new reality.

While my observations of these reactions are entirely subjective, sociological researchers Marie Bruvik Heinskou and Lasse Suonperä Liebst draw our attention to objective ways of measuring the feelings that unfold during social engagement in ritualization (2016). In particular, Porges' landmark work[6] adds new tools and methods to the scientist's toolbox.

RITUAL ANCHORS MEMORIES AND TIME

Interestingly, Levine prescribes this process of oscillation between intense emotions for the resolution of trauma in the therapeutic context.[7] Based on the observation that pain and pleasure cannot be felt simultaneously, he advises *titrating* strong feelings and *pendulating* between painful and pleasurable memories. This is exactly what a competent celebrant instinctively does during a ceremony. Although Levine has never applied this part of his theory to ritualizing, he does assert: 'The tranquil feelings of aliveness and ecstatic self-transcendence that make us fully human can also be accessed through ritual. This way they become enduring features of our existence' (2005, p.xvii). This process is reinforced by memory.

Recent neuroscientific research by Karim Nader's research shows that, contrary to what we previously thought, memories are not permanent:

---

6   'Porges helped us understand how dynamic our biological systems are. He gave us an explanation why a kind face and a soothing tone of voice can dramatically...help people shift out of disorganised fearful states... If physiological mind-brain-viscera communication is the royal road to affect regulation, this invites a radical shift in our therapeutic approaches...to anxiety, attention deficit/hyperactivity disorder, autism, and trauma-related psychopathology... The polyvagal theory legitimates the study of age-old collective and religious [sic] practices such as communal chanting, various breathing technics, and other methods that cause shifts in autonomic state' (van der Kolk 2011, p.xvi).

7   Levine refers to this moving back and forth between emotions as pendulation, 'the primal rhythm expressed as movement from constriction to expansion – and back to constriction, but gradually opening to more and more expansion... The perception of pendulation guides the gradual contained release (discharge) of "trauma energies" leading to expansive body sensations and successful trauma resolution' (2010, p.80). He uses the acronym TRIPODS to describe this process in healing trauma: Titrating, Resourcing, Integrating, Pendulating, Organizing, Discharging, Stabilizing.

His mentor Joseph E. LeDoux explains that the 'brain isn't interested in having a perfect set of memories about the past...instead, memory comes with a natural updating mechanism, which is how we make sure that the information taking up valuable space inside our head is still useful. This might make our memories less accurate, but it certainly makes them more relevant to the present and the future [i.e., adaptive]' (LeDoux quoted in Levine 2015, p.141). Since memories are not fixed, recall during ritualization has the potentiality of switching off the fear generator and interrupting the somatic loops that involve negative repetitive thoughts, emotions, images or actions. Rituals reflect our concept of time, how it passes and what that passing means. Appropriate ritualizing in a safe setting is an opportunity to relegate painful sensations from the past to the past by updating a memory based on new information. Upgraded sensations, in particular smell,[8] form rescripted memories and emotions that, when accessed anew during ritual, empower rather than overpower. 'In this way', remarks anthropologist Matthieu Smyth, 'ritualizing a lifecycle passage, or even a seasonal event, serves as a benchmark or reference point among a series of lesser points. It reassures us that we have indeed moved on from one phase to another, and that the transition has truly been completed; it inaugurates a new reality within which we can evolve in peace' (2014).

---

8   According to Amanda White, research technologist in the Psychiatry Department at Penn State College of Medicine, the olfactory bulb has direct connections to two brain areas that are strongly implicated in emotion and memory: the amygdala and hippocampus. Interestingly, visual, auditory (sound) and tactile (touch) information do not pass through these brain areas. This may be why olfaction, more than any other sense, is so successful at triggering emotions and memories (White 2015).

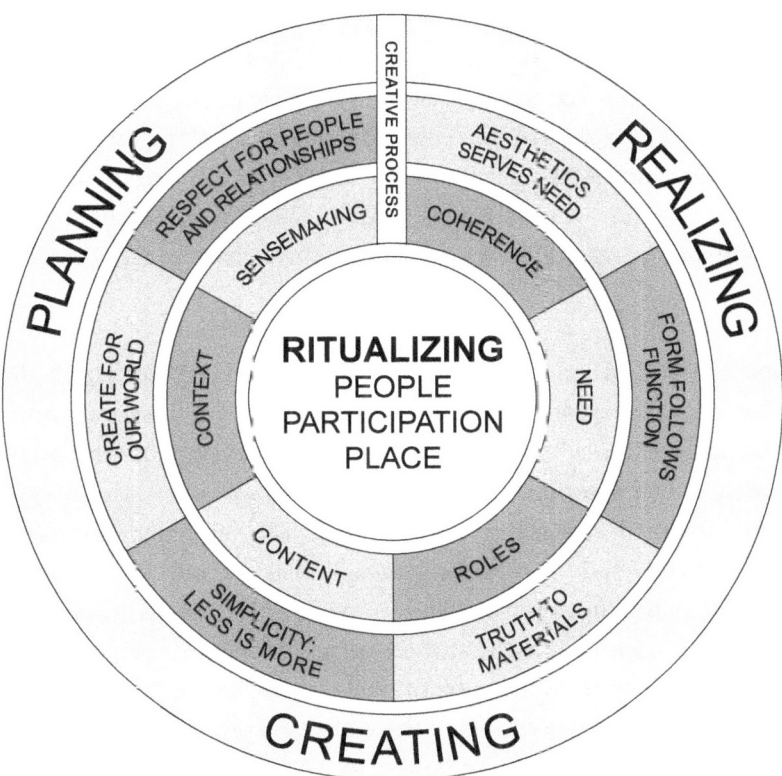

Figure 4.2. Creative process of ritualmaking

Figure 4.2 illustrates the application of the creative process to the creation of secular ritual. The threefold process involves planning, creating and realizing (see the outer ring). The six basic rules of ritual design form the acronym CRAFTS (see the second ring). Ritual design is buttressed by six supports: need, roles, context, content, sensemaking and coherence (see the third ring). At the heart of each ritual is a person or people, an event, a transition or an occasion (see the centre). These concepts are developed more fully in my book, *Crafting Secular Ritual: A Practical Guide* (2017).

RITUAL AS A CULTURALLY STRATEGIC WAY OF ACTING IN THE WORLD

Ritualizing is a social activity that contributes to our capacity as human beings to celebrate joyful moments and spring back after hardship. 'Unlike in recent centuries, in which rituals [were] set by hierarchical societies,' Levine observes, 'we moderns need to participate directly in the creation of our own transformational experiences through ritual' (2005, p.xvii).

The function of traditional ritual

Traditional ritual brings people together for a ceremony; the social gathering that follows is just as important. Our sense of taste enhances a sense of belonging and conviviality. When people first feel that traditional rituals are no longer appropriate, they typically try to get their institution to adapt its rituals to suit their needs. Fiancés ask their religious leader or mayor to do or add 'something special' so that the traditional wedding ceremony has meaning for them. Upon the death of a non-religious relative, families request that there be no mention of religion or god during the funeral. As a rule, traditional ritual is designed to take people smoothly from the planning to the realizing phase. Established ritual components were created and then evolved over a period of time; they require participation but no creative input from the adherent. The desire to actively create one's own transformational ritual experience is at cross-purposes with the institution's function as guardian of ritual tradition.

Ritualizing in multicultural contexts

Another common reaction to the sentiment that traditional rituals are unsuitable involves borrowing or stealing – depending on one's perspective – rituals that seem to work for other cultures.[9] This is not a new phenomenon. Throughout the history of humankind, ritualmaking has been enriched by cultural exchange. Sinologist Nicolas Standaert

---

9   Many indigenous peoples are insulted by Westerners' appropriation of their rituals. Ironically, appreciation for tribal rituals increases at a time in human history when it is rare, if not impossible, to find people who remain unscathed by the impact of Western culture.

explores a 17th-century example of cross-cultural ritual exchange between Europeans and Chinese people during the funeral of an Italian Jesuit priest called Matteo Ricci (1552–1610). Ricci's funeral lasted well over a year, as traditional Christian rites were grafted onto established Chinese practices to reinvent funerary rituals. Standaert's analysis of the mechanics of two-way cultural interaction exchange[10] is pertinent, not only to Ricci's colleagues and their Chinese converts, but also for 21st-century contexts where people also find themselves 'in-between' traditions. Standaert stresses the importance of 'the internal coherence of rituals that are created anew as a result of [cross-cultural] encounter… By "coherence" is meant that in the eyes of [the ritualmakers], the new creation fits internally together, makes sense, and is considered effective' (2008, p.212). Without a doubt, throughout the ages, creating rituals that fit these three conditions has always required time, skill and rigour.

The risks of do-it-yourself ritual

The fanciful, copy-paste approach too often associated with emerging ritual is rarely satisfying and not without risk. Ritologist Ronald L. Grimes observes:

> Like traditional rituals, do-it-yourself (DIY) ritual can result in complicity, empty gestures, people having to do something they resist doing. In either case, deep-seated resentment can lie under the surface of ritual acts. If DIY rituals are really going to meet our needs, they have to be made up out of the familiar, not the exotic: metaphors that make sense to us, language that reflects the way we see the world, and symbols with which we have a history. Start with your own broken teacups, the stuff in your backyard, keepsakes in the backs of drawers. Begin there, not with someone else's rituals. (Grimes 2016)

---

10   Standaert presents four analytic frameworks for understanding the role of cross-cultural exchange in ritualmaking: transmission, reception, invention and interaction, and communication. He describes the fourth framework as 'not a *radical* alternative to the other frameworks, but rather it builds upon those previous frameworks…it helps to reveal the internal coherence of rituals that are created anew as a result of the Chinese-European encounter' (2008, p.212).

SENSEMAKING[11] IN RITUALMAKING

The couple who believe that they must *give meaning* to their wedding ceremony may spend hours trawling the internet, sifting through wedding vows, ready-made poems or readings; they may take symbols from cultures that are foreign to them. Most find it more rewarding to sit face-to-face, perhaps over a glass of wine or on a sunny terrace, in sincere discussion about what the transition means to them separately and as a couple. The real challenge they face is how to nudge out what being married means *to them*.

One newly married couple I worked with told me:

> We had little idea of the work involved when we contacted you. But, what we do remember about our wedding was the ceremony: the preparation was crucial. For us, it meant an eight-month long process that gave us the opportunity to ask ourselves questions and put words on how we experience our relationship. Pronouncing the vow we wrote ourselves in front of our nearest and dearest made it official. The symbolic gestures of our promise were meaningful because they made sense to us and to our guests. When we left [the place where the ceremony was held] we felt married. When we got home, it felt real. Now, we cannot imagine having done it any other way; it was so right for us.

This couple made their personalized wedding ceremony 'from scratch', yet it was not *creatio ex nihilo*. The process involved setting aside time to explore the meaning that is tucked away in the nooks and crannies of their own lives and cultural traditions. The values they share were 'decoded' into words and gestures. The couple negotiated the wording of their commitment to their common goals in a joint wedding vow. Every aspect of their ceremony communicated these shared values to their guests: vow, words spoken, symbols, choice of guests, venue, decorations,

---

11   Sensemaking is the process by which people experience and make sense of their experiences. While the search for sense has been studied by several disciplines under a number of names for centuries, the term 'sensemaking' has marked scientific research since the 1970s.

food and drink. It was the coherence of these elements that rendered the wedding ritual meaningful for them and their entourage.

People with pluricultural origins may need to delve deeply into their multifaceted heritage and draw upon several traditions simultaneously to achieve a sense of wholeness in their ritualmaking. Since they belong to these cultures, their use of traditional texts or practices is not only legitimate but it is also meaningful, respectful and coherent with their identity.

Some occasions, such as when a newborn is not expected to live, leave little time for deep interactive planning. Yet even then there is no reason to resort to a chaplain or other people's rituals. I encourage young parents to consciously make this time special by being an island of safety for their baby. Leave no room for regrets. Touch, authentic words and taking in each other's smells contribute to savouring each moment. Clinical psychologist and rolfer (bodyworker) Pedro Prado affirms that meaning-making involves not only the mind and the body: 'Meaning is an individual and cultural factor. When we are going for meaning...we are also going for how the individual shares it with others' (Prado and Allen 2005, pp.25–28). Even an ephemeral 'community' composed of a nurse and a parent contributes to humanizing a tragic situation. One couple held their newborn, shared their hopes and sorrows, and tied a colourfully braided ribbon to the baby's ankle to mark her connection to their 'clan'. It made more sense to them than a few drops of water sprinkled by clergy they might never see again.

Expectations for sensemaking and authenticity are higher for reinvented and customized ritual, observes sociologist Margaret Holloway. She quotes a mourner leaving a funeral as saying: 'Funerals aren't nice but it couldn't have been nicer' (2015, n.p.). Emerging rituals need to feel right to be right. In order to feel right, ritualizing must touch the body's 'felt-sense' and effect a 'felt shift'[12] (Gendlin 1962, p.44). Making ritual that

---

12 'A felt sense is not a mental experience, but a physical one, a bodily awareness of a situation or a person or an event. [It is] an internal aura that encompasses everything you feel and know about a given subject at a given time – encompasses it and communicates it to you all at once rather than detail by detail' (Gendlin 1962, p.44).

feels right involves *seeking*, *creating* and *taking meaning* (Holloway 2015). People *seek meaning* through their choices about the different aspects of the ceremony such as music, readings, dress and symbols. They then use these elements to *create meaning* for themselves and those present at the ceremony. *Taking meaning* from a ceremony marks the transition and anchors it in daily life.

> **Guidelines for repackaging ritual**
>
> - Authenticity, not parody of others' rituals
> - Voluntary, not imposed
> - Theatrical, not theatre
> - Artistic, not Art
> - Celebration, not a party
> - Therapeutic, not therapy
> - Playful, not a game
> - Time-out-of-time, not time-out

THE SECRET TO REPACKAGING CONTEMPORARY RITUAL

Ritual needs to be repackaged today as an alternative culturally strategic way of acting in the world. The secret to making secular ritual that effectively meets our most profound human needs lies in a creative process based on coherence and authenticity. This calls for theory that focuses on the experiencing body. Ritual is not a game, but it can be playful; it is not therapy, but it can be therapeutic; it is not theatre, but it is theatrical; it is not Art, but it is artistic.[13] The process I use as a celebrant to ritualize lifecycle transitions can be summarized as personalized *accompaniment* that leads to the creation of ritual that makes sense because it is based on *authenticity*, *affect* and *coherence*.

---

13 While I have used these formulas for years with clients and in celebrant training courses, I was delighted to discover recently that Ronald L. Grimes presents his students with a table of similar formulations to stimulate discussion about ritual. See Chapter 8 'Mapping Ritual' in his book *The Craft of Ritual Studies* (2014).

CONCLUSION

We live in a dislocated society at the cusp of an era of inevitable change. The challenges of our ultramodern world require that people everywhere 'do something' to remain human and connected with others. Like the ancients, we do this by conscientiously engaging in playful, artistic and ritual pursuits. As a culturally strategic way of acting, ritual is basically communal and emotional: it makes us feel less alone, more supported, inventive, proactive, safe and alive. Fitting secular ritual represents a unique and profoundly humanizing and civilizing force that fixes us – individually and collectively – firmly in present reality.

We create and harness the power of ritual as we celebrate a marriage, welcome a child into the family, mark a youth's coming of age, a graduation, a birthday, a seasonal festival or honour the dead with a funeral. By acknowledging our joys and sorrows together, we strengthen our attachment and emotional attunement and fashion landmarks in time and space that help us make sense of our lives, our relationships and the world around us. To achieve this end, our ritualmaking must obey the highest laws: respect for people, relationships and the Earth. Body-based secular ritualizing is capable of enhancing our social bonds, transforming us into caring groups and fostering organic communities that promote social and even ecological and geo-political stability.

REFERENCES

Asad, T. (2003) *Formations of the Secular: Christianity, Islam, Modernity.* Cultural Memory in the Present Series. Stanford, CA: Stanford University Press.
Bell, C. (1997) *Ritual: Perspectives and Dimensions.* New York: Oxford University Press.
Dissanayake, E. (1992) *Homo Aestheticus: Where Art Comes From and Why.* New York: Free Press.
Dissanayake, E. (2016) Personal correspondence.
Gendlin, E. (1962) *Experiencing and the Creation of Meaning.* New York: Free Press.
Gordon-Lennox, J. (2017) *Crafting Secular Ritual: A Practical Guide.* London: Jessica Kingsley Publishers.
Grimes, R.L. (2014) *The Craft of Ritual Studies.* Oxford: Oxford University Press.
Grimes, R.L. (2016) Personal correspondence.

Heinskou, M.B. and Liebst, L.S. (2016) 'On the elementary neural forms of micro-interactional rituals: Integrating autonomic nervous system functioning into interaction ritual theory.' *Sociological Forum 31*, 1.

Holloway, M. (2015) 'Ritual and Meaning-Making in the Face of Contemporary Death.' Keynote Lecture Symposium: Emerging Rituals in a Transitioning Society. Utrecht: University of Humanistic Studies.

Jonte-Pace, D. (2009) 'Foreword: Notes on a Friendship.' In C. Bell, *Ritual Theory, Ritual Practice*. New York: Oxford University Press. [Originally published in 1992; Foreword appears in OUP 2009 edition.]

LeDoux, J.E. (2015) cited by P.A. Levine in *Trauma and Memory: Brain and Body in a Search for the Living Past: A Practical Guide for Understanding and Working with Traumatic Memory*. Berkeley, CA: North Atlantic Books.

Lenoir, F. (2012) *La Guérison du monde*. Paris: Fayard.

Levine, P.A. (2005) 'Foreword.' In M. Picucci, *Ritual as Resource: Energy for Vibrant Living*. Berkeley, CA: North Atlantic Books.

Levine, P.A. (2010) *In an Unspoken Voice*. Berkeley, CA: North Atlantic Books.

Levine, P.A. (2015) *Trauma and Memory: Brain and Body in a Search for the Living Past: A Practical Guide for Understanding and Working with Traumatic Memory*. Berkeley, CA: North Atlantic Books.

Porges, S.W. (2012) Interview with William Stranger at Dharma café, 6 June. Available at https://vimeo.com/44146020, accessed on 3 February 2016.

Prado, P.O.B. and Allen, D. (2005) 'Co-laborare.' *Structural Integration 33*, 1, 25–28.

Scaer, R.C. (2001) *The Body Bears the Burden*. Philadelphia, PA: The Haworth Medical Press.

Scaer, R.C. (2005) *The Trauma Spectrum: Hidden Wounds and Human Resiliency*. New York: W.W. Norton & Company.

Scaer, R.C. (2012) *8 Keys to Body–Brain Balance*. New York: W.W. Norton & Company.

Schirch, L. (2005) *Ritual and Symbol in Peacebuilding*. Bloomfield, CT: Kumarian Press.

Smyth, M. (2014) Private communication.

Standaert, N. (2008) *The Interweaving of Rituals. Funerals in the Cultural Exchange between China and Europe*. Seattle, WA: University of Washington Press.

van der Kolk, B.A. (2011) 'Foreword.' In S.W. Porges, *The Polyvagal Theory: Neurophysiological Foundations of Emotions, Attachment, Communication and Self-Regulation*. New York: W.W. Norton & Company.

van der Kolk, B.A. (2014) *The Body Keeps the Score. Brain, Mind, and Body in the Healing of Trauma*. New York: Viking Books.

White, A. (2015) 'Smells ring bells: How smell triggers memories and emotions.' *Psychology Today*. 12 January. Available at www.psychologytoday.com/blog/brain-babble/201501/smells-ring-bells-how-smell-triggers-memories-and-emotions, accessed on 5 August 2016.

5

CASE STUDY: A NORDIC RITE OF PASSAGE COMES OF AGE

Jeltje Gordon-Lennox

Confirmation as a rite of passage for coming of age has deep roots in traditional Nordic culture. For hundreds of years Nordic state churches held the key to adulthood. Until 1849, young people could not legally marry, hold adult jobs or even wear adult clothing until they had been approved by their parson and confirmed by the church in a public ceremony. While confirmation remained a significant sign of the passage from youth to adulthood in all Nordic countries until the early 1900s, it is no longer obligatory. Furthermore, young people now have a choice between a religious or secular confirmation. Each year about 17 per cent of all young Norwegians,[1] 8.5 per cent of Icelandic youth,[2] 1.5 per cent of Finnish youth[3] and a smaller percentage of young people in Denmark and Sweden are confirmed in humanist or secular ceremonies.

---

1   Human-Etisk Forbund, the Norwegian Humanist Association (NHA), supplied these statistics for 2016.
2   Siðmennt, Félag Siðrænna Húmanista, the Icelandic Ethical Humanist Association (IEHA), supplied these statistics for 2016.
3   According to Tuomas Rutanen of the Finnish Prometheus Camps Association (Prometheus-leirin tuki ry), 1.5 per cent or 853 Finnish youth attended the humanist camps in 2015.

As in the past, young people aged 14 to 16 wear special clothes at the ceremony, and their family members come from afar to celebrate in family festivities planned long in advance. The biggest change in this old Nordic tradition is the non-religious content of the secular confirmations and the fact that the venue is no longer a church building but a concert hall, a medieval castle, a municipal cinema, a cultural centre or a city hall or community building.

The confirmation tradition – whether religious or humanist – is now so interwoven into Nordic culture and society that it has become an integral part of strong family traditions in the countries that formerly comprised the Kingdom of Denmark: Norway, Iceland and Denmark. This study examines the evolution of non-religious confirmation ceremonies in these three countries.

HOW DID THIS CHANGE COME ABOUT?
A bit about the history of confirmation

In order to understand the importance of confirmation in Nordic society today, we must take a brief look at the origins of confirmation. In the early years of the Christian Church, three Sacraments of initiation – Baptism, Confirmation and Eucharist/Communion – were celebrated together by bishops for adult catechumens at the Easter Vigil. Over time, the three sacraments were associated with separate moments in Christian life. As Christianity spread northwards with the Romans and much of Europe became Catholic, confirmation began to be practiced at adolescence rather than infancy. During the Middle Ages, it became known as the sacrament of (spiritual) maturity. In 1308, the catechism of the Roman Catholic Church warns: 'Although Confirmation is sometimes called the "sacrament of Christian maturity", we must not confuse adult faith with the adult age of natural growth, nor forget that the baptismal grace is a grace of free, unmerited election and does not need "ratification" to become effective.' As Christianity spread northwards with the Romans and much of Europe became Catholic, confirmation began to be practised at adolescence rather than infancy. During the Middle Ages, it became known as the sacrament of (spiritual) maturity. Youth, confirmed between the ages 12 and 15, were regarded as old enough and ready to live active, responsible Christian lives.

Confirmation in Nordic countries

The history of confirmation in the Nordic countries and their associated territories is inextricably intertwined. From about 1397 to 1523, Denmark, Sweden (which then included Finland) and Norway, together with Norway's overseas dependencies (Iceland, Greenland, the Faroe Islands and the Northern Isles) were joined under the Union of Kalmaris. Although the states legally retained their sovereignty, one single monarch, the King of Denmark, directed most of their policies. With the breakaway of Sweden in 1523, the Union of Kalmaris was effectively dissolved.

In 1536, King Christian III joined the Reformation movement and imposed Lutheranism on his extended kingdom, which then covered an area that now constitutes most of Denmark, Norway and Iceland. The King – like his favoured theologian – rejected confirmation as a sacrament, and it fell into relative disuse. Some Lutherans, however, followed Luther's advice to retain confirmation as a public rite for children.[4] The practice reappeared late in the 17th century in a somewhat different form under the influence of Pietism. This Protestant movement from Germany, with its strong emphasis on individual devotion, paved the way for compulsory confirmation.

King Christian VI reintroduced the confirmation of youth in 1736 as a legal and religious rite. Compulsory confirmation contributed to a rise in the level of literacy and to the institution of regular schooling throughout the Kingdom. As from 1814, the School Law applied free, obligatory education for all children from six or seven years old and until their confirmation seven years later. All young people aged 14 to 19

---

4   'Urge magistrates and parents to rule well and to send their children to school...train children to be pastors, preachers, clerks [also for other offices, with which we cannot dispense in this life], etc. . Since the tyranny of the Pope has been abolished, people are no longer willing to go to the Sacrament and despise it [as something useless and unnecessary]' (Luther 1529).

– regardless of their social status or gender – were required to learn the catechism by heart. Catechetical teaching usually took place during the winter months and was followed by a public examination ceremony held on a Sunday three to four weeks after Easter. The successful 'confirmands'[5] received their first communion and acquired civil rights that included the right to wear adult clothing, marry, become an apprentice, a soldier, a witness or a godparent. Those who failed the examination spent another winter studying and were examined again the following year. Those who did not succeed in passing the examination by age 19 could be punished with a prison sentence or even forced labour.

Although the Danish–Norwegian union was dissolved in 1814, Iceland remained a possession of Denmark until 1944. As from 1849, the Constitutional Act of Denmark ensured the freedom of thought and religion in Denmark and its territories. Confirmation continued to be an important rite for Nordic society, but it was no longer the determining factor for access to civil rights.

HUMANIST CONFIRMATIONS IN NORWAY
LENE MÜRER IN COLLABORATION WITH SIRI SANDBERG AND INGER-JOHANNE SLAATTA (NORWEGIAN HUMANIST ASSOCIATION)

Until 1911, Christian confirmation was compulsory in Norway. In 1951, the Norwegian Humanist Association (NHA) established a secular alternative so that non-religious youth could confirm and keep their integrity; 34 confirmands chose this option and participated in the ceremony in Oslo. Every year since then, Norwegian youth have had the option of doing a humanist or a church confirmation. Moreover, the NHA has used its vast experience with humanist confirmations to guide some of the associations in neighbouring countries as they put secular confirmation ceremonies into place for their youth.

In the early days, humanist confirmations were not well received. When the Minister of Church Affairs accepted the NHA's invitation to

---

5   A confirmand is a person, usually a young person, who has begun the process of becoming a candidate for confirmation or affirmation of baptism.

attend that first ceremony, the Norwegian Parliament debated the issue for two hours. Fortunately, times have changed. While the majority of 15-year-olds are still confirmed in the Lutheran tradition, a growing minority of youth today opt for a humanist confirmation to celebrate their coming of age. Some 10,000 young Norwegians participate in humanist confirmations each year.

Figure 5.1. The first humanist confirmation in Norway (Oslo, 1956)
'I remember the day of the confirmation. The outfit I wore, with a pretty blouse, a purse and a fancy umbrella. An actor read a poem, an opera singer sang and the town orchestra played. The ceremony was lovely. It was hard to make a different choice than what was the norm, but I have made untraditional choices later too which have influenced my life.' (Gry from Oslo was a confirmand in 1957.)

The humanist programme

The young people who choose to do a humanist confirmation come from all socio-economic backgrounds and represent a wide range of the cultures present today in Norway. The confirmands hail from the entire country; from big urban areas such as Oslo, Bergen and Trondheim, from the small towns in the south with their white painted wooden houses, and from the sparsely populated areas in the far north where the Sami communities live. Some of the youth genuinely want to learn more about the humanist perspective. Others come to discuss issues and topics important to them in their lives. Not all are so serious: many come for the festive ceremony. More recently, young people participate because humanist confirmation has become part of their family tradition. After 65 years, humanist confirmation may well be a tradition for several generations of a humanist family! There are, of course, those who are mostly interested in the gifts they will receive at their family gathering. Most of the confirmands want a humanist confirmation for a mixture of reasons. For all, confirmation represents a proud moment for the young people and their families.

Figure 5.2. Youth number 250,000 in a humanist confirmation in Norway (Arendal, 2016) Stina (sitting in the chair) is from Arendal, Norway. The young people with whom she prepared for her confirmation in 2016 are standing around her. The poster she holds states that she is the 250,000th Norwegian to be confirmed in a humanist ceremony. In speaking about her experience Stina said: 'I have learned a lot about humanism and human rights, but I have learned even more about myself.'

The course

In preparation for the confirmation ceremony, the youth participate in a course designed to awaken the confirmands' curiosity. It gives them a starting point for discussion and learning about humanism, their own life stance and human rights. Helping the confirmands structure their often unstructured thoughts and clearly expose their opinions in a safe, social environment is a big task. The main objective of the course is not to supply easy answers, but to encourage reflection and critical thinking. It represents one step on the path to adult life. It is also a support for young people as they face the challenges of daily life.

Figure 5.3. A course in humanist confirmation in Norway (2012)
'I remember the thought-provoking discussions from the course. It felt like a good place to learn to discuss. We had course leaders who were enthusiastic and managed to engage the youth in discussion. I got to know other young people who I would not otherwise have gotten to know.' (Helga was confirmed in Manial in 1986.)

Volunteers who receive special training in how to guide discussions with teenagers lead the course. They have an array of appropriate exercises at their disposal, and aim for a practical approach rather than the more theoretical methods used at school. Among the confirmands' resources for discussion is an illustrated book with texts and quotations called

Think About It! (NHA 2012). Some confirmands use the book during the course while others read it in their own time.

Figure 5.4. The humanist confirmation ceremony in Oslo in 2002 took place at the town hall

Three subjects are a mandatory part of the course: humanism, critical thinking and human rights. With this as a basis, the young people in each group usually influence the content of their course. With support from the leaders they explore who they are and how to determine what is important and right for them and their life. The leaders often get the young people started with exercises or questions that get the discussion going on a concrete level. Once engaged, the youth are often capable of taking the discussion to more abstract levels. Some groups tackle friendship, identity and personal boundaries. Others talk more about ethics and social responsibility.

The young people are supported as they examine their own and others' attitudes critically. They learn that it takes courage to stand up for their opinions but also to change their mind. An important step in becoming a critical thinker is to ask questions. The course may well leave them with more questions than answers.

Figure 5.5. A confirmand in traditional Norwegian dress has her photo taken with her family after the humanist confirmation ceremony in Oslo, Norway (2014)

The ceremony

At the end of the course, the youths celebrate their confirmation with a festive, solemn and dignified ceremony. Humanist confirmations are held on Saturday or Sunday, mainly from late April to late May. Families gather to see their young people, in formal dress, take a step towards adulthood. The ceremonies focus on the young person's importance to family and society: on what it means to make good decisions, to get support from adults, to take a stand in important matters, and to contribute to making the world a better place. It includes processions, speeches addressed to and from the confirmands, music, singing, reciting poetry and awarding diplomas. After the ceremony, most of the parents honour their child's coming of age with a big family celebration.

> People believed I might end up in hell, and would pray for me. Some of my family did not attend my confirmation. I think my confirmation has made me stronger and made it easier for me to make hard choices later on in life.
>
> > (Grethe, the first humanist confirmand from the town of Namsos, Norway in 1976)
>
> Last year I met an old acquaintance who told me that I am one of the few people he knows that is still true to the values and ideals of my youth. I am really proud of that. Too many people just float along and never think about who they want to be. Be critical, ask questions and take responsibility for your actions!
>
> > (Gøril, confirmed in Bodø, Norway in 1981)

CIVIL CONFIRMATIONS IN ICELAND
BJARNI JÓNSSON (SIÐMENNT, THE ICELANDIC ETHICAL HUMANIST ASSOCIATION)

In 2017, Siðmennt, the Icelandic Ethical Humanist Association (IEHA), celebrates 29 years of civil (secular) confirmations in Iceland. The confirmation programme, which grew out of parents' desire to give Icelandic youth an alternative to religious confirmation, brought about the founding of the Association, which officially dates to 1989. It now provides secular ceremonies for all of the major transitions in life.

Participation in the humanist confirmation programme is open to all youth; membership is not a requirement. In fact, the Association actively discourages parents from enrolling their children into the organization before they are 16. The Association's mission statement, which was adopted in 2005, is based on the 2002 Humanist Manifesto of the International Humanist and Ethical Union (IHEU). Nonetheless, unlike the Christian confirmation, secular confirmands are not required to adhere to any dogma or to take an oath.

> We especially appreciated the philosophical content of the preparation course; the focus on the child and his or her position in society, responsibility, moral awareness and concepts such as justice, friendship, fairness and more were discussed on a peer basis.
>
> (Sigurður, father of a young person confirmed by Siðmennt)
>
> The civil confirmation course (especially ethics/philosophy) was excellent with its emphasis on tolerance towards other religions and life stances. The ceremony was also wonderful; grandparents who had been very sceptical about civil confirmation were ecstatic!
>
> (Margrét, mother of a young person confirmed by Siðmennt)

On average, 300 Icelandic teenagers participate in the secular confirmation programme every year. There are 12 to 14 classes every winter for those in cities. Those who live in outlying areas can take the course in two intensive weekends. The teachers of the programme are usually philosophers. In preparation for their civil confirmation, young people meet in groups for discussions about ethics, personal relationships, human rights, equality, critical thinking, relations between the sexes, the prevention of substance abuse, scepticism, protecting the environment, getting along with parents and being a teenager in a consumer society. In short, they learn about what it means to be an adult in contemporary society, and how to take responsibility for their own views and behaviour.

The course is crowned with a formal graduation ceremony in the spring. There may be anywhere from 7 to 12 ceremonies in various parts of the country. During the ceremony, some of the confirmands perform music, read poetry or give speeches. Prominent members of Icelandic society also speak about the importance of their coming into adulthood. All of the confirmands receive diplomas. Well over 3000 Icelanders have now chosen this alternative to religious confirmation. By the spring of 2017, approximately 35,000 guests will have attended a civil confirmation ceremony in Iceland.

In addition to a long-standing working relationship with the NHA, the Association recently engaged in an inter-Nordic network of Humanist Associations as well as with the British Humanist Association (BHA).

Figure 5.6. Humanist confirmation ceremony in Reykjavik, 24 April 2016
The humanist confirmation ceremony was held in a cinema called Haskolabio. The words 'freedom, human dignity and shared responsibility' are written on the screen behind the group of young confirmands.

Figure 5.7. Humanist confirmation ceremony in Copenhagen, 30 May 2015
The confirmation ceremony portrayed here took place at the Black Diamond concert hall in the Royal Library in Copenhagen.

> **Objectives of Danish humanist confirmation**
>
> The aim of the secular confirmation programmes is to strengthen humanist values in society. Humanist confirmations are open to all young people who want to examine their life stance, that is, their relation with what they accept as being of ultimate importance. This involves the presuppositions and theories upon which such a stance could be made, a belief system and a commitment to potentially working it out in one's life.
>
> The course is intended to strengthen young people's capacity to think independently and to act ethically. It encourages:
>
> - developing insights into one's own experiences, actions and behaviour
> - reflection and critical questioning
> - awareness of the one's life stance
> - circumspection, respectfulness, tolerance and responsibility.
>
> The ceremony is designed to give young people an opportunity to formulate their life stance and to get support from their family and society in living up to their ideals.

SECULAR CONFIRMATIONS IN DENMARK
MARIE LOUISE PETERSEN (DANISH HUMANIST SOCIETY)

Nothing reflects the meaning of confirmation to the Danish better than the phrase *At træde ind i de voksnes rækker*, which states that the young person literally 'has stepped into the ranks of the adults'. Confirmation is still the main mark for Danish youth of their transition into adulthood today. Yet these young people are much less likely to opt for a humanist confirmation than their equally secular Nordic neighbours. This is in large part due to the history of confirmation in Denmark.

Non-religious confirmations appear and disappear

In 1909, obligatory public examination was outlawed and youth were confirmed as long as they regularly attended the preparation courses. At that time, approximately 98 per cent of the Danish were members of the official church (*Folkekirken* or the People's Church). The first civil confirmation took place in 1915 in Copenhagen; four girls were confirmed in this ceremony organized by the Association Against Church Confirmation. The group, later known as an association for Civil Confirmation, was founded by a working-class party called the Social Democrats, which fought for the separation of church and state. During the 1930s, nearly 2 per cent of Danish youth chose to be confirmed in a civil ceremony. In the 1970s, the popularity of both civil and Christian ceremonies declined and, in 1992, the Association was disbanded (Kaiser 1992).

Around the same time, a number of young people began to organize their 'non-firmation'. This minimalist formula, which remains popular today, involves skipping the ceremony and just having a party. The traditional family party is such an important event that many Danish parents will celebrate their child's 15th birthday with a big gathering, whether or not there is a confirmation ceremony.

Humanist confirmation

In 2008, Humanistisk Samfund, the Danish Humanist Society, was founded with assistance from its sister organization in Norway, the NHA. Providing humanist ceremonies was given high priority – in particular, for funerals. The first humanist confirmation was organized in 2010. The event represented hours and hours of volunteer work that began with long discussions about what to call the ceremony. The Danish group wanted to avoid potential confusion and the irrefutable religious connotations of the old term, but in the end, decided to follow the Norwegian lead and call their ceremony a humanist 'confirmation'.

Eleven youths from all over Denmark travelled to Copenhagen for that first humanist ceremony; the next year the number doubled. In 2012, thanks to the involvement of qualified volunteers like Annette Bøgh, a mother with a degree in philosophy, there were enough young people for two ceremonies. Annette says:

I committed myself to building up the humanist confirmation course in West Denmark because I felt strongly about being able to offer this option to my son and other young people in West Denmark! I'm still part of it and I enjoy it. Our family is not religious – however, I think that rites of passage are valuable for all young people, regardless of their view on life.

In May 2016, three ceremonies were held in two parts of Denmark for a total of 92 confirmands. The humanist confirmation is now the Danish Humanist Society's most popular offer.

The humanist programme

The Danish built their humanist programme for coming of age ceremonies on the traditional and new models. Preparation takes place during the winter and in the early spring. The course is held over two intensive weekends in a scouts' hut or at a youth hostel. Danish youth explore issues related to humanism, human rights, ethics, identity and critical thinking. Optional subjects include sexuality, alcohol and drugs. Discussions are enhanced by group work, role-playing, games, drawing, singing and physical exercise; there are a few short lectures.

The ceremony takes place on a Saturday in early May. Each confirmand can bring a maximum of nine to ten guests. In 2016 it was held in the concert hall of the Royal Library in Copenhagen and in a historical theatre in Aarhus in Jutland. The ceremony, which lasts about an hour, includes singing and a speech from a well-known person. One of the most moving moments is when the confirmands describe in their own words what humanism means to them. Each confirmand is called up by his or her full name, presented with a certificate for the course, the Human Rights Declaration and a rose. At the close of the ceremony, the assembly sings as all of the confirmands stand together at the front. The assembly then rises and applauds as the young adults exit in a procession. Afterwards there is a small reception for the families while pictures are taken of the confirmands and their course leaders. Most families leave rather quickly to get ready for their big family gathering. Unique to Denmark is a countrywide celebration called 'Blue Monday' (Blå Mandag),[6] when the confirmands skip class to show off their new status and clothes, and just have fun.

A paradoxical relationship between church and state

One of the reasons for the ambivalent attitude towards secular confirmation lies in a persistent paradoxical relationship between the 'state' religion and the Danish state. According to a recent survey, the percentage of church members dropped from 81 per cent in 2010 to 78 per cent in 2015. Few church members are regular churchgoers, and at least 35 per cent say they do not believe in God.[7] It should be noted that church membership is conferred by baptism (usually infancy), not by confirmation. Once a person is registered as having been baptized, they are considered a member of the church and are subject to church tax.[8] People must take special action to renounce their membership.

Furthermore, children in schools run by the municipalities receive instruction in Christian studies throughout their primary and lower secondary school education.[9] Teachers are free to give instruction in world religions or philosophy, but there is no obligation to do so before the eighth grade when the students are 13 to 14 years old, the age when most students are confirmed. Danish teens, like those everywhere, have busy schedules. By law, the school system must facilitate teens' preparation for church confirmation by allowing them to participate in these courses during school hours. According to official statistics, nearly 70 per cent of all Danish youth opt for church confirmations. Whereas some rural

---

6 The Blue Monday tradition in Denmark seems to date back to the 18th century. Most schools give the confirmands the day off from classes. Together with their classmates, they put on their 'Second Day Clothes' and go to town to enjoy themselves, spend money and may end up partying. Sometimes this includes drinking alcohol. In many schools they get lectures and pamphlets about how to have a safe Blue Monday.
7 See http://politiken.dk/debat/analyse/ECE1004535/saadan-ser-danskerne-paa-gud-og-kirke, accessed on 29 June 2016.
8 Danish church tax varies from 0.5 to 1.2 per cent of gross salary, depending on the rules of the municipality where the citizen lives.
9 Praying and preaching have not been permitted during lessons about Christianity since 1975.

regions register church confirmations for 84.5 per cent of the youth, in the region around Copenhagen the percentage drops to 40.6 per cent.[10]

> Since I never really believed in God, I was interested in a humanist confirmation. To me humanism basically means that you trust in humankind and are convinced that people can take responsibility for their own lives – without any approval from god or an almighty power. Of course, I also wanted a confirmation party with all the trimmings. I'm glad I could take the confirmation course and be confirmed in a ceremony. I got exactly what my friends got, only without God.
>
> (Katinka, confirmed in 2010 in Copenhagen)
>
> I enjoyed my confirmation – every bit of it. I can feel the difference: People who know I confirmed say: 'he has passed that age'. Now, when I discuss politics, I feel like I am taken more seriously. For me, the high point of the ceremony was delivering my short speech. I really sensed that I was trusted with a great responsibility. Wearing my first suit for the ceremony added to that feeling of going through a transition. Doing 'Blue Monday' together with my class was also really important. It is something we will always remember.
>
> (August, confirmed in 2013 in Aarhus, West Denmark)

REFERENCES
Luther, M. (1529) *Small Catechism*. English online translation available at http://bookofconcord.org/smallcatechism.ph, accessed on 16 May 2016.
Kaiser, B. (1992) *Ind i de Voksnes Rækker: En Bog om Konfirmationen*. Copenhagen: Gad.
NHA (Norwegian Humanist Association) (2012) *Think About It!* Oslo: NHA.

---

10   Some 47,746 young people (14–15 years old) were confirmed in the *Folkekirken* in 2014. See www.km.dk/folkekirken/kirkestatistik/konfirmerede, accessed on 29 June 2016.

6

MULTICULTURAL WEDDING CEREMONIES

VENTURING INTO THE WORLD OF DIVERSITY

Andrés Allemand Smaller

Do you know what makes me angry? The challenges facing couples from different backgrounds who decide to get married and have a wedding ceremony.

Caitlin and Nabil are one such couple. And a great one too. Their friendliness, warmth and obvious commitment to each other impress me. I appreciate how they openly explore the different dimensions of their relationship and express their shared values. Their decision to get married seemed perfectly natural to them. Unfortunately, like so many couples nowadays, they soon realized that the very diversity they cherish in their relationship was problematic when it came to organizing a fitting wedding ceremony.

Caitlin is a British Catholic, raised in the Netherlands. She hardly ever goes to church but she does believe in God, and she would have loved to have a traditional wedding. Nabil comes from a Moroccan Muslim family, but he considers himself an agnostic, who just happens to be quite fascinated by Buddhism. As much as he loves his family, Nabil enjoys living in a cosmopolitan city like Geneva, Switzerland. This is where Caitlin and Nabil met and fell in love.

Neither a religious wedding nor a secular ceremony seemed right for the couple. Caitlin cannot have a Catholic wedding with her Muslim groom, and a Muslim ceremony with a Christian bride is just as unthinkable. Conversion is not an option either. They love each other as they are, *with* all their differences, not *in spite* of them. They want to be true to themselves and to each other. Pretending to be something they are not – particularly on an occasion as important as their wedding day – was simply out of the question. A Buddhist ceremony might seem like an option, but it did not make sense to Caitlin. As for Nabil, he felt that a strictly religious wedding would be meaningless anyway.

What about a secular ceremony, one that does not involve a religious representative? In Switzerland, couples must first be married at the town hall. No symbolic wedding – religious or otherwise – can be celebrated before the couple has their civil wedding certificate in hand. Many people are quite satisfied with this short ceremony during which a civil servant reads the Swiss legal provisions for marriage; sometimes the civil servant adds a reading that he or she particularly likes. The bride and groom and their witnesses then sign the wedding contract.

Although Caitlin and Nabil enjoyed their civil ceremony, they wanted something more. They wanted a ceremony that would make them *feel* married. They needed to be able to express their unique relationship and commit to each other in a celebration of their union, in the presence of all of their relatives and close friends. They could, of course, ask a secular celebrant to help them organize a symbolic ceremony. However, Caitlin made it clear that it would be frustrating for her to have a secular wedding in which her faith was ignored; in fact even a ceremony with just one or two religious references would not do. Nabil, too, sensed that they needed a wedding that took into account their complex reality. For these reasons, they also ruled out organizing a Catholic-Muslim wedding with an 'interfaith' celebrant from the US; they do not experience their life together as a blend of their religions.

So what should they do? They want a ceremony that genuinely reflects who they are as individuals and a couple. Is that too much to ask? It is surprising, shocking even, that people like Caitlin and Nabil are led to believe that their situation is so complicated and problematic. What they want is rather simple: to feel that they can be themselves, that they can be authentic, as they commit their lives to each other, from the bottom of their hearts. Therefore, the kind of wedding ceremony that feels genuine for people like Caitlin and Nabil and their guests revolves around the couple's values, their passions, their plans for the future, as well as the cultures they come from, the languages they speak, the places where they grew up or where they chose to settle down, local traditions, religions to which they feel attached (however slightly)…

In my opinion, this should be true of any wedding. But since it is not, I have given it a name: I call this a 'multicultural wedding ceremony'. It is the kind of ceremony that takes into account each and every defining aspect of the couple's complex identity, including elements from their religious cultures. The celebrant's role is to create a ceremony that suits their reality, instead of forcing the couple to 'fit into a box', be it religious or not.

I find it deplorable that this kind of wedding ceremony has not yet become common practice in Geneva where I live, an international city that is home to so many supranational institutions, businesses and non-governmental organizations. Roughly one-third of the population is composed of foreigners, another third is made up of second-generation immigrants and the rest hail from all four corners and language groups in Switzerland. When people meet for the first time, talk effortlessly includes explanations about one's family origins. Diversity here is mainstream. Multicultural couples are the norm.

Although not every city in the world is as international as Geneva, multicultural couples are no longer the exception in our global world today. Like Caitlin and Nabil, they have defined their own spirituality and values without necessarily relating to the institutions of their original religions. Furthermore, the internet has transformed the concept of 'community'. People share their opinions, their beliefs and their values, with a large network of generally like-minded 'virtual friends'. They do have a spiritual life and reflect on the meaning of their existence, but they may not formally identify with any organized group or institution.

Furthermore, although they do not usually follow the lead of an authority figure, they may be inspired by several of them simultaneously.

While this all makes fascinating study for researchers, it remains a real challenge for multicultural couples. Society seldom responds adequately to their reality. By definition, tradition evolves more slowly, and this is particularly true when familiar – in this case, religious – institutions are in crisis. Nonetheless, this is not a sustainable situation. Society needs to adapt to its own evolution.

This question is not just theoretical; it represents a real personal concern for me. I grew up in a society that values diversity, surrounded by people who are all genuinely searching for meaning in their lives. My wife and I had to deal with the absence of a suitable solution for our wedding ceremony. The same was true for many of my relatives and friends. Our loved ones are Christian, Jewish, Muslim, Buddhist, Hindu, agnostic and atheist. Why on earth should all these people be deprived of a genuine wedding ceremony? This is why, over the last five years, I have made it my mission to create multicultural ceremonies for the couples who need them. With each couple, we design a unique wedding ceremony that truthfully reflects their beautiful and complex reality.

To be frank, however, the situation of multicultural couples was not my primary concern when I trained as a secular celebrant. I was initially driven by my frustration with a society – Swiss, in this case – that offered atheists and agnostics only the option of a short civil ceremony at the town hall. I felt compelled to prove that a more symbolic ceremony – one with no allusion to religion – could be very powerful. I soon found out that there were many celebrants out there doing atheist ceremonies – especially in Anglo-Saxon countries – and that it was indeed a formidable option for many non-religious couples.

However, as a trained celebrant, my ideas about what a non-religious wedding ceremony should be like were constantly challenged by the situations of the couples who called on me for a wedding ceremony. I was asked to do weddings for an Ethiopian Orthodox and a Swiss atheist, an American Hindu and a Swiss agnostic, a Celtic groom and an Ismaili bride... It soon became apparent to me that believers and non-believers intermarry not out of ignorance but because they accept a partner who deals with existential questions differently than they do. Unless one or the other is radical about their religion, the couple does not let this difference keep them apart. The question at that point became *how* could I best help them create a perfectly genuine multicultural wedding?

HOW DOES IT WORK?

How does one create a multicultural wedding ceremony that actually works? How indeed does one intertwine different cultures and traditions into a ceremony in such a way that it does not end up looking like a cheesy mishmash or a distasteful patchwork? Even more risky is the challenge of introducing elements from the couple's different religious traditions, without being disrespectful or ending up with a ceremony that resembles a parody of a religious wedding. This is a serious and legitimate concern.

To be truly convinced that it works, I believe one needs to actually experience such a wedding. The kind of feedback I get from the newly-weds' close relatives – many of whom had been discreetly or vociferously sceptical before attending the ceremony – is proof that such a ceremony can feel real and respectful. The father of a Hindu bride told me he was proud of his daughter for having organized such a meaningful ceremony. The aunt of a Jewish bride, who was disappointed that her niece was 'marrying out of the community', came to thank me after the wedding. She told me that hearing her niece publicly express her strong attachment to her Jewish roots really touched her. An atheist groom who had at first resisted the idea of a symbolic ceremony became excited when he realized that he would finally be able to express his love for his dear Christian Orthodox wife before their friends and family…

Every wedding is unique because every couple I work with is unique. Yet I can identify ten guidelines for creating a multicultural ceremony. These recommendations stem from one core principle: be absolutely genuine in everything you say and do. I insist that the couples I work with not only keep this in mind, but that they use it as the main criteria as they compose their ceremony. Every aspect of the wedding must reflect who the bride and groom really are. As their celebrant, I consider myself their ceremonial spokesperson.

GUIDELINES FOR A MULTICULTURAL WEDDING CEREMONY

1. The couple write their own vows

This is my number 1 rule, because it automatically stimulates an appropriate mindset. I half-jokingly tell the couple that their wedding ceremony is ready when they have finished writing their vows. Everything else is just a decor for them to express their commitment to each other. This is a bit of an exaggeration, of course. But the couple gets the idea: nothing is more genuine than their personalized vows. I encourage them to use their own words, rather than to try to produce brilliant poetry. Whatever it is they promise to each other, it must sound sincere. To help them find what they would like to say, I make them define separately what their commitment is about, in very practical terms. What kind of couple do they hope to be in the future? What do they need to do in order to make that happen? What qualities do they value the most in their relationship, and how do they intend to preserve them? Which challenges do they expect to face, and what makes them confident that they will overcome the obstacles together? Usually, the bride and groom end up writing separate vows, using their own words and expressing their different personalities. They also love to keep them secret until the ceremony. However, I always suggest that they both conclude on an identical sentence. They are not just different individuals promising different things; they are also a couple making a deal.

The process of writing vows defines the spirit of the ceremony. Throughout our working sessions, I remind the couple that their commitment is at the centre of their unique wedding, and that every other 'ingredient' must feel just as genuine.

2. Explore non-religious symbols and rituals first

As a celebrant, it is my job to help the couple spot the rituals that will make them *feel* that they are actually getting married. This involves a gut feeling, not just a rational thought. Since they are not used to the 'language' of rituals, many couples simply rush to their religious tradition to find ideas. The attraction is almost irresistible, if only because tradition feels familiar. Does that mean that these rituals are the most appropriate for the couple? Not necessarily. There are so many other ways to symbolize the union of two people! Feeding each other, sharing a drink, washing or kissing each other's hands, exchanging personal gifts, lighting a candle together, singing a duet, painting something together, planting a tree, packing a suitcase... The list is endless. There are so many creative ways to symbolize this transition from single to married!

I present couples with photographs of non-religious rituals instead of talking about them. They react immediately to the images. Suddenly their imagination is stimulated. They can imagine, for instance, how it would be to have their guests sitting in circles around them, rather than in rows. One bride thought of feeding chocolate to the groom and receiving cheese in return. A couple from different countries asked their relatives to bring water from a lake and symbolically poured this element from their different 'sources' onto a plant.

Once a couple can imagine a few alternative rituals, they relax and do not rush to religious symbols anymore. The latter will only be chosen if they are really meaningful to the couple. In this way, the selection of both secular and religious symbols becomes all the more genuine.

3. Keep an eye out for unexpected material

In my experience, the richest material can take very unexpected forms. Let me give you an example. A very sporty Australian couple came to me for a ceremony. The bride was of Jewish origins and the groom was nominally Catholic. They shared many values, but when it came to organizing a wedding ceremony, it was very clear to her that she would need several traditional Jewish rituals in order to *feel* that she was getting married. He observed that his bride's sense of belonging to her community was as strong as his was weak. He was uncomfortable with the very thought of adding a Catholic ritual. So I asked him, what 'culture' would he use to express his values? He seemed clueless…

As they talked about their life together and about their separate passions, I soon realized that the groom became particularly inspired whenever he spoke about surfing. I must confess that, at first, I was a bit annoyed by the cliché of the 'Aussie surfer'. Gradually, as I listened to him, his enthusiasm fascinated me: he described his sport as if it were an art, a science, a way of life for him. It was all about choosing the right spot and the right wave. Deciding when was the right moment to jump and then when to stand up. Keeping your balance. It was about the thrill of those few exhilarating seconds when you are on top of things. But it was also about dealing with the many frustrations of falling short, and that unquenchable yearning to keep on trying, again and again and again. Suddenly, it hit me: this was not just about surfing. The groom was clearly expounding on his philosophy of life: the perpetual search for balance; being able to acknowledge vulnerability; the capacity to persevere and to make endless efforts to make things work; the ability to read the signs; the will to learn and grow. In a way that was not immediately obvious to the groom, this was also his philosophy about his marriage. And most importantly, this was the culture that was closest to his heart. From there on in, we had all we needed to balance the bride's Jewish culture with the groom's surfing culture.

Another couple created a beautiful ritual blending the Ukrainian bride's attachment to her Christian Orthodox tradition and the atheist groom's emotional connexion to the land his family owns in Tuscany. At the ceremony, the bride's parents stood up and offered the couple a traditional Ukrainian wedding bread called *korovai* as well as a small bowl filled with salt. The groom's children from his first marriage then came forward with the typically Italian *focaccia* bread and a bowl filled with oil from the olive grove he had planted years ago on his family's land. Surrounded by their closest relatives, the bride fed the groom a mouthful of *korovai* dipped in salt, and he fed her a mouthful of *focaccia* dipped in oil. The symbolism was powerful, but it was also a lot of fun. All their relatives and friends were smiling, and some had tears in their eyes.

4. Spot the most suitable religious rituals

As I noted earlier, rituals involve a gut feeling, not just rational thought. Even if you define yourself as an atheist, you may still relate on an emotional level to the original religious culture of your family. I like to tell couples that if symbolism is the 'language' of social rites, each tradition has its own 'grammar'. We are usually most comfortable expressing ourselves in our mother tongue; it should not come as a surprise that we find it easiest to relate to rituals from our own background. Even a bride who feels estranged from her parents' religion may find that she understands this language because it speaks directly to her emotions. This is important to acknowledge because the couple should *feel* married at the end of the ceremony. What exactly is the turning point? For a Christian groom, it could be the moment he sees the bride in her white dress. For a Hindu, it could be when the couple circles the fire. For a Muslim bride, it may be when she has her hands dyed with henna tattoos. It could also be many other gestures or moments, since each person is different and unique.

Having said that, it is not always easy to know which ritual will feel right, because few people realize how strongly they feel about their religious culture. They can tell me if they believe or not, if they practise or not, if they feel a sense of belonging or not...but they rarely accurately evaluate their attachment to religious rituals. To help couples spot the right symbols, I ask them to do a simple exercise. Each person receives a typical order of ceremony for a wedding from his or her tradition of origin. I ask them to highlight any aspect of the ceremony they would feel was missing if it was not incorporated into their wedding ceremony. I insist that they should feel free to leave it blank. Often, it is only when people study the order of a traditional wedding ceremony that they begin to measure their level of attachment to their religious culture. Whether or not people officially adhere to their tradition, it is not unusual for them to feel strongly about several religious rituals. One British groom, with no religious background to speak of, realized that as he was growing up he had been influenced by mainstream culture and felt quite attached to some Anglican wedding traditions, if only because he may have seen them in some English TV series. He was, in fact, influenced by a religious culture but had no awareness of it.

Interestingly, many wedding rituals that people consider religious are, in fact, cultural traditions. There are examples of this from traditions the world over. The different wedding traditions found throughout the Arab world are only one instance of this. The religious moment in a Muslim wedding ceremony is short and discrete, which leaves room in the wedding ceremony for many customs that reflect local cultural diversity. These customs are meaningful, even to an atheist.

5. Sort through the essential 'ingredients' of the ceremony

At the end of this process, couples usually end up with a long list of ideas for their ceremony. There is generally too much material for their wedding. In my view, this is a good thing because it forces the couple to look deep into the meaning of each symbol or ritual in order to determine which ones make the cut. Usually the couple quite naturally balances out their different cultures and values to produce an accurate 'picture' of who they are together and what their commitment means to them. My role as a celebrant mostly involves helping them focus on the different moments in their wedding ceremony. How do the bride and groom want to enter the ceremonial space? How should their guests be welcomed? How and when are their backgrounds and values expressed? How will they pronounce their vows? How is their union symbolized? How do they want their blended community to show they approve? How do they want the ceremony to end, and how will they step into their 'new life'?

6. At the ceremony, name the elephant in the room

The guests at the wedding need to know at the outset why the couple called upon a celebrant who specializes in multicultural ceremonies. For many people, there is no such thing as a non-religious wedding rite, unless it is a civil wedding at the town hall. It is important that the guests understand that this ceremony is not an anti-religion statement. On this very special day, as the couple commit their lives to each other, they want to be completely truthful with themselves, each other and their guests.

When I introduce myself at the start of each ceremony, I announce that it is not a religious wedding, and that I am neither a priest nor a pastor nor any other kind of religious representative. This may seem obvious, but it cannot be taken for granted. When I make this statement, I notice a shift in the audience. Suddenly, people feel included rather than excluded from the ceremony. This was confirmed to me when two Jehovah's Witnesses thanked me after the wedding ceremony, not only for having declared that I am neither a priest nor a pastor, but also for adding that I was not an 'elder' or a 'brother' either (titles assigned to Jehovah's Witnesses leaders). The groom had told me that he grew up in a family that belongs to that community, although he now considers himself an atheist. Acknowledging the groom's Jehovah Witness background during the ceremony made his relatives and friends feel welcome *as they are,* and it freed them to assume rather than hide their faith. In the end, this little rule of mine has become an efficient tool. In general, people tell me they start feeling comfortable the minute I, as a celebrant, acknowledge them.

Sometimes, there is a hidden dimension to my welcome phrase. One day, as I explained to a couple what I was planning to say at their ceremony, the Muslim groom insisted that I declare: 'I am neither a pastor nor a priest, neither an imam, nor a rabbi.' The reference to the rabbi was in fact a veiled homage to his deceased Jewish grandmother who had converted to Islam in order to marry his grandfather. Many of the relatives did not know about her origins and he did not want to use the occasion to publicly reveal them, but he did want to evoke her memory at this symbolic moment in his life.

7. Remind the guests that they are the couple's 'community'

What is expected of the wedding guests? It is also important to say at the outset that the bride and groom did not simply invite guests to their wedding, but that they bring their communities together for this occasion. In the past, their villages may have joined them in celebrating their marriage. Nowadays, those 'villages' have gone global; people come from around the world to be present. Yet the meaning of the wedding has not changed. This is why I ask the audience to stand up when the couple walks in; with this simple gesture, what seems to be a disparate crowd suddenly starts identifying itself as the couple's community.

During the ceremony, I invite the guests to witness the couple's commitment, but also to 'walk the couple into marriage', to help them *feel* what is actually happening. In this way, the guests support their friend or relative in the spirit of this unique wedding. In my experience, when the guests feel welcome, and they sense that the wedding ceremony corresponds to the couple's expectations, they are happy to assume this role. It helps that the couple's intentions are made very clear and that all are aware of what is at stake. The majority of guests respect the couple's choice and enjoy the celebration. There is then no reason for anyone to be against a multicultural wedding. When the couple and I debrief several weeks after their ceremony, I ask them if they heard any criticism; the answer has always been 'no'. Any guests who do feel unhappy about the ceremony probably keep it to themselves.

8. Religious rituals may be performed, but not by the celebrant

I have made it clear that the bride and groom are encouraged to express their beliefs, values and personal codes about what life and marriage means to each one of them. Yet whenever a religious aspect is included in the ceremony, it is essential that a person who belongs to that religious group perform it – not the celebrant. I am convinced that the celebrant has to play a neutral role that is respectful of the beliefs of all of the guests. In order to preserve this role, he or she cannot have a hand in any religious elements performed during the ceremony. It also has to do with authenticity: religious ritual feels genuine only when it is performed by a member of the appropriate religion.

While it may be relatively easy to involve a guest in the reading of a religious text or prayer, in the singing of a religious song or in bearing a religious object that will be used by the bride or groom, there are definitely limits to what may be done. For instance, only a Catholic priest may bless a cup of wine and only an Orthodox priest should crown the heads of the bride and groom. In such cases, I prefer to mention the ritual without enacting it. If the couple feels very strongly about including such a ritual, a friend or relative should bear and present the cup of wine to the couple. The celebrant must then explain that this act is only a *reminder* of a religious tradition, and concentrate on why it is so important for the couple to include it in their wedding ceremony.

In the case of the Jewish bride I mentioned earlier on, we determined that it would be best if her father blessed the wine cup and invited the bride and groom to drink from it. Later, four of the bride's Jewish friends stepped forward and read the traditional seven blessings. They felt so at ease that they spontaneously started singing the blessings rather than just saying them. Many of the guests joined in, making it an emotional moment for everyone. Towards the end of the ceremony, the bride's father wordlessly placed the wine cup next to the groom's foot and indicated to his son-in-law that he could crush it with his heel. The fact that the bride circled seven times around the groom when she entered the ceremonial space and then the couple stood under a *chuppah* (traditional Jewish canopy) clearly needed an explanation, which brings us to the next rule...

9. Explain briefly what each religious ritual means *to the couple* in this context

Keep in mind that guests who do not belong to a particular culture may not understand references made to it during the ceremony. How a traditional ritual is introduced is extremely important. Any such ritual should be preceded by a short explanation so that all of the guests know what is happening and why. The goal is to help the guests feel included in the ceremony. In fact, it is interesting to note that many religious people know relatively little about the historical significance of their rituals.

The celebrant cannot, and should not, pretend to know what a religious ritual means to a practitioner. Ritual customs often have multilayered meanings, some of which may be contradictory or even controversial. For instance, there are many different explanations about why the Jewish bride circles the groom seven times. Even rabbis are not in agreement. My opinion is that this kind of information is unnecessary and irrelevant to the wedding ceremony. The only explanation that really matters is what the chosen symbol means to the couple in the context of their multicultural wedding ceremony. In the case of the Jewish bride and the atheist groom, I relayed to the assembly the couple's interpretation of the circling as a mark of their never-ending love (circle) and of the intimate space they share. I also explained that the *chuppah* represented the couple's desire for a home that protects them and their relationship (the ceiling) yet remains open to the world (no walls).

Moreover, some rituals may be common to several cultures. For example, the British Catholic bride (at the outset of this chapter) particularly liked the Celtic hand-fasting ritual, because it reminded her of her Irish grandfather. The groom liked the idea too, but he was even happier when he heard that a similar ritual is sometimes practised in Buddhist weddings. After the ceremony, one of the groom's relatives remarked that a similar ritual is performed during weddings in some parts of Morocco, the groom's country of origin.

10. Smile

This may sound cheesy, but I smile during the ceremony to reassure the guests and the couple that everything is under control, so that they can relax and enjoy the occasion. People are not yet familiar with multicultural wedding ceremonies, so they can feel a bit nervous when the ceremony begins. However, the uniqueness and meaningfulness of such ceremonies make them exhilarating. Couples truly take ownership of their wedding and their guests can sense it. They are often very moved to see how much time, energy and thought the bride and groom invested to make this ceremony – and the whole day – very special for everyone.

IN CONCLUSION:
A NEW 'RITUAL GRAMMAR' IN THE MAKING

What have I learned in my journey into the world of diversity? The tradition of getting married does not seem to suffer from the crises of religious institutions. Weddings and religion do not need to be coupled; they are two very different things. For centuries, of course, religion was the main way to marry. Even today, we still use, understand and react emotionally to rituals expressed through religious 'grammars'. Nevertheless, even couples who are completely estranged from religion do want a meaningful wedding ceremony. They crave for a social rite that will help them *feel* the transition from single to married. They may not be religious, but they do have values and a 'community' formed by their loved ones. They mainly need a celebrant to help them discover this and to support them as they define the meaning they want to give to their union, as well as the rituals and symbols they wish to use in order to express their commitment in the most genuine way.

Organizing multicultural ceremonies has also made me realize that a new global 'ritual grammar' is in the making. In our interconnected world, theoretically at least, we can hear about everyone else's wedding, see their pictures and read the comments of their friends. This does not, however, seem to be leading us to a unified model for weddings. A world of diversity means that most people are 'polyglots' when it comes to rituals – they can understand and relate to several 'symbolic languages' at the same time. They acknowledge that their identity is complex and therefore they are prepared to choose the rituals that seem to express the most accurately who they are, deep down, and what they intend to do as a couple.

Everywhere, couples want to tailor their unique, authentic ceremony. I am happy to say that I can now see exactly how to help them do that.

I am not angry anymore.

7

CASE STUDY: A FUNERAL CEREMONY FOR A VIOLINIST

Christine Behrend

INTRODUCTION

I became an independent funeral and wedding officiant relatively recently after a career in qualitative marketing research. During my first three years in this new role I have created and led a number of ceremonies throughout French-speaking Switzerland, and have been confronted with a variety of issues in ceremony design. One regular challenge in funerals has been to design a ceremony that is simple and easy to follow, yet effectively pays tribute to the deceased's life, personality and achievements. This is especially true when the person led a rich and complex life. In addressing this problem, I have found that objects can play a valuable role as symbols, and can powerfully encapsulate different dimensions of a person's activity or accomplishments. It also provides a visual focal point during the ceremony. In the funeral ceremony described below, designed for a Swiss violinist and violin teacher, Victor, the violin itself was used. It was a universal symbol that could be immediately recognized by all present and carried a strong emotional charge.

The approach I chose was to make a distinction between two fundamental dimensions of Victor's music-making:

- On the one hand, the physical aspects – in particular, the violin as a tool and a physical extension of the musician himself.

- On the other hand, the immaterial aspects: the music Victor had created, the love of music he had inspired, the emotions of his music-making and the know-how he had passed on to his students in the course of a long teaching career.

The violin illustrated both these aspects. During the ceremony, as the celebrant and other speakers remembered Victor and paid tribute, the violin was symbolically 'alive', that is, it was played at various moments throughout the ceremony by one of Victor's former students.

At the time of committal and final farewell, the violin symbolically 'died', that is, it fell silent and was placed in its case alongside the coffin. The empty case had been open and visible by the coffin from the start of the ceremony in anticipation of this moment.

The silencing of the violin, symbolizing the death of its owner, made it easier for those present to 'move on' and to focus on the immaterial legacy. The violin had been a vehicle for creativity, passion, emotion and dedication; these were the elements that continued to live on after Victor's death. Not only would they be remembered; they would continue to be active in the music of the students whom Victor had trained as violinists and who, in turn, would train their own students, generation after generation.

FUNERAL CEREMONY FOR VICTOR, VIOLINIST AND VIOLIN TEACHER

Before the start of the ceremony, Victor's empty violin case is placed beside his coffin.

Music
'*The Well-tempered Clavier*' by Johann Sebastian Bach. Recording by Glenn Gould.

Opening words by celebrant
Welcome to this farewell ceremony… My name is C.B. I am an independent celebrant and am conducting this ceremony today on behalf of Victor's wife and son, Margarida and Leo.

We have come together to celebrate the life of Victor S., a life that began exactly 72 years ago and which has just come to its close. Victor did not belong to any religious institution or movement, and consequently this ceremony does not follow any established tradition. Our ceremony has been designed to reflect Victor's values, passions and personality...

As you know, Victor was a professional violinist and also taught the violin. His life was steeped in music. His musical tastes ranged from Gregorian chant to electronic music, from Beethoven to Brassens. But throughout his life he held a strong and steadfast attachment to the music of Johann Sebastian Bach... During our ceremony, Sophie M., a former student of Victor's and today a professional violinist, will play some extracts from Bach's Sonatas and Partitas for solo violin. These were some of Victor's most renowned concert pieces, but he also loved to play them alone in the evenings at his home in the village of B. The instrument Sophie is playing was Victor's favourite violin and it accompanied him throughout his long career.

Music
'*Partita*' by Johann Sebastian Bach.

Eulogy read by celebrant
Victor was born on...1941 in... At the time of Victor's birth, war was raging throughout Europe, but the future musician was unaware of it. His parents, Aline and Paul, were farmers. From his earliest childhood, Victor rose early and accompanied his father to the stables to milk the cows, marvelling at the sunrise and the birdsong. 'Those who do not rise at dawn,' he used to say, 'miss the best part of the day.' It was perhaps thanks to this childhood, spent among the treasures of nature and the protective love of his parents, that Victor developed the simplicity of heart and the natural capacity for happiness that many envied him.

As a child Victor was a dreamer; as a teenager he was an idealist outraged by the injustice and inequality of the contemporary world. At the age of 17 he wrote two articles in the school magazine protesting against the nuclear arms race and expressing anxiety about the Cold War between the United States and the Soviet Union.

Music entered Victor's life by chance when he was ten. After a snowstorm prevented his father from collecting him from a friend's birthday party, Victor had to spend the night at his friend's place. This turned out to be a stroke of good fortune, because it was on that evening that Victor heard classical music for the first time in his life. He was bewitched by the beauty of what he heard, and from that day on remained captive to the spell of music. He always remembered exactly what music he heard that first evening: it included Maria Callas, the great Swedish tenor Jussi Björling and Benjamin Britten's *War Requiem*. In the space of a few hours, Victor discovered his calling and took the decision to devote his life to music.

In vain his parents suggested he take over their farm. In vain they encouraged him to train for a safer job, at least as a fall-back. Victor launched himself, body and soul, into music. Violin lessons at Lausanne Conservatory from 1952 to 1959, while Victor was still at secondary school, were followed by professional classes at the same Conservatory and then a two-year scholarship to the Julliard School of Music in New York, which he attended from 1963 to 1965.

Back in Lausanne in 1965, he embarked on his dual career, that of concert violinist and teacher, which lasted for more than 40 years, until Victor retired in 2006. Those 40 years brought a wealth of experience. His career had too many facets to be recounted here, but we can re-trace three main stages: Sinfonietta de Lausanne from 1966 to 1995, Baroque-Four string quartet from 1986 to 2006 and the Ensemble Intercontemporain from 1995 to 2006. You may have heard Victor in one of the many concerts he gave, both inside and outside Switzerland. Leo has set up a blog that gives many insights into Victor's musical career and includes excerpts from his interpretations.

Alongside his career as a concert artiste, transmitting music to others was very important to Victor. Teaching meant that he could never become complacent. He was moved by a strong desire to share – he wanted others to partake in the incomparable pleasure of music-making. And he loved rising to the challenge of planting the seed of music in a child's spirit and nurturing the young plant until the child grew into an accomplished musician.

Music was not the only passion in Victor's life. In the early 60s, Margarida was studying biology at Lausanne University and living in digs close to the Conservatoire, just above Victor's favourite café, the Chat Gris, where she also went every day. They exchanged glances, then a few words, then long conversations... From sharing opinions and experiences they ended up sharing their lives. Their love stood the test of two years of separation while Victor was in New York. They married on January 15th 1966 and never left each other's side.

Victor was a strong defender of humanitarian and pacifist causes. One of his commitments was to Amnesty International, of which he was a long-standing member.

A talented individual and outstanding musician. Victor inspired several generations of musicians and won over the public with the power and beauty of his interpretations.

A man of high standards, Victor demanded a lot of his students and was impatient with laziness or lack of commitment. Those pupils might find him curt or abrupt

An accomplished teacher, Victor always gave warm encouragement to his students and always congratulated them on their progress.

Generous and warm-hearted, Victor openly shared his music and know-how, and the door of his house was always open to those who came to chat, play music or drink a glass of white wine.

Sensitive and considerate, Victor always thanked Margarida for the happiness they had built together.

A father, Victor raised his son Leo with firmness and at the same time with great affection.

No longer among us, Victor died suddenly on October 15th in his sleep, from a heart attack.

A man of exception, Victor leaves us with countless memories.

We will now observe a quiet moment to allow each of you to remember Victor as you yourselves knew him and what you shared with him. Sophie and Johann Sebastian Bach will accompany us. After this moment's silence, Margarida will talk to us about Victor.

Music
'*Partita*' by Johann Sebastian Bach.

Tribute by Margarida
Victor, I have spent my life with you, and now you are gone. I am in shock, I cannot quite understand what has happened, nor why. If you were here, you would explain it to me, but you are no longer here. I feel emptiness and sadness.

Yet at the same time I feel enormous gratitude. What you gave to me, no one else could have given. The life we lived together I could not have lived with anyone else. I thank you from the depth of my heart.

And in my sadness I find consolation. Although you are no longer by my side, I remember you vividly. I will always remember how you asked me to marry you by playing Jacques Brel's '*Ne Me Quitte Pas*', because at that time you were very shy. I remember the look of astonishment on your face when you met Leo for the first time, just after he was born. I can still hear the grating sound of your string as you tuned them before extracting your music from them. I will never forget the way your fondue always went wrong but you always insisted on making it yourself anyway. And the tenderness with which you played a Fauré lullaby to soothe an injured bird.

This, and so much more, was you. I thank you from the depth of my heart.

Presentation by celebrant
The next piece of music is the second movement of Bach's '*Double Violin Concerto*'. It was chosen by Margarida and Leo not only because it was one of Victor's favourite pieces but because the interweaving of the two violins symbolizes man and woman, life and death, sadness and happiness. The recording is of Victor himself and the British violinist F.B.

Music
'*Double Violin Concerto*', *2nd Movement* by Johann Sebastian Bach.

Presentation by celebrant

Our two next tributes are from the world of music: first, Stéphane B., a violinist who played alongside Victor in the Lausanne Sinfonietta. And then, Barbara G., one of Victor's students.

Tribute by Stéphane

The most talented musicians often fall into one of two categories. Either they have inflated egos and look down on everyone else, or they are surprisingly generous and unpretentious. Victor, you belonged 200 per cent to the second category. You were moulded from the same clay as the Barenboims and Menuhins of music, passionate about the beauty of music but equally passionate about sharing your enthusiasm and expertise with other. You always displayed the greatest respect not only for the great and mighty but also for the frail and the unknown.

You were brilliant to play alongside in the orchestra. I remember the concert when you played with such gusto that your bow flew off and landed in the audience, creating an effect as dramatic as it was unintended. And the time when the percussionist behind us dozed off, and you gently woke him up, much to the disappointment of some of our colleagues who were gleefully anticipating his misfortune. When the orchestra was engaged in a battle with a visiting conductor, very famous but erratic and ill tempered, you became the orchestra's spokesman and worked out an agreement.

I speak on behalf of all your colleagues, from the recent and distant past, when I say that we will miss you enormously, not only for your qualities as a musician, but even more for your qualities as a human being.

Tribute by Barbara

It is quite a few years ago that I was one of Victor's students, but I remember those lessons as clearly as if they were yesterday. When I arrived in the little room behind the German church, I felt not only expected but truly welcome. Victor always asked me how I was, not out of convention but because he was genuinely concerned for my wellbeing. Initially, it was my parents who insisted on my taking violin lessons; I didn't want to. But very soon Victor created in me a true love of music and took me on a journey of musical discovery spanning many centuries and many different countries. An excellent teacher, he was uncannily good at detecting even minor impediments. At one point he corrected my posture just very slightly and the tone of my violin instantly improved, as if by a miracle. He had the patience of an angel and as long as I tried my hardest he always encouraged me.

His teaching made a tremendous difference to my life and I am happy to be able to pay tribute today. If all teachers were like Victor, the world would be a better place.

Music
'*Chaconne*' by Johann Sebastian Bach, played by Victor's former student Sophie.

Separation and closing words by celebrant
We have celebrated Victor and the life he lived. The time has now come to say farewell.

[Margarida and Leo come forward, take the violin from Sophie's hands, place it in the case and put the case back by the side of the coffin. Then they return to their seats.]

Victor is dead, and his violin has fallen silent. But as we have heard during this ceremony, Victor leaves precious and enduring memories among those who knew him. His love of music and humanitarian values form a living legacy. The emotions he created with his violin playing leave lasting imprints. The talent he fostered in others will in turn create fresh emotions, and so the cycle will continue for generation after generation of musicians.

[A few moments of silence.]

As Victor himself requested, his body will be cremated… His ashes will be scattered on Lake Geneva, below his beloved village of B.

[Invitation to the reception after the ceremony.]

As you leave the room, you will again hear Bach's '*Goldberg Variations*', this time in the interpretation of Uri Caine, much loved by Victor.

Music
'*Goldberg Variations*' by Johann Sebastian Bach. Recorded by Uri Caine.

8

CASE STUDY: A MEMORIAL AND A WEDDING ROLLED INTO ONE HUMANIST CEREMONY

Isabel Russo

Humanist Ceremonies™ is the growing network of over 300 celebrants trained and accredited by the British Humanist Association (BHA) to take non-religious ritual, namely funeral, wedding and naming ceremonies, throughout England, Wales and Northern Ireland. The BHA promotes humanism as an ethical and fulfilling non-religious approach to life involving a naturalistic view of the universe. It supports the belief that our morality derives from recognizing the need we have to live together in communities happily and peaceably, a conviction which naturally leads to the concern that we should be responsible for our actions – and that our actions should contribute to the happiness and the welfare of others as well as our own.

People with humanist beliefs and values are profoundly supported in identifying and expressing those beliefs and values in the thousands of humanist ceremonies that we provide every year. The roots of Humanist Ceremonies can be traced as far back as the 1890s, when members were meeting the emerging need for non-religious ceremony on a voluntary basis. However, it is only since the 1980s that we have worked to formalize our provision, with intensive training and quality assurance for our celebrants, as well as the fostering of a network that works collegially as a community of practice.

At a time when people are moving away from a religious outlook, humanist ceremonies are becoming increasingly popular. However, every situation is unique, and our celebrants are well versed in being able to take on atypical requests. One such request that I would like to focus on for the purpose of this chapter called for a memorial and a wedding to be performed in the same ceremony.

In November 2014, the BHA was approached with an unusual request on behalf of a long-standing BHA member. The gentleman's partner had died after a long illness, a year before same-sex marriage became legally recognized in England in December 2014. This meant that whilst the couple had been able to register their civil partnership in 2005, they had not been able to fulfil their dearly held wish and promise to each other to marry. The request now was that we find a celebrant who would be willing to conduct a marriage ceremony, combined with a memorial service.

We immediately rose to this challenge and turned to Jill Satin, an experienced humanist celebrant trained in both weddings and funerals, who fully embraced the work ahead.

Our celebrant met with her client many times, and over a few months was able to create a script that was at the same time an acknowledgment and a 'sealing', but also a letting go.

To add to an already unusual set of circumstances, our celebrant faced an additional challenge: her client had also embarked on a new relationship which he requested be recognized within the ceremony. In so many ways, the ceremony that she was crafting did not, and could not, 'make sense' – and this is why it is such a good example of the work that we do.

When the celebrant delivered the ceremony in central London on a cold but beautiful twilight January evening to a close group of family and friends, she said by way of introduction:

> Our ceremony today is part memorial; part a conversation about love, grieving and loss, and ultimately a celebration of commitment and finding renewal and new love. In other words, a journey through the complexity and joys of the rich tapestry of life.

And in relating the event to me months afterwards, our client wrote:

> I would describe the ceremony as the second happiest day of my life, a time for dark reflection but principally for the joy of finding that the bitterness of knowing that so many radiantly happy experiences could never be repeated, was changing into a greater calm, serenity and gratitude... It was an event where, Janus-like, we all looked back and forward – an occasion that has taken me beyond an abyss and into the light.

The success of the ceremony proved that well-crafted, authentic ritual unconstrained by the protocol and precepts of religious ceremony is perfectly able to hold and reflect the extreme complexities of human experience in a way that does not feel onerous or formulaic. If we agree that successful ritual marks and facilitates moments of profound transition from one state of being to another, with words and actions that resonate with all those involved, then this was most definitely a ritual that 'worked'. And it is perhaps a useful exercise to reflect on some of the choices that the celebrant made that ensured such success.

THE UNUSUALNESS OF THE CEREMONY AND THE CHALLENGE IT PRESENTED WERE HONESTLY ADDRESSED

The opening words of a ritual set the tone of the ceremony and the expectations of those taking part. For a successful ritual to take place it is crucial that those words resonate as being authentic to the subject matter as well as inclusive to those listening. In this case, the celebrant made the choice to address the unique nature of what was to follow, and any feelings of uncertainty or anxiety that there might be around it, in her opening words:

> Now I'm sure that some of you are just a little bit uncertain about today, about what we're really trying to do and what the focus and point of it all is. So allow me to explain...

It is interesting to note the warm and conversational nature of her tone as she acknowledges the understandable uncertainty in the room. Later, the celebrant is again frank about the unusualness of the situation, helping to dispel any sense of pretence or the need to politely suspend disbelief from those taking part:

> Normally when I am asked to conduct a marriage ceremony I have both partners available to me. I ask them both to answer many questions and to think with me about why they are entering into a marriage contract. I am more than slightly hampered in this case as dear Lyndon is no longer with us, but I am sure he would have been hugely touched at Bryce's determination and love, and Bryce has been able to distil for me what Lyndon would have thought with candour, accuracy and humour.

Humanist ceremonies are frequently described as being 'refreshingly honest'. With religious dogma, protocol and process removed, we are able to sensitively acknowledge and accept the more challenging parts of humanity, putting them into the context of the whole person and the whole situation.

THE BROADER HISTORICAL AND POLITICAL CONTEXT WERE REFERENCED

One of the critical elements in the construction of this script was the need to address the situation that the much wished and hoped for marriage between Bryce and Lyndon had been made impossible by forces that were beyond their control. This was not a wedding ceremony born out of the acceptance of a protocol that mapped out how they could express their love, but one born in response to the understandable fury that Bryce felt at the prejudice and political injustice that had barred his and Lyndon's right to validate their love in the way they wanted. That context and the anger generated by the injustice of the wider political landscape needed to be expressed, and the celebrant did so by again honestly addressing the issue, and talking candidly about gay rights and the history of same-sex civil partnership and marriage:

> Nine years ago same-sex couples in the UK finally had the right to have a legal ceremony which registers them in a civil partnership. However, they were not allowed to marry. Just last month on December 10th 2014 same-sex couples were granted the right to convert their civil partnership to a marriage allowing a registrar to declare 'husband and husband' or 'wife and wife'. Finally there is formal national recognition to a hugely important issue that lesbians and gays have been seeking: the right to validate their union in a society that is often resistant to change.

The celebrant could not change history for Bryce and Lyndon. She could not undo generations of prejudice, or bring Lyndon back from the dead to create the wedding ceremony that they had so dearly wished for, but she could address Bryce's needs by making sure that his and Lyndon's struggle and story were told – and heard.

THE CELEBRANT AND CLIENT WORKED COLLABORATIVELY

Bryce was at the heart of this ritual, and therefore it was crucial that he had a voice throughout. The celebrant ensured this was so, meeting and speaking with Bryce frequently during the creation of the ceremony. Ritual commonly explores changing identity, signposting and supporting the passing from one identity to another. In this complex ceremony, Bryce was at one and the same time acknowledging his journey into widowhood after a relationship of 37 years, celebrating his newly attained identity as Lyndon's husband and announcing his emerging identity as a partner in a new relationship. No attempt was made to link these different identities, but Bryce was able to give voice to all three. And literally so, as he was given the opportunity to read his own words throughout the ceremony.

The rawness of his loss was not avoided for the comfort of those listening:

> Unable to eat or sleep I became a walking skeleton. Elderly ladies offered me their seat on the underground. And when death finally came, once an initial numbness had worn off, a new universe of pain began…

The depth of his love for his husband was not toned down for the comfort of his new partner:

> Our relationship evolved over the years into something as natural as it was intense…above all, to quote my youngest niece, we were 'comfortable' with each other. 'You were,' to quote a friend, 'the most married couple I have ever known, joined at the hip and impossible to consider separately.'

And the joy of having found somebody new to love and be loved by was not suppressed by a sense of duty to what had gone before:

> …his loving and welcoming Indian family, so different to my own and Lyndon's warring set-ups, has made a huge difference to my life. It is full is of laughter and wit and once we passed an initial politeness barrier became increasingly ribald and mischievous. I respect his wonderful intelligence and human perception, something so much more important than mere 'cleverness'.

THOSE GATHERED HAD AN ACTIVE ROLE

In non-religious ceremony, it is not God who bears witness to the ritual taking place, but the community of family and friends – those people who have shared with the protagonist other significant life moments and in doing so, forged the human ties of friendship, trust and compassion. Bryce's ceremony took place at a venue that had huge significance to him – the home in which he had shared his life with Lyndon – and it was witnessed by those people who were enduringly significant to him who, as he says:

> ...had remained close and steadfast during a seemingly unbearable sadness and grief.

The celebrant ensured they knew they had an active role to play and acknowledged their roles both as witnesses at a wedding:

> It is your presence here which gives this ceremony its special significance; for it is an outward symbol of the love between Bryce and Lyndon that has led Bryce to make his declarations, in the presence of all of you, the people whom he most loves and respects and whose friendship he most values. You represent his wide circle of friends and family and your support in the future will be all the richer for having been here today.

And also as mourners at a memorial:

> Bryce and Lyndon's family and friends have had to face a personal journey through grief, and it has been different for each of you. There was no one else like Lyndon in the whole world, and there never will be again. You loved him. And the price we pay for the joy of loving someone is the terrible pain we face when they die. Lyndon was special and different for each of you, and so your grieving for him will be individual and special as well.

Alerting the gathering to the active role they had to play as witnesses rather than as watchers imparted an understanding that the ceremony and its success was a shared responsibility. This in turn gave rise to a conscious sense of participation and engagement in the room, the outcome of which was a magnification of the impact of the ritual.

THE 'MISSING' PERSON WAS POWERFULLY RECREATED

Whilst the celebrant acknowledged that the ceremony was unusual in that one of the key people was not present, she nevertheless evoked a powerful sense of Lyndon throughout the ritual, describing how he looked, how he sounded, what he wore, and sharing the stories, memories and words that Bryce had used to recreate Lyndon for her in their meetings.

She also gave Bryce the space to talk deeply about who Lyndon was for him – and to reflect on the occasion of their civil marriage, which he did with intricate detail and joy.

In 're-creating' Lyndon, the celebrant achieved the dual effect of reclaiming the person that he had been before he was diminished by illness and death – a powerful function of a successful memorial. She also 'brought him into the room' so that as the ceremony developed and Bryce took his vows to Lyndon, Lyndon was vividly present in the hearts and minds of those who were bearing witness.

WHAT MARRIAGE MEANT IN THIS CONTEXT WAS SPECIFICALLY EXPLAINED

A sentiment often expressed at a humanist wedding ceremony is that whilst marriage is embedded in our culture and is widely regarded as a common undertaking, no two marriages are ever the same. Each marriage, and therefore each wedding, is entirely unique to the couple, and so it follows that the foundation, aspiration, language and action of both wedding and marriage are for the couple alone to define.

In the course of this wedding and memorial ceremony, the celebrant encouraged Bryce to explore what his first 'marriage', the civil partnership, had meant to the couple before then arriving at the kernel of meaning of the current marriage ceremony. As well as focusing on the meaning the two men had given their relationship when Lyndon was alive, the wider meaning of the day of the civil partnership itself was powerfully evoked. As we know, Bryce and Lyndon were one of the very first couples to take part in a same-sex civil partnership. The event itself was therefore not only a deeply personal landmark moment for them; it was also a very public landmark moment that was destined to be shared on the world platform. Again the celebrant encouraged Bryce to use his own words to describe the event:

> ...and so our Partnership took place before an ever-helpful Westminster Council in Marylebone Town Hall. Our subsequent escape with our witnesses, Sylvia and her late husband Rupert was

blocked by a sensationally large press gathering from the British newspapers and journalists from Greece, Spain, Canada and, startlingly, Russia. Our picture appeared on the front of *The Times* and *The Guardian* and, alarmingly, on the front of the Moscow paper. That night Lyndon sang in the Gay Men's Chorus in the Barbican, where our marriage was announced before thousands to deafening applause. Changed times!

By the light it shone in contrast, the vivid explanation of the first ceremony and of the public platform on which it was held brought clarity to the identity of this second, intimate, deeply personal and private marriage ceremony. The celebrant skilfully bridged the two by touching on the quote commonly attributed to André Maurois: 'A happy marriage is a long conversation which always seems too short.'[1]

The foundations and aspirations of this memorial marriage were then made clear in word and in symbolic action. The celebrant reflected that this marriage ceremony was an acknowledgement of the work the two men had put in to make their partnership a success, and that it was a confirmation of their love of over 37 years. The climactic moment of the ceremony took place as Bryce made his promises to Lyndon, promises of love and respect, and of a lifelong commitment to cherishing everything that they had shared. Bryce charged his wedding ring with the words:

> Lyndon, I will wear this wedding ring with pride and as a symbol of my respect, affection and love for you. It is a symbol of everything we have done together, and it will always be a reminder of all the wonderful times we have had and my deep gratitude.

Having sealed his commitment to cherishing the past, the ceremony's final component was then addressed as Bryce's new partner was acknowledged and welcomed and the future was shaped as a safe and happy place for Bryce to step into. Before he died, Lyndon had made Bryce promise that

---

1   André Maurois, born Émile Salomon Wilhelm Herzog (1885–1967) was a French author. He speaks about marriage in his *Memoirs 1885–1967*; the book was translated into English by Denver Lindley and published by Harper & Row in 1970.

he would, in time, seek a new love to bring him happiness. This promise was touched on by the celebrant, and then consolidated as she drew the ceremony to a close. She observed that Lyndon would have been the first to raise a glass to the commitment to the past as well as to toast Bryce's future, wishing him a sense of completion and every happiness with his new partner. The sense of both opening and closing chapters was therefore fully accomplished in a ceremony that managed to achieve the recognition and confirmation of a love of 37 years, as well as the fulfilment of a dearly held wish and a promise to marry against all odds. This was a stabilizing anchor for Bryce as he committed to the memory of what he recognized as the love of his life, yet was also able to acknowledge and accept his present step into a new future and a new relationship.

As one friend at the end of the ceremony put it: 'I think it was the strangest but also the nicest wedding ceremony I have ever been to.'

CONCLUSION

For Bryce, the process of creating and enacting this ceremony brought him a powerful sense of healing, closure and renewal. He was able to grapple with the deep emotional and psychological experiences that the past years had visited upon him, and was supported in being able to articulate, shape and harness these experiences in a way that resonated with his deepest values and aspirations.

For me, the only golden rule to effective ritual, however simple or complicated the circumstances, is for it to be crafted in accordance with the belief system of the person for whom it is being constructed. The rest of the work requires sensitivity, pragmatism, creativity and a strong grasp of the direction of travel, but as long as the central sensemaking tenet is in place, then there is no limit to what can be achieved or to the nuances and complexities of contemporary living that can be expressed.

In a contemporary society, where there is an increasing recognition that physical, emotional and psychological transitions need to be articulated and acknowledged without the dogma and precepts of a religious script, we are facing the emergence of new ceremonies for a new age.

Alongside unique and creative funeral, wedding, naming and coming of age ceremonies are adoption, divorce, menopause, and gender change ceremonies, all examples of emerging rituals that have their roots in our collective contemporary journey and that are starting to push tentatively to the surface.

In an ever-changing world, where the tectonic plates of belief, politics, technology and identity are constantly shifting, it is up to each individual, should they wish, to carefully define that which has heart and meaning for them, and to map their lives according to their values. Ritual always has been and always will be key to this process.

I am very grateful to both Bryce Morrison and Jill Satin for their willingness to so generously share both the content and the experience of this ceremony with me.

PART III

RITUALIZING IN INTIMATE SPACES

9

RITUAL AS RESOURCE

HEALTH AND TRANSFORMATION IN THE TWENTY-FIRST CENTURY

Michael Picucci

Although the word 'ritual' may carry old religious, diplomatic and military connotations for some, others interested in establishing new modes of healing have embraced it and reclaimed it in a rational and creative context, with much success. Ritual, retooled, is being brought into service as an energetic resource for individuals, relationships, intentional communities and groups. This chapter proposes the use of ritual as a human technology ideally suited for personal and cultural transformation, creativity, balance and healing. There are numerous ways to apply this technology to one's daily life and the results can be astounding, bringing some to describe its efficacy as 'magical'.

In essence, the function of ritual is to assist one in accessing internal resources of energy from the physical, emotional, intellectual and spiritual, all of which are interconnected and accessible by an unseen but universal 'source energy'. This singular energetic web is superficially difficult to access by 'left brain only' rational constructs, but it is readily available through 'right-and-left brain' ritual processes. These rituals access the unconscious as a doorway to a deeply hidden life force. Hereafter, we will refer to this universal life force as 'source energy'.

In my practice, I have found ritual to be an elegant process for dissolving deep-seated and often unrecognized bio-energetic blocks to health, wellbeing and transformation. Unblocking may relate to formulating new healing energies, accessing greater intellectual or creative energies for problem-solving, or intensifying visionary and spiritual energies.

Ancient wisdom concerning the performance of rituals emerged from a world in which time was experienced slowly and people were consciously connected to the energy and vibrations of the universe. To remain healthy, unblocked and balanced, individuals living a fast-paced lifestyle need to relearn how to live in the present moment and reconnect with this energy. Our immediate connection to 'source energy' emanates from the Earth we live on and from the cosmos in which it is embedded.

By becoming fluent in the use of these energies, individuals, groups (permanent or not) and communities can develop profound ways of calling on universal resources to facilitate a variety of transformative experiences.

TERMS USED IN THIS CHAPTER

Ritual usually refers to a ceremonial rite, or an action sanctifying a certain process. Here we expand its meaning to include not only physical actions, but also mental and energetic processes such as intention and visualization. In the field of anthropology, a 'rite' generally involves visible, that is, externally observable action only. For our purposes, a ritual may also be non-observable, such as a thought, an image, or a word filled with intention and directed to initiate qualitative change or to achieve a certain outcome. In a real sense, ritual is a 'tool', a spiritual fulcrum or pulley for assisting individuals and groups who wish to discover more satisfying ways of being and manifesting.

Source energy refers to the life force that exists everywhere, throughout all space and time (see Figure 9.1). It is the prime mover or actuating force behind everything in existence. It is the energy that invisibly connects the individual to the earth, to everyone and everything in the universe. It makes up our own essence, that innate, hidden vibration of the universe which in Taoist literature is called *chi*. It is the mysterious force that animates us, and the various energies we look to as life-giving, including those in the spiritual, mental, emotional and physical domains. Because of its universality, 'source energy' offers not only the possibility of personal healing and insight, but also collective healing and conscious evolution.

Felt sense is understood as the here-and-now physical (somatic) sensations associated with various mental constructs, core memories and imagery. 'Felt senses' are the interface between the self and 'source energy'. When we develop the ability to access and use 'felt sense' as a tool, it helps us transmute our intentions into effective action in the everyday world.

Intention is a forward-moving force to achieve a specific desire, result or outcome. In any transformational ritual, intention must be present. Ritual gives power to our intentionality and helps us focus it like a *vajra*, the 'Thunderbolt' symbol used in Tibetan magic, representing the force of truth. Intention directs the energy created by ritual towards a specific desire or result. In fact, anecdotally, our experiments with shared intentionality have often led to outcomes far greater than we 'intended'.

Resource refers to any positive memory, person, place, object or action that creates a soothing or calming feeling in one's body. This internal, and indeed integral, resource is at the foundation of ritual and what makes it so effective.

The curious observer self is an unseen part of a person, which perceives all experiences (thoughts, feelings, felt senses, etc.) without judgement or agenda. The 'curious observer self' perceives, knows and records all we see, do and feel with a curiosity that comes from the deepest level of selfhood. It is also wiser than our linear, binary, logical thinking brain.

Each of these terms describes an element of ritual that we have found to be essential for utilizing it as a transformational tool. In combination, these six elements constitute a remarkably powerful gateway into the old 'reptilian sectors' and limbic brain, unlocking long-forgotten powers for visualizing and manifesting change. By grounding in the *felt senses*, tuning into *source energy* and bringing three elements to the fore, *intention*, *resource* and our *curious observer self*, we can create powerful rituals re-engineered and updated for our times, and which can be harnessed for the greater good.

In a nutshell, the process is quite simple: connect with *source energy*, create an *intention* concerning desired outcomes, bring in *resources* and the *curious observer self* to the specific task at hand, and witness the alchemy and results as they come to fruition.

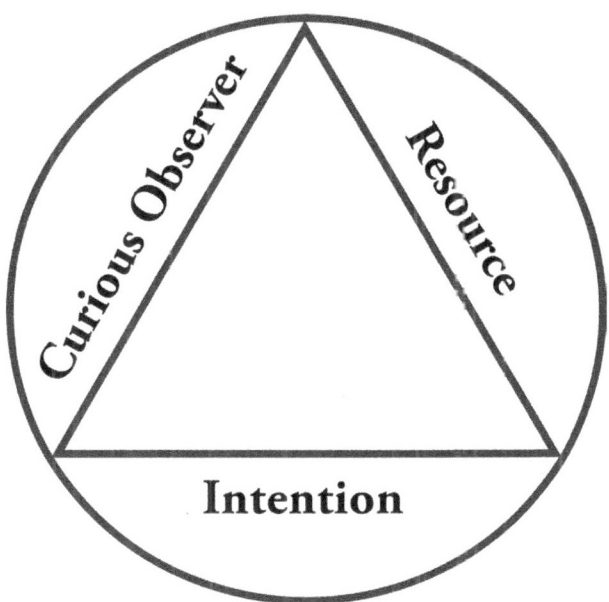

Figure 9.1. Source energy

CONNECTING WITH SOURCE ENERGY

'Source energy' is the universal power behind all effective ritual. The nature and design of any specific ritual allows this energy to be customized and directed towards any given intention. For our purposes, accessing 'source energy' begins the process. By closing the ritual with an expression of gratitude for the gift of connection – in remembrance that within the source energy we are all one – we end with it as well. The initial steps are outlined below:

1. Grounding, tuning into, focusing on and integrating 'source energy'.
2. Amplifying 'source energy'.

3. Engaging and directing 'source energy'.

4. Expressing gratitude.

The last step returns us to the mundane and simultaneously confirms our connection with the numinous, or divine. By consciously moving through these preparatory steps sequentially, one can set the stage for incorporating the other elements for the ritual.

The first step in the process is to relax and let go of tensions and previous frames of mind. This can be called 'grounding' and broken down into four steps all its own: grounding, tuning in, focusing and integrating. All four are especially helpful to anyone attempting to access the power of ritual for the first time. All four help those involved 'tune into' the sacred space within, by bringing attention to the body's felt senses. By directing attention inward toward an awareness of the body *in the moment*, individuals are able to access their innate intelligence. Starting with their own body's unique connection with 'source energy', men and women are ultimately able to discover their unique vibration within the cosmos and tap into a greater field of intelligence not limited by the everyday consciousness.

There is a relationship between innate intelligence and feelings of wellbeing. When one is 'in touch' with the inner self, it allows access to the body's inherent wisdom. This relationship, explored in earlier times by traditional shamans, is still practised in traditional communities around the world. The term 'felt sense' encapsulates numerous modes of awareness otherwise difficult to put into words. After grounding, tuning in, focusing, and integrating, we ramp up by breathing with the energy, then amplifying it, then focusing without distraction on the purpose of the ritual. Then the energy is clearly directed, sometimes with an accompanying gesture that triggers the unconscious mind and 'felt senses' to engage fully with the intention at hand. We then remember to give thanks.

By mindfully working through the steps to access 'source energy' as described here, anyone can develop an intuitive system for responding to a particular situation and coming up with specific solutions. This ability can at times appear to border on 'magic', an unusual ability to influence the course of events by using hidden or supernatural forces. It is not uncommon for transformative ritual to bring sudden and unexpected changes, reminiscent of the kind of healing associated with shamanism.

Those who are without access to traditional or religious rituals that create a connection to this energy can learn, or relearn, alternative methods for accessing it through simple grounding exercises. Two traditions that incorporate excellent grounding exercises are the formal mindfulness practices of meditation and yoga. Those without these practices can also accomplish body grounding relatively quickly by following the steps below:

1. *Grounding.* Sit calmly, expanding the awareness of 'now'. It helps if you can observe sensations while grounding, noticing the parts of your body that touch whatever you are sitting or lying on, and allowing them to be. Eventually, you come to realize that you are being held in space. You may even subtly experience gravity's wonderful role in all of this.

2. *Tuning in.* Softly, half-close your eyes to minimize visual distraction. After a minute or two, shift awareness to the natural breath. Observe the in and out of it, noticing that it takes little or no conscious effort. Your body knows how to breathe by itself, so allow each breath to be perfect in that moment.

3. *Focusing.* If the mind begins to chatter (as it has been conditioned to do, aka 'head noise'), imagine respectfully setting the interruptions aside. The linearity of the mind is remarkably effective for language, creativity, wonderful stimulation, productivity and logical or rational constructs. But remember that this noisy little mind was not organically designed to observe, much less control, the more complex workings of felt human experiences and consciousness. Although one can approach that level of integration in higher states, at times it is better to enjoy the easy flow of mundane existence and trust in the source.

4. *Integrating.* Invite your consciousness to focus on the body, becoming aware that this consciousness is one's entire self and

therefore larger than the mind. Become comfortable with this new awareness and the subtle contentment that it brings.

5. *Breathing.* Slightly reorient your focus to the natural breath. Observe the in and out of it, remembering that breathing is expansive by nature, and an ideal way to visualize the amplification of source energy. When breathing consciously, you are connecting to the opposite of fear. The more attention you can give to the breath, the more you move into a state of calm non-attachment in relation to everyday personal and cultural realities. Therefore, the primary tool for tuning into 'felt senses', for developing and strengthening a connection between the earth and ourselves, is breath. By bringing air into the lungs, the body opens to life and to the amplification of resources and possibilities.

6. *Amplification.* Place both hands over the heart, one over the other. Begin to notice an uptick of inner strength and mild elation. Utilize whatever visualizations or emotions you desire in order to amplify the flow of source energy into your sacred space and your body. Remember to stay grounded in the 'felt senses'. Bring your attention to the soles of the feet and notice the sensation of contact between your feet and the floor or ground. Importantly, feel gravity!

7. *Directing.* Now that you are deeply relaxed and integrated as one with 'source energy', and have stored up a reservoir of life-affirming energy as well, it is time to direct that energy towards your chosen goal. Set forth the intention that all obstacles, inner resistance and debate against achieving a certain intention will disappear without difficulty and undue effort. Directing the 'source energy' is akin to planting a seed, knowing that it will grow according to its own nature. It is important to acknowledge that creative processes take time and are subject to cycles of drought and spurts of growth. A specific concluding action may be used, such as snapping, pointing or crossing the fingers, clapping, holding

'three fingers' together or 'knocking on wood'. As well as helping to close the ritual, these types of physical actions connect us to former times when the forces of nature were ceremonially invoked using such gestures.

8. *Gratitude.* As stated before, offering gratitude is a splendid way to complete any ritual. It is also a good 'ego check', returning us to everyday reality while humbly honouring the mysterious aspects of ritual and the numinous or divine qualities of 'source energy'.

THE KEY TO RITUAL: INTENTION

Just as connecting with 'source energy' opens up the process of ritual, intention provides the focus or direction of energies for following through to the ultimate goal, through each of the steps, each of which can be called an intention of itself. Once the purpose or ultimate goal of the ritual has been decided upon, it is beneficial to state that intention simply, consciously formulated in an inner language, whether in the mind or spoken aloud. Some might call this a 'vision statement'. Formulation of an idea in thought, word or speech focuses 'attention to the matter'. With this singularity of focus, a concentration of purpose is created, and an inner vision emerges that provides direction, like an archer's single-minded attention on the bull's eye. Indeed, our use of intention is not novel. According to the Oxford English Dictionary (OED), the definition of 'intention' speaks to the idea that what is perceived by the intellect is *rendered* by intention. In the same OED entries, from a theological perspective, the validity of a sacrament is dependent on three aspects: matter, form and intention.

Simply put, no intention, no ritual!

BRINGING IN THE POWER OF RESOURCES

Another essential element involves opening oneself to opposite pairs of energies in the body. This I call the dance of opposites, and it is the key to generating energetic fields and vibrations. The opposites referred to here are the opposing energy forces (both flowing resource energy and unpleasant constrictive sensations) at work in our lives and in the world around us. They may include negative memories and the fear they engender. When conflict is felt, it is important to note it rather than to dismiss it. It is only when we become aware of that felt sense of conflict or constriction hidden within our energetic blocks in the body that healing can occur. Fundamental to therapeutic healing is this concept of inviting both pleasurable/expanding and troubling/constrictive energies into the healing process in a new and cordial way. In many indigenous cultures there are no 'bad' energies, only those that are respectfully transformed. By pursuing a more integrated way of living, we can embody a wholeness that utilizes every dimension of our being, which includes situations we experience as contradictions, duality and paradox. A paradox is a situation or statement that appears to be contradictory, but is not. Embracing these realities helps the linear mind comprehend the nature of wholeness, which is anything but linear. In developing the capacity to comfortably hold opposite energies at the same time, individuals can access otherwise unrecognized unconscious resources.

Energy stored in memory and the body is a resource energy that can be accessed through practice. Many who seek help from stress disorders soon reveal that they were conditioned to focus on their problems, deficiencies and on what needs to be corrected. They may not have been acculturated to look at the moments of blessings or the gifts they've received. Many deprecate such moments, because they are either not honoured by their culture or are seemingly ephemeral and fleeting. Yet these energetic resources for healing are still alive in their living memory and can be utilized as valuable transformational tools.

It may be helpful for individuals to compose a written inventory of inner and outer blessings as they begin to use 'ritual as resource' practice. By naming and sensing these resources, they gain and access power within themselves. It is important to orient one's thinking about these resources without regard to past or present, because energy healing happens outside of linear time.

It is also important to dwell not only on the pleasurable memories themselves, but also on the bodily sensations they engender. When we recall a pleasant moment, we feel good. It helps to think of pleasant memories as accumulating rather than as occurring only in the past, or as something that has ended. By bringing expansive memories of pleasant things that are lodged in the past into contact with the perhaps constrictive energies in the body in the present moment, the individual becomes aware of both simultaneously. This can also happen in the reverse, bringing a pleasant sense of the body in the present into contact with constrictive senses from the past.

Linking the powerful energy of good memories with the goodness of 'source energy' of the present helps individuals make deep contact with their innate intelligence. As soon as individuals evoke such imagery, they bring a sense of spiritedness to their lives because in its most granular aspects, ritual both attracts and is made from spirit, that which enlivens both our souls and the universal source which ritual links us to.

When learning to connect with this self-healing capacity, it is helpful to note that slow is fast. When an individual takes in a breath of spirit, the body will generally relax, allowing observations to emerge that are clear and informed in nuanced and subtle ways. 'Slow is fast' may seem contrary to contemporary or social conditioning, but it makes sense if one is to dive deeply past unconscious blocks and into the levels of awareness that lie beneath them. It is the slow movement of consciously directed mental activities that resonates with the autonomic nervous system, bringing a calmer resolution to this practice. It can be difficult to open up to the unknown, especially in very busy times. However, by recognizing this rhythm, individuals are better able to trust their own experience, and for personal ritual, this is seminal. Energy systems build organically. There is no rush; evolution is long.

THE ENIGMA: CURIOUS OBSERVER SELF IN ACTION

Now that the intention for the ritual has been chosen and amplified, and resources have been evoked and brought to the process, the next step is to surrender to the 'felt senses' of the body, and suspend the thinking mind. Allow the curious observer to simply notice that we have a mind (often noisy and distracting) as well a body that is alive. Having arrived at this profound state of awareness, the next step is to relinquish control of the little self and just let it go, bringing the focus of attention to the heart, to emotions, and whatever emerges without attachment. The 'curious observer', like a sprite sitting on a shoulder, comes into focused attention but remains detached, witnessing and recording what is ebbing and flowing in the body.

CLOSING THE RITUAL

Gratitude completes the ritual and acts as a seal for the experience. The goal is to retain gratitude and carry it into daily life. To keep the all-loving energy of ritual accessible, it is important to express gratitude for each step of transformation, whether small or large, thankful each time a weight is lifted, or a shift is made toward balance. This is why ritual is ended with thanks, just before coming to closure. By doing so we acknowledge a return from the sacred back to ordinary space, bringing gifts of ritual energy to our daily challenges and to those around us.

PUTTING IT TOGETHER: RITUAL IN ACTION

A young man who came for counselling needed to ask for a raise at his job, but was struggling to find the resolve to do so. He was successful and accomplished in many areas of his life, yet he kept running into an internal block, becoming tongue-tied whenever he approached his supervisor. John (not his real name) agreed to go through the steps of complete ritual. After a short grounding exercise, he gave the ritual the name 'The Job Raise Ritual'. He verbalized his intention to articulate 'myself fearlessly and respectfully and ask for what I want'. We then moved through the embodiment of energies, both constrictive and expansive, and all the powerful internal alchemy that brought into the process. All the while his 'curious observer' surveyed with detached interest what was occurring on various levels of his body and awareness, without judgement. On conclusion of the ritual, he experienced a release of the constrictions with the expansion of good energies and feelings in his body. We sealed the experience by expressing gratitude for the gifts of clarity, insight and courage. This increased awareness and the felt senses that it engendered stayed with him for a long time. He used the memory and recalled experience to shepherd himself successfully through negotiating a salary that he felt provided a sense of dignity for his labours. As a result, John connected with his desires and in the process experienced a reconnection with his soul or higher self as well.

EVERYDAY USES: RITUAL IN ACTION
Personal energetic transformation

Personal ritual is a powerful vehicle for transformation, as illustrated above. With practice, this can be done without guidance. The participants in ritual should come to the process with humility and willingness to allow their body's innate intelligence to work with 'source energy' to manifest. Compassion for self is helpful, as the individual will then better accept and trust the processes involved. Doing rituals in this manner requires entering into a holding zone with self-respect while acknowledging the existing realities of others and our world. Doing personal or collective (group) ritual when hearts, minds and resource energies are aligned is like entering a powerfully charged twilight zone. It is helpful to create a sacred or consecrated space of one's choosing, a quiet, maybe candle-lit room, or a space outdoors in nature. For those on the go, a morning shower can become a sacred space for a daily ritual.

Individual ritual

The individual can apply the general aspects of this resource to their own particular need. Ritual can also be used in the face of life-threatening illness, either for oneself or for loved ones, as it is beneficial during times of loss, death and bereavement. But it is also beneficial during daily activities and routines.

In a communing ritual, one holistically enters into communion with the totality of all life, all resources, and simultaneously sending and receiving conscious and unconscious messages. Personal ritual can be explored in actively energetic terms, incorporating music and dance as well. The experience of communing deeply with all life can be at times far more satisfying than an experience of meeting one's needs with worldly success. Communing ritual can be incorporated into any workshop or group setting with remarkable qualitative results (see the Further reading section at the end of this chapter).

Any type of ritual involves the act of connecting and communicating with unseen realities. Let everything be as it is, unless it causes discomfort. Creating space for everything and anything respectfully opens the inner ears as wide as they will stretch, listening to whatever comes back. In that place of compassion, we often find words, language and symbols that arise from the heart and body.

These practices are adaptable, and can be modified as each feels the need, and can be shortened to fit into one's daily existence on a regular basis. For example, I make use of ritual before beginning or working on publishing projects, starting the process with attention to breath, invoking nature and creating a formal intention. Another acquaintance begins a typical day by going outdoors, standing in contact with the raw earth, facing east towards the rising sun and sprinkling a pinch of cornmeal into the air and onto the earth while voicing a personal prayer to the sun itself, the sky above, the four directions, and the earth beneath, giving genuine thanks for the opportunity of the day, and asking for help in feeling or accomplishing whatever that day's intentions are.

In fact, it can appear that traumas pop up in our life's journey to assist in connecting with the divine, as much as it may appear to be the opposite. Sometimes in the midst of day-to-day travails and misfortunes, other worlds are opening so that source energies can flow in. Ritual can even prepare the way for acceptance of one's own death.

In Alcoholics Anonymous, individuals are instructed in the 'Serenity prayer' to accept the things that cannot be changed, and at the same time told not to 'sweat the small stuff'. Hence, ritual used either in everyday small stuff situations or life-shaking ones can help the individual face challenges serenely without wearing out emotionally. At least one part of ritual's power in overcoming trouble is its ability to access information beyond the reach of the rational mind, by reconnecting with 'source energy', with an expansive consciousness that results from the exercise.

TRAUMA HEALING RITUALS

One critical aspect of trauma is that it is about loss of connection – to ourselves, to our bodies, our families, to others, and the world around us. However trauma occurs, whether a single event or a series of events, it can result in a fundamental deregulation of the nervous system. It can happen slowly, over time, and so we sometimes adapt to these subtle changes without even noticing. This outline of the ritual practice can be harnessed and customized for any transformational work, but its efficacy is particularly evident when dealing with the healing of trauma. Concomitantly, the healing of trauma will help strengthen one's intuitive, innate intelligence.

How do these blockages develop? Based on years listening to clients' stories and modelling the 'curious observer' for them, I put together a scenario that most people can relate to, one that explains the build-up of such bio-energetic blocks to these innate resources. As we grow up, we typically receive messages that all expressions of need are either good or bad. We decide which of our personal characteristics are acceptable to society and which ones need to be hidden. As a result of how we, as humans, are wired, some of the characteristics that we considered bad never went away. They created their own domain in the dark corners of our personalities, and eventually took on lives of their own. These dark corners constitute what Carl Jung in his writings labels the 'shadow'. Because the shadow-self retains enormous hidden energy, it can become a warty goblin lurching around the repressed regions of our psyche and out of our conscious management. The shadow-self can be a 'dumping ground' for all the characteristics we disown, so honouring and accepting our own shadow is a profound spiritual discipline. Ritual allows individuals to tap into the hidden energy of this cloaked self. When familiar with their shadow, individuals are less likely to be locked in isolation and at the mercy of hidden forces, and more likely to connect and 'be resourced' by this energy, just when it is needed most. This reunion of the concealing shadow and revealing light aspects of us is referred to as 'integration'.

Transforming trauma requires fusing the energy frozen in what could be called the trauma vortex of the central nervous system with its polar opposite energy in the healing (or resource) vortex. Any methodical endeavour to integrate the shadow-self in this way will be well worth the grapple. In maturity, an individual can responsibly handle an integration experience that couldn't have been dealt with in earlier years. It is the dance of these opposite energies that generates new energy streams and connections with 'source energy'.

Every person is larger than their own unconscious, and therefore capable of integrating all the paradoxical aspects of the self. This is true both of aspects that are primitive, contradictory, devouring, destructive or weak, as well as those that more reliably reflect the true self. The point is to make the self so large that all parts can coexist peaceably beyond just those that we bring to the world and those that we cloak.

RELATIONSHIPS: POWER OF TWO RITUAL

Ritual can be useful in attracting and sustaining a life partnership and all couple relationships. Energy as a component in relationships can be affected by a ritual practice.

In this ritual, we create a third, unseen entity when we choose to bond with another person. This generally happens during the first three months to a year of being with a partner. One entity is the individual, another is the individual's partner, and the third is unseen, the relationship itself. Once the third entity forms as an energy field, it represents the best of both partners as well as their contradictions. The relationship becomes larger and paradoxically more fragile than either of the pair involved.

Before a couple is able to achieve the alchemy and unity they may desire, each partner must first learn to dissolve traumas left from earlier primary relationships, the foremost of which is with their parents. Remember that most relationships make sense mainly as learning experiences, and ritual enhances the learning portion, turning them into 'oh yes' rather than 'oh no' experiences.

The Power of Two Ritual requires a regular commitment of time, typically involving committed and periodic sessions. Repetition of the ritual helps to address and remove the barriers that invariably arise. Although immediately rewarding, these sessions produce subtle and perhaps radical transformations in the union, and couples should set aside breaks in between sessions to notice and integrate these changes.

A basic Power of Two Ritual

1. One partner volunteers to be the reader, selecting appropriate opening and closing prayers, poems or other texts for the session.

2. The other partner becomes the convener, who arranges the timing of the session and the setting of the ritual space. An appropriate object should be selected (wood branch, feather, stone, etc.), simple in design and light enough to hold in the hand when speaking. The person who holds the object has the floor, free of interruptions.

3. Before the session, each partner may create a list of three paradoxical, contradictory areas of personal sensitivity within the relationship. Both lists are brought into the ritual space.

4. The session begins as each party states an intention to support a healthy and vibrant relationship.

5. The ritual begins with at least one minute of conscious breathing, allowing the everyday noise of the mind to subside. Partners may sit facing each other close enough for the knees and lower legs to touch, holding hands, and looking into each other's eyes.

6. The reader should slowly begin with a prayer or passage that supports the highest good of each, of the union and of the outer world. That person then passes the talking object to the 'convener'.

7. The convener speaks first, always using personal experience and 'I' statements, taking up to ten minutes. The other partner practises silent, active listening, thereby energetically creating a safe space for the speaker.

8. The listener is also the timekeeper and should signal to the speaker when the first nine minutes have passed. A pre-selected word, such as 'ho', 'hai', or 'yes' is used when the speaker is finished, to signal that the sharing was received.

9. The first speaker then passes the object to the partner, who repeats the ten-minute sharing, as above, without comment on the previous presentation. The object is then passed back to the first speaker. This speaking and passing protocol – to end one speaker's time and begin another's – is continued throughout the sessions.

10. The first speaker, using 'I' statements, now takes five minutes to express what it was like to share earlier, as well as what it was like to listen to the partner's sharing.

11. The second speaker reflects, as above, also in a five-minute block.

12. If appropriate, a short break can be taken at this point.

13. After reconvening, the first speaker shares what he or she listed as three paradoxical areas of personal sensitivity surfacing in the relationship. The pattern of ten minutes of sharing followed by five minutes of feedback is repeated.

14. The reader then closes the session with a prayer or appropriate poem or passage. Props used in setting the sacred space are respectfully collected and stored, and the space is returned to its everyday use.

15. The partners should schedule a time, perhaps even a month into the future, for the follow-up session. In the interim, it is important for the individuals to reflect quietly and to consider what has been learned and integrated, again grateful for new awareness and energies.

The goal in this regular, periodic ritual is to honour 'the third entity' by orienting both partners in the relationship in the same direction with the same intentions. Practised with conscious commitment on a periodic basis, ritual can help partners maintain an open, healthy and increasingly energetic relationship.

CONCLUSION

These basic principles of energy-based ritual, as briefly described here, offer a new twist on an ancient technology, opening new doors to personal transformation and balance. Through ritual, we are able to open ourselves to otherwise unknowable and invisible realities, inviting us to find new ways of seeing, feeling, doing, thinking and indeed, being in the world. Knowing without knowing, we experience the flux between the uncertainty of life and an intuitive sense of certainty about what feels right in the heart, a place where real transformative action can occur. The flow of energy and information is quickened and our capacities for joy, creativity and healing increase. It is through this use of energy that we find a comfortable level of connectivity with ourselves, with others, with nature and with a remarkably intelligent and cooperative universe. In short, ritual allows access to an ancient magic that modern-day research and conventional healers are just beginning to understand. It is an exciting moment in the history of psychotherapy, joining past, present and future together, and uniting traditions at the root of all world cultures in the name of healing and self-transformation.

FURTHER READING

Gendlin, E. (1982) *Focusing*. New York: Bantam.
Levine, P.A. (1997) *Waking the Tiger*. Berkeley, CA: North Atlantic Books.
Levine, P.A. (2008) *Trauma Healing: A Pioneering Program for Restoring the Wisdom of Your Body*. Lewisville, CO: Sounds True.
Picucci, M. (2005) *Ritual as Resource: Energy for Vibrant Living*. Berkeley, CA: North Atlantic Books.

10

SENSING THE DEAD

THE ROLE OF EMBODIMENT, THE SENSES AND MATERIAL OBJECTS IN THE RITUALIZATION OF MOURNING

Joanna Wojtkowiak

Ritualization in post-secular societies has changed significantly over the last few decades. As traditional religious rituals decline, new or re-invented rituals have emerged. The focus of ritual theory too has shifted from ritual as tradition – for the most part *religious* tradition – to ritual as a domain that is 'conceived as occupying cultural space alongside other cultural domains such as politics, art, or religion' (Grimes 2014, p.343). This dynamic perspective of ritual acknowledges the fact that ritualizing may be either religious or secular, or both. 'Ritualizing'[1] refers to the deliberate, active and intuitive activity of ritualmaking (Grimes 2014; Lukken 1999). The act of ritualmaking puts the accent on ritual innovation and experience; it also draws attention to the importance of embodiment in ritual. How we experience the world around us through our bodies – what Thomas Csordas calls the body as 'being-in-the-world' (1994, p.10) – has often been neglected. Yet this is the point of departure for any analysis of ritual

---

[1] Ritual has many definitions in the literature. Grimes cites more than 60 in the appendix of his book *The Craft of Ritual Studies* (2014). He uses the term 'rite' to refer to 'specific enactments located in concrete times and places'; this set of actions is widely recognized by members of a culture. 'Ritualizing' he refers to as the 'act of cultivating or inventing rites' (2014, pp.192–193). Yet rather than giving inclusive or exclusive definitions of ritual, he prefers to describe about 16 family characteristics, of which he identifies and expounds on four central qualities: embodied, condensed, prescribed and enacted.

because embodiment is the most basic and perhaps most important part of ritual participation.

In this chapter, I use theoretical insights and recent research to analyse in detail the practice of private ritualizing during mourning in Western contexts, with an emphasis on the Netherlands. The question addressed is: What is the role of embodiment, the senses and material objects in the ritualization of mourning in post-secular society?

Central to the theoretical framework of this article are Ronald L. Grimes' concepts of ritualizing and ritualization and Thomas Csordas' idea that 'culture is grounded in the human body' (1994, p.6) and that bodily experience is 'the existential ground of culture and self' (1994, p.269). In the first part of this chapter I address how our post-secular and pluralistic context affect the expression of grief. Second, I look at the material dimension of mourning, in particular, ash objects[2] and the deceased's personal belongings. Third, I examine the role of embodiment, the senses in the material dimension of ritual. To conclude, I compare the insights from this theoretical inquiry with the practice of contemporary ritualmaking by professionals and non-professionals.

MOURNING IN POST-SECULAR SOCIETY

Death is a universal human experience and an ultimate concern (Yalom 1980). When confronted with the loss of a loved one, the meaning of life is often challenged by that experience (see Baumeister 1991; Park 2010). Ritualizing this loss is a cultural response to existential concerns; it initiates a social and psychological transition in the grieving process (Romanoff and Terenzio 1998). Traditionally, this response was defined in religious terms determined by the group into which one was born. In contemporary post-secular society, traditional collective narratives are replaced by a plurality of beliefs that force mourners to search for new ways to preserve the memory of their dead.

---

2   Ash objects are articles that contain the ashes of the incinerated body of the deceased.

Following a 'ritual emptiness' in the second half of the 20th century, a 'ritual revival' observed in the 1980s and 1990s brought about remarkable ritual innovation. Certain social groups such as LGBT groups (lesbian, gay, bisexual and transgender) and celebrities unwittingly became pioneers in the field of ritual innovation as they looked for alternatives to the traditional church funeral. Funerals of famous people emphasized the personality of the deceased and their personal wishes. Western countries, such as the UK, US, New Zealand and the Netherlands, also saw a rise in emerging rituals around death (Garces-Foley 2002; Garces-Foley and Holcomb 2005; Walter 2012; Wojtkowiak and Venbrux 2009).

The Netherlands is a good example of ritual innovation. While the majority of the Dutch population belonged to a religious institution (61 per cent) in 1970, only 30 per cent regularly practised their religious affiliation by 2012 (de Hart 2014). The labels 'religious', 'spiritual' or 'secular' are complex and not mutually exclusive, particularly in the pluralistic and post-secular Western context (Ammerman 2010; Molendijk 2015). 'Pluralism refers to the idea that there are many valid responses or answers to any significant questions about the nature of reality' (McLeod 2013, p.51). Although the majority of the Dutch population is now religiously unaffiliated, this does not necessarily mean that people consider themselves aspiritual or areligious. Surveys of personal spirituality and religiosity give a more diverse image of Dutch society. Among the unaffiliated, 20 per cent describe themselves as religious (Becker and de Hart 2006) and 26 per cent as spiritual, which includes beliefs in the transcendent (Kronjee and Lampert 2006).

RITUALIZING MOURNING
Grief experiences and the senses in symbolic relationships

The longstanding conviction about mourning that was conceptualized by Freud (1985 [1917]), known as the grief work hypothesis, holds that mourners need to work through their grief, let go of the deceased and move on with their lives. A recent shift in grief literature and therapies recognizes the healthy side of maintaining a symbolic relationship with the deceased, and integrating this new bond with the deceased into one's daily life (Walter 1996). Mourners can be very creative in how they preserve a symbolic relationship with deceased loved ones; their ritual repertoire can be broad.

The bereaved may perpetuate their relationship with deceased loved ones by remembering their birthday or the anniversary of their death, visiting the grave[3] or participating in collective remembrance rituals, pursuing activities they enjoyed together, talking about them and holding on to objects that serve as reminders (e.g., photographs, jewellery, clothes). These examples represent an increasing secularization and individualization of beliefs and ritual practices around death.

The symbolic bond with the dead can also take sensorial forms as when the mourner feels the presence of the deceased during post-death encounters (Gibson 2008; Klugman 2006; Nowatzki and Kalishuk 2009). Widows (50 per cent) and parents (80 per cent) frequently experience an encounter with their deceased relatives, most often in the months following death. Survey research shows that these occurrences – which cut across gender, age and religious affiliation – are remarkably sensorial experiences: visual, auditory and even tactile.

The bereaved also recount asking for advice in the evening and having an answer in the morning. It is not always clear to them whether the response came from a 'good night's sleep' or from advice actually received from their deceased relative. Sometimes the answer lies somewhere between these two options, which seems to suffice for mourners with no strong views on what happens after death.

Research interview data reveals that these encounters with the dead often strengthen beliefs in an afterlife (Wojtkowiak and Venbrux 2010). Regardless of whether the contact was understood by the bereaved as literal or symbolic, most insist that it felt positive and comforting.

---

3   In the Netherlands, research (*n*=514) shows that while a majority (70 per cent) of mourners commemorate their loved ones (most often on the deceased's birthday or on the anniversary of their death), only a small minority (9 per cent) visit the grave often or regularly (de Jong and Kreting 2006); some 65 per cent never return to the graveside. Although the study does not give reasons for this overall decrease in traditional memorial practices, we hypothesize that it may be related to individualization, growing geographical mobility and families' increasingly busy lifestyle that leaves little time for grave maintenance.

On the whole, mourners relate positive associations and emotions when recalling their encounter. It makes them feel more connected with their loved one and leaves them with a sense of healing in their grief process.

The fact that transcendental beliefs are not always clear-cut – especially for people who have experienced post-death encounters – leads us to include the role of 'belief' in studies about how people ritualize mourning. Understanding and sorting people's ideas about what happens after death is difficult. First of all, people do not always know what they believe; among those who do, many are unable to articulate their thoughts. Second, the categories of 'belief' or 'believing in something' are complex (Bull and Mitchell 2015, p.5). In the Netherlands we observe a decrease in traditional Christian beliefs about the afterlife (e.g., bodily resurrection) and an increase in other ways of thinking about what happens after we die (e.g., reincarnation) that include uncertainty and an openness to metaphysical explanations, as well as a firm but broad understanding of the 'soul' (Bernts, Dekker and de Hart 2007). It is particularly important to take belief into account when creating rituals for a group of people who may have very different ideas about what happens after death. We conclude that, for our contemporary society, even a fuzzy spirituality may be comforting.

Pragmatic pluralism and materials in symbolic bonds

It is interesting to note that relatively few mourners return to the cemetery to honour their dead. As the number of cremations rises, the number of visits to the gravesite decreases.[4] A popular exception to this trend began about ten years ago with a secular variant of an All Souls' Day celebration that now takes place in Dutch cemeteries in early November (van der Lee 2008). Those who do honour their dead today with visits to the cemetery often decorate the grave with many different sorts of symbols, such as crosses, statues of Mary and Buddha, as well as with personal belongings. Ammerman (2010) argues that worldviews are plural, that people have

---

[4] In 2015, 63 per cent of the Dutch population chose cremation; this parallels the situation in the UK. Interestingly, the majority (45 per cent) of those who choose cremation said that their decision was motivated by a desire to avoid burdening their families with the maintenance of a grave (van Keulen and Kloosterboer 2009).

always taken meaning from various sources – secular, humanist, spiritual and religious. Dutch cemeteries are an example of the proliferation of this kind of 'pragmatic plurality' (2010, p.156). The private memorials in homes – maintained by about 30 per cent of all Dutch households – also reflect a plurality of ritual symbols (Wojtkowiak and Venbrux 2009, 2010).

Material and sensory experience plays a central role in the mourning process. Conserving and ritualizing with material objects that belonged to the dead is another mourning practice that symbolically perpetuates ties with them. The bereaved may wear the deceased's clothing or jewellery or use their tools or other articles that belonged to them. Research by Australian scholar Gibson (2004, 2008) reveals that these items may be significant in the mourning process as 'transitional objects'. Much in the same way that children use transitional objects like teddy bears to stay connected with their parents, the bereaved may use personal articles as a link with the deceased. Smell is an especially powerful sense in mourning; wearing, touching and smelling the deceased's clothing gives immediate access to memories of that person (Gibson 2008). Mourners who wear the deceased's jumper or hug it to themselves describe how they sense the presence of the deceased. The notion of transition also means that, eventually, bereaved people come to accept that as the smell fades away, they stop wearing the clothing. The meaning of the object changes, as it goes from being a reminder of grief, pain and sorrow to a source of comfort and connection with their deceased loved one. Photographs of the deceased, also significant to the grief process, are visual reminders of the relationship (Wojtkowiak and Venbrux 2010). The impressive diversity of these symbolic bonds is confirmed by research done elsewhere (see Benore and Park 2004; Klass, Silverman and Nickman 1996; Unruh 1983).

How the bereaved pursue their relationship with their loved one is considered highly personal, and not something to be shared with the outside world. Mourners rarely want others, especially strangers, to know what an object means to them (Heessels 2010). Similar reactions are seen among mourners who maintain a memorial for the deceased in their home. While they often take time for thinking about or talking with the deceased, this ritual activity is kept in the private sphere (Wojtkowiak and Venbrux 2010).

Ritualizing with cremains

The practice of cremation in the Netherlands bears fuller examination because it opens up new avenues for ritualization. Legally, the bereaved have the right to take the urn with their loved one's ashes home with them. This option offers more creative alternatives for ritually dealing with the cremated remains (Heessels 2012) that go beyond the traditional practice of scattering or burying the ashes. Cremated remains, referred to as 'cremains', may be integrated into a piece of jewellery, turned into an object known as a 'cuddle stone' or added to a painting or even a tattoo (Heessels 2010). Wearing, holding and touching these objects is often a conscious intentional activity that helps mourners feel connected to the deceased. Through ritualized handling of the ash object, the bereaved intentionally draws his or her attention to the object and consciously connects with it. While for many mourners the cremains creation remains an object, for others it incarnates the deceased. When Heessels studied the significance of these material representations to the bereaved, she discovered that even when only part of the ashes are preserved in an ash object, it represents the whole person. Some mourners talk to the deceased as they handle the object. Others may use the deceased's name when referring to the object. These examples underline the importance of the senses and embodiment in the practice and study of ritual.

RITUAL AS EMBODIED EXPERIENCE

Ritual is attention-grabbing (Moore and Myerhoff 1977); it creates a focus in time and space. As attention is directed towards the ritual experience, the senses are heightened.[5] Earlier in this chapter, we saw how the bereaved use their senses (e.g., touch, sight, smell) to engage with their loved one through material objects. Their connection with the deceased is experienced through their body, either by sensorial post-death encounters (visual or auditory) or through interaction with material objects that represent the dead person, and in some cases is considered to be

---

5   Unless, of course, one is not paying attention, preoccupied or bored, which would make the ritual less 'effective'.

that person. During these private ritualizations, the body becomes the agent for the experience of mourning. This sensory experience involves a conscious connection that may have transformative potential.

As noted above, we experience the world around us through our bodies (Csordas 1994). In his classic work, psychologist William James (1981) defines the body as being part of the self, more specifically as the most intimate part of the material self, followed by our attire and the physical environment, such as our home. While James sees the body as the reflective part of the self, Csordas gives the body a more active role as an 'experiencing agent' (1994, p.3). In order to appreciate the difference between the body as a reflective self or an experiencing self, we must consider the conceptual difference between 'the body' and 'embodiment'.

Csordas sees the 'body' as a biological, material entity and 'embodiment' as 'the way we engage with the world' through 'perceptual experience' (1999, p.145). This distinction clarifies how culture, and therefore ritual, can be understood and detected in methodological research. When studying the 'body', the focus is on how the body represents culture. This view contributes to definitions of culture where a system of symbols, including the body, can be read as a 'text' (Csordas 1999, pp.146ff). Studying culture from the perspective of 'embodiment' underlines the body as the primary source of experiential and existential meaning: it is how we make sense of the world. In the case of private mourning practices, we find that mourners take meaning from these embodied sensorial experiences. Grief becomes more bearable and a positive connection is made with the deceased loved one.

In Csordas' (1999) view, Western – more specifically Euro-American – culture often focuses on visual imagery in the study and experience of cultural life, but bodily experiences are just as important. Body imagery is a state of sensory experience where the body (being-in-the-world) links events, experiences and hence creates meaning (making sense of being-in-the-world). The situations cited above of meaningful material and sensory encounters with the dead are examples of embodied imagery in the case of grief. This state, which appears as a mixture of different sensory experiences (e.g., tactile and visual), requires a person to be in a 'somatic mode of attention' (Csordas 1999, p.151). During mourning, this somatic mode seems to be accessed more easily and ritual can stimulate that too. The somatic mode of attention is activated during ritual as attention and the senses are focused on the ritual experience, which is perhaps also why ritual is often connected to meaning-making.

Studying culture, and therefore ritual, from the embodiment perspective means focusing on the *bodily experience*, the way bodies move and interact (being-in-the-world with others). Gergen affirms that 'it is through collaborative action that all meaning emerges' (2009, p.53), which is also how embodiment 'works' in ritual too. Bodies are not only representations of meaning, but create meaning while experiencing the world. Interaction or collaboration with others is important. For some people the 'other' or 'others' may be transcendent powers. It might also be an imagined other (e.g., such as discussed in dialogical self theory; see Hermans 2002). As I illustrate in this chapter, material objects and sensory experiences with the deceased may also serve this function. The distinction between body and embodiment is important to the understanding that mourners do not necessarily see objects and sensory encounters only as figurative representations of the dead, but also as literally physical or sensory connections with the dead. This brings us back to our concern about pluralistic beliefs about the transcendent in post-secular society as well as pluralistic beliefs about embodiment: objects can initiate sensory experiences of the dead.

EMBODIMENT FROM A NEUROANTHROPOLOGICAL PERSPECTIVE

A material object that is used in ritualizing is thus not just a decorative or inanimate lifeless thing. As noted above, objects can be very meaningful to mourners; they stir up sensory experiences. We not only see objects in ritualizing; we experience them. Objects are given meaning through ritual activity, as well as through their biographies (Kopytoff 1989). Kopytoff argues that the meaning of objects also lies in their social biography: a pen may be very important to me because it belonged to my grandmother.

The pen may have little or no monetary value, but it has emotional value to me. In the same way that people have biographies, so do objects, especially objects that belonged to the dead (Gibson 2004, 2008). According to Grimes, 'objects are not just "there". The senses mediate them to humans through the brain' (Grimes 2014, p.273).

The neuroanthropological perspective (e.g., study of the brain) underscores the role of the experiential in ritual. 'Ritual shapes the brain by providing experiences rather than transmitting messages' (Bull and Mitchell 2015, p.5). This means that the primary goal of ritual is less the communication of a message than the transmission of an experience. Understanding the meaning of the experience may take time; it can also change in the course of time. The meaning and biography of an object also changes in the course of time. During the grief process, the funeral urn may be moved from a prominent place in the living room to a more private spot in the bedroom, for instance. Studies on post-death encounters show that most of these sensory experiences occur shortly after death and then decrease significantly with time (Klugman 2006).

Ritual participants bring diverse messages, attitudes or conceptions of life and death into ritualizing today. Even within the same family, people may have different views on the afterlife. This diversity of perspectives in contemporary society today can be brought together by a focus on the deceased person's life, values, relationships and attitudes. Moreover, this diversity of views reinforces the importance of experience in ritualmaking today. The ceremony that is focused on the deceased feels right (Holloway et al. 2013).

CONCLUSION: INSIGHTS FOR CONTEMPORARY RITUALMAKING

What can we learn from the role of embodiment, the senses and material objects in the ritualization of mourning and contemporary ritualmaking?

First of all it is important to note that the cases of ritualized mourning presented in this chapter are not hypothetical constructs but real situations that arose in the private sphere. The insights gained from these research cases are significant for contemporary ritualmaking. Embodiment as a way of engaging with the world is crucial for understanding ritual; in fact, it must be considered as fundamental to ritualizing. In practice, this means that, rather than focusing primarily on the message and meaning of certain actions and symbols, sensory and perceptual experiences are central to ritual understanding.

How can the sensory and material dimension be consciously introduced into ritualmaking? Smell, for instance, can be a very powerful sense during a funeral. The deceased's favourite perfume can be sprayed in the room where the ceremony takes place. Flowers or any other fragrance that the mourners associate with their loved one may also scent the room.

The material and sensory dimensions are important considerations during the grieving process because they create a connection with the deceased. Maintaining such bonds with a deceased loved one is considered useful for healthy grieving (Romanoff and Terenzio 1998; Walter 1996). Engaging with material objects that belonged to the deceased has transformative potential, both for meaning-making and as a healing context in which to deal with grief. As research shows, most often these objects represent a private, intimate link between mourners and their deceased loved ones.

When crafting remembrance ceremonies, the bereaved can bring an object into the ceremony that reminds them of the deceased. Material objects or keepsakes can be integrated either privately or publicly into the ceremony. Thus, the bereaved have an opportunity during the ceremony to share a story about the object and in this way talk about their relationship with the deceased. Those who may not necessarily want to show their object to others may find meaning and comfort just by discretely holding the object and taking time for their own private memories.

Furthermore, as we saw in Gibson's research (2008), as the biography of the object changes, it can be re-ritualized and given another place in the mourner's life. The meaning of material or 'melancholy objects' (Gibson 2004) changes over the course of time, and it is important to consider this when crafting rituals.

Timing matters to ritual: at what point in the grieving process does the ritual take place? It makes a difference if the ceremony takes place soon after death, during the funeral, or at a memorial service months or years later. In each case, the ritual will have a different tone or message; an object will have taken on other meanings. What is the purpose of the objects in the ritual? Is it to remember the deceased and feel a connection with the deceased? Or is the intention of the ritual to transform the relationship, and thus the object, in order to introduce a new phase in the mourner's life? These questions need to be considered whenever one is creating tailor-made rituals.

Last, embodied experience, that is, how we engage with the world (Csordas 1993), is crucial to ritual. Our senses are important stimuli for having a meaningful ritual experience. These insights are essential to the crafting of new rituals. From this perspective, ritualizing involves balancing ritual elements (e.g., sounds, text, action) as well as different sensory experiences. Ritualizing is an intuitive process that takes place in a dialogue with the bereaved. This requires a sensitive approach towards mourners when exploring possible meanings and messages, all the while keeping in mind the form of the ritual and the importance of embodied experiences.

REFERENCES

Ammerman, N. (2010) 'The challenges of pluralism: Locating religion in a world of diversity.' *Social Compass 57*, 154–167.

Baumeister, R.F. (1991) *Meanings in Life.* New York: The Guilford Press.

Becker, J. and de Hart, J. (2006) *Godsdienstige veranderingen in Nederland. Verschuivingen in de binding met de kerken en christelijke traditie.* Werkdocument 128. Den Haag: Sociaal Cultureel Planbureau.

Benore, E.R. and Park, C.L. (2004) 'Death-specific religious beliefs and bereavement: Belief in an afterlife and continued attachment.' *The International Journal for the Psychology of Religion 14*, 1, 1–22.

Bernts, T., Dekker, G. and de Hart, J. (2007) *God in Nederland, 1996–2006.* Kampen: Ten Have.

Bull, M. and Mitchell, J.P. (eds) (2015) *Ritual, Performance and the Senses.* London: Bloomsbury Academic

Csordas, T. (1994) 'Introduction.' In T. Csordas (ed.) *Embodiment and Experience: The Existential Ground of Culture and Self.* Cambridge: Cambridge University Press.

Csordas, T. (1999) 'Embodiment and Cultural Phenomenology.' In G. Weiss and H.F. Haber (eds) *Perspectives on Embodiment: The Intersections of Nature and Culture.* New York: Routledge.

de Hart, J. (2014) *Geloven binnen en buiten verband. Godsdienstige ontwikkelingen in Nederland.* Den Haag: Sociaal en Cultureel Planbureau.

de Jong, G. and Kreting, J. (2006) 'Ode aan de doden. Opinieonderzoek over dood en uitvaart.' *Kaski, onderzoek en advies over religie en samenleving.* Nijmegen: Radboud Universiteit Nijmegen.

Freud, S. (1985 [1917]) 'Rouw en melancholie.' In T. Graftdijk and W. Oranje (eds) *Freud.* Amsterdam: Boom. [Originally published in 1917.]

Garces-Foley, K. (2002) 'Funerals of the unaffiliated.' *Omega 46*, 4, 287–302.

Garces-Foley, K. and Holcomb, J.S. (2005) 'Contemporary American Funerals: Personalizing Tradition.' In K. Garces-Foley (ed.) *Death and Religion in a Changing World.* New York: M.E. Sharpe.

Gergen, K.J. (2009) *Relational Being. Beyond Self and Community.* Oxford: Oxford University Press.

Gibson, M. (2004) 'Melancholy objects.' *Mortality 9*, 4, 285–299.

Gibson, M. (2008) *Objects of the Dead. Mourning and Memory in Everyday Life.* Carlton, VIC: Melbourne University Press.

Grimes, R.L. (2014) *The Craft of Ritual Studies.* Oxford: Oxford University Press.

Heessels, M. (2010) 'From Commercial Goods to Cherished Ash Objects: Mediating Contact with the Dead Through the Body.' In E. Venbrux, T. Quartier and J. Wojtkowiak (eds) *Body, Performance, Agency and Experience.* Wiesbaden: Harrassowitz Verlag.

Heessels, M. (2012) 'Bringing home the dead. Ritualizing cremation in the Netherlands.' Unpublished PhD thesis, Radboud University, Nijmegen.

Hermans, H.J.M. (2002) 'The dialogical self theory as a society of mind: Introduction.' *Theory Psychology 12*, 2, 147–160.

Holloway, M., Adamson, S., Argyrou, V., Draper, P. and Mariau, D. (2013) '"Funerals aren't nice but it couldn't been nicer." The making of a good funeral.' *Mortality 18*, 1, 30–53.

James, W. (1981) *The Principles of Psychology.* London: Macmillan & Co.

Klass, D., Silverman, P.S. and Nickman, S.L. (eds) (1996) *Continuing Bonds. New Understandings of Grief.* New York: Routledge, Taylor & Francis Group.

Klugman, C.M. (2006) 'Dead men talking: evidence of post death contact and continuing bonds.' *Omega Journal of Death and Dying 52*, 3, 249–262.

Kopytoff, I. (1989) 'The Cultural Biography of Objects.' In A. Appadurai (ed.) *The Social Life of Things: Commodities in Cultural Perspective*. Cambridge: Cambridge University Press.

Kronjee, G. and Lampert, M. (2006) 'Leefstijlen en zingeving.' In W.B.H.J. van de Donk, A.P. Jonkers, G. Kronjee and R.J.J.M. Plum (eds) *Geloven in het publieke domein. Verkenningen van een dubbele transformatie*. Amsterdam: Amsterdam University Press.

Lukken, G. (1999) 'Rituelen in overvloed.' *Een kritische bezinning op de plaats en gestalte van het christelijk ritueel in onze cultuur*. Baarn: Gooi en Sticht.

McLeod, J. (2013) 'Developing pluralistic practice in counselling and psychotherapy: Using what the client knows.' *The European Journal of Counselling Psychology 2*, 1, 51–64.

Molendijk, A.L. (2015) 'In pursuit of the postsecular.' *International Journal of Philosophy and Theology 76*, 100–115.

Moore, S.F. and Myerhoff, B.G. (eds) (1977) *Secular Ritual*. Assen, Netherlands: Van Gorcum.

Nowatzki, N.R. and Kalishuk, R.G. (2009) 'Post-death encounters: grieving mourning and healing.' *OMEGA Journal of Death and Dying 59*, 2, 91–111.

Park, C.L. (2010) 'Making sense of the meaning literature: An integrative review of meaning making and its effects on adjustment to stressful life events.' *Psychological Bulletin 136*, 2, 257–301.

Romanoff, B.D. and Terenzio, M. (1998) 'Rituals and the grieving process.' *Death Studies 22*, 8, 697–711.

Unruh, D.R. (1983) 'Death and personal history: Strategies of identity preservation.' *Social Problems 30*, 3, 340–351.

van der Lee, I. (ed.) (2008) *Allerzielen Alom: Kunst tot herdenken. [All Souls Around: Art for Remembrance.]* Zoetermeer: Meinema.

van Keulen, M. and Kloosterboer, M. (2009) *Rapport: Hoeveel vaart zit er in je uitvaart?* Amsterdam: TNS Nipo Business and Finance.

Walter, T. (1996) 'A new model of grief: bereavement and biography.' *Mortality 1*, 1, 7–25.

Walter, T. (2012) 'Why different countries manage death differently: A comparative analysis of modern urban societies.' *The British Journal of Sociology 63*, 1, 123–145.

Wojtkowiak, J. and Venbrux, E. (2009) 'From soul to postself: home memorials in the Netherlands.' *Mortality 14*, 2, 174–158.

Wojtkowiak, J. and Venbrux, E. (2010) 'Privates Spaces for the Dead: Remembrance and Continuing Relationships at Home Memorials in the Netherlands.' In A. Maddrell and J.D. Sidaway (eds) *Deathscapes: Spaces for Death, Dying, Mourning and Remembrance*. Farnham: Ashgate.

Yalom, I.D. (1980) *Existential Psychotherapy*. New York, Basic Books.

11

FOOD AND RITUAL

Lindy Mechefske

For over 55 million years, mankind and his earliest ancestors have roamed the planet in search of one thing – FOOD.

From the earliest primates to the appearance of *Homo sapiens* approximately 195,000 years ago, finding food and water has been critical to our survival. We are hardwired to think about our next meal, the need is encoded in our DNA. We eat because it is a biological necessity, because food is life. But food is also about hunger and yearning; about memory and love; about life and death; and about community, belonging and the powerful connections between us.

From farm to food processing factory, from restaurant to home table, from market stall to superstore, food is the world's largest single industry. And with a global population set to reach 9.7 billion by 2050 (UN 2015), food needs will be set to be among the most pressing of all issues facing the planet. Food is, quite rightly, the topic *du jour*.

It is hardly surprising, then, given both our history and the fundamental and perpetual biological necessity to eat, that we are so preoccupied with food. And neither is it surprising that food and ritual have become so interwoven that they are virtually inseparable.

It is the way that we eat that is governed by a long history of entrenched and evolving rituals. These rituals include everything from the method with which we hunt, fish, garden, gather, shop for, and prepare our food to the number and order of meals per day, the timing of meals, and even the predictable order of courses within a meal.

Rituals decree the types of food we consume at what meal, the hygiene of every step along the way, from source to table, including washing our hands before we eat, the implements that we eat with, the lighting and background noise levels the places we gather to eat, and whom we eat with. Rituals prescribe the appropriate social etiquette and manners and even the clothing we wear to different meals. Rituals dictate whether we slurp or burp or employ quiet bodily control, whether we guzzle or sip, eat dinner at 5pm or 'fashionably late' at 8pm, eat in silence like Queen Victoria or fully immersed in noise and conversation. It is ritual rather than nutritional logic that accounts for the order and timing of meals. If nutrition played a more substantial role in the timing of meals, we would perhaps eat our biggest meal of the day, typically dinner, first thing in the morning. Rituals even influence our sense of taste.

It could easily be argued that the relentless necessity of eating has shaped our profound need for the system of rites we attach to food, and that food and food rituals affect our daily life more than any other single aspect of our existence.

Humans are the only animals that cook their food. But our need to eat pre-dated fire and therefore cooking. It pre-dated ordered civilization. And it pre-dated any form of organized religion. So although all these things – the discovery of fire, the evolution of man from primitive primate to modern *Homo sapiens*, and the advent of organized religion – brought about new food rituals, none of them are entirely responsible for the myriad of rituals that we act out each day as we gather, prepare, serve and eat our meals.

EATING AS A SOCIAL ACTIVITY

Food is a way of telling our stories. Our earliest memories often involve food. We cannot think about the important dates in our lives without remembering the food involved. Food stories are fundamental – the real stories of our families, our communities, and of our lives.

Almost all our major cultural, social, secular, and religious celebrations are linked in some way to food. Many of our celebrations began in religious contexts but over the years have evolved into wider cultural and social spheres – and in many cases what were once highly ritualized religious celebrations have moved towards becoming mainstream, secular celebrations, often centred on food.

North American Thanksgiving is an excellent example. In Canada, the first Thanksgiving dates back to 1578, when English explorer Martin Frobisher was on his third trip to the Arctic, searching for the Northwest Passage. Storms and calamities plagued the expedition, separating the fleet of ships. When they met again in what is now known as Frobisher Bay, expedition minister, Robert Wolfall, administered communion and delivered a sermon on thankfulness. Canadian Thanksgiving rituals have evolved from that early, historical prayer ceremony to a traditional and largely secular feast. The highly ritualized Thanksgiving feast still celebrates the harvest and remains centred on the principle of gratitude, but is almost universally partaken of by the entire nation, regardless of faith.

Many other historical, religious celebrations are now celebrated in increasingly secular ways. Easter and Christmas in North America, for example, are celebrated in both cultural and religious contexts. At the same time, there is a growing global awareness of the major religious celebrations of all faith celebrations including, for example, Passover, Ramadan, Diwali, Baisakhi, Kwanzaa and Solstice. Understanding the food-related feasting and fasting rituals associated with these and other religious and cultural events around the world is a bridge to building a global sense of community.

And while food is often at the centre of religious and cultural rituals, it is also at the centre of so many other life events including weddings, funerals, childhood birthday parties and New Year's celebrations. Eating is a profoundly social activity the world over. It is a vehicle for all of our relationships and much of our socialization process is built around food. We eat with our kindred. We foster new and old relationships through food. We have an innate craving to come together around food. We brunch and *do* lunch. We attend banquets. We go for coffee. We throw dinner parties. We picnic and potluck; we take tea; and we break bread together. We celebrate birth, life and death with food. We care for people through food. We heal with food. We revel and party at all of life's events with food, and we do it together. 'We use eating as a medium for social relationships: satisfaction of the most individual of needs becomes a means of creating community' (Visser 1991, p.ix)

The social aspect of eating begins in earliest infancy, moments after a baby enters the world and first latches onto its mother's breast. By necessity of design, babies are held close to their mother who, miraculously enough, can provide all the nourishment that a rapidly growing baby requires. Unable to fend for themselves, babies are entirely dependent on their mother and family for their survival. And unlike babies in the animal kingdom, human babies remain dependent on their families for food for years. Food is our first symbol of love and security.

Once children are old enough, one of the first rites of passage is to have their friends over to share food – often for a birthday party or other special occasion – or to partake of food at their friends' homes. Young children understand that what we eat on these social occasions matters greatly. It would be unthinkable for most six-year-olds living in the Western world to eat snails, oysters, eel, blood sausage or offal of any description at a birthday party. Children learn quickly that food is a powerful symbol of who we are; that pizza or something similarly popular, and an iced birthday cake served with candles ablaze are the socially acceptable foods on these occasions. This is the very definition of ritual – something done as part of a ceremony no matter how small; always done in a particular situation and in the same way each time; something done in accordance with social custom or normal protocol.

Even though the birthday cake remains a ritual throughout most of our lives, cropping up long after the days of childhood birthday parties, once children move into adolescence and young adulthood food continues to play an important role in social development and relationships. From coffee dates to popcorn at the movies to dining out, dating often revolves around food and beverages. Young adults begin to define themselves by the foods they eat.

Where we live and with whom we eat, and even the degree of familiarity of the person with whom we eat, all play a large role in how we eat, the types of food we eat, and how much we eat. Eating has long been part of the human mating ritual. Though in general we have a natural tendency towards eating approximately the same amount that others around us are eating, and usually partake of similar foods, the tendency is disrupted when men and women eat in front of a stranger of the opposite sex – whereupon both sexes tend to eat less (Salvy *et al.* 2007).

Eating is such a fundamental social activity that in some cultures it is considered unacceptable to eat alone. In Thailand, for example, eating alone is said to be unlucky. In South Korea dining solo in public is discouraged, and so important is dining together that the Korean word for family actually translates to 'those who eat together'. All over the world, the kitchen is the heart of the home, and food is at the heart of the community.

SENSE OF TASTE AND RITUALS

What we eat and the way we eat it is a potent symbol of identity. We cannot think of 'cavemen' without thinking of hunting and gathering. We cannot think of Australia without the 'barbie', Japan without sushi, Germany without sausages and beer, Italy without pasta, Britain without fish and chips, India without curry, or France without wine, cheese and croissants.

Jean Anthelme Brillat-Savarin, the French lawyer, politician, gastronome and writer, once said, 'Tell me what kind of food you eat, and I will tell you what kind of man you are' (2011 [1949] p. 15). Yet the person in the Paris café lunching on a classic sole *meunière* accompanied by a crisp Chablis is not fundamentally any different from the American in a roadhouse eating a hamburger and fries washed down with Coke. Or the Indian at work in Mumbai eating rice, flat bread, dal, curries, yogurt and pickles from a dabba or tiffin box. All are, after all, part of the same genus, *Homo*. Each is merely conforming to a ritual sense of taste that is informed by their ethnic, national, religious, social and cultural conventions.

The varying tastes of different nationalities are due to many factors including cultural rituals such as the amount of time allotted for meals. But tastes can also be influenced by practical matters such as what is locally available, and so, therefore, what one is used to eating. While food can be an indicator of nationality, it can also be an indicator of social class, wealth, status, worldliness, and cultural and religious background. And so in this way, social, cultural and geographic factors all influence not just what we eat, but also our sense of taste.

Curiously, our sense of taste has little relation to our nutritional requirements. If only nutrition played a bigger role in our sense of taste, perhaps we would crave a lot more seaweed, sardines and flax seeds and a lot less in the way of sugary treats, pastries, potato chips and chocolate. If nutrition was a primary factor in taste, we might not live in a world where we are simultaneously overweight and malnourished; and where, for the first time in history, there are more overweight people than underweight (Popkin 2007).

Recent research instead points to ritual as having an important impact on taste. Professor Kathleen Vohs, a marketing and consumer behaviour researcher, noticed when she opened a bottle of wine with a screw top that the taste did not seem to match that of a corked bottle. She hypothesized that the missing ritual of unwrapping the foil from the bottleneck and then removing the cork adversely affect her enjoyment of the wine. Vohs went on to co-author a study in which individuals were asked to perform a set of small rituals and then report their satisfaction levels.

In one experiment one group was instructed to unwrap a chocolate bar, break it in half and re-wrap the second half, then eat the first half before going on to unwrap the second half and eat it. This group consistently reported higher levels of enjoyment than the test group who simply unwrapped the chocolate bar and ate it all at once. Similarly, a group of participants who performed an identical set of gestures before eating carrots (banging their knuckles on the table, closing their eyes and taking a deep breath), reported a higher level of enjoyment of their carrots than the test group who participated in non-ritual, random gestures before eating their carrots. The results confirmed the hypothesis that rituals affect taste (Vohs *et al.* 2013). It doesn't really matter that the rituals don't make particular sense – banging knuckles on the table should not logically affect the taste of the carrots consumed immediately afterwards. In fact, this only further cements the importance of rituals, which are, after all, merely pervasive cultural inventions.

There are a multitude of rituals performed before eating including pouring drinks, taking our places at the table, placing our serviettes, not commencing eating before the hosts, and in many cases, saying a ritual blessing, grace or offering of thanksgiving. All of these routine activities before a meal are thought to have a similar effect to that found in Vohs' research, that is, they are believed to enhance the appreciation of the food, and not just because of delayed gratification.

Offering some sort of blessing or even slowing down enough to merely think about gratitude prior to eating may be particularly rewarding in terms of how the food tastes, since both gratitude and acknowledgment have been shown to have a powerful effect on our brain chemistry, and hence on our perception. In fact, the effects of mindfulness rituals before eating go further than merely making us appreciate and enjoy our food more; they also improve our digestion. Research has shown that if we eat in a relaxed, more mindful state, we tend to eat less food and digest it better. Conversely, conflict, criticism and stress have all been shown to trigger the sympathetic nervous system that slows down and impedes proper digestion (Albers 2003).

Almost all cultures and religions offer some sort of prayer or meditation on thanksgiving before a meal, even if only done on ceremonial occasions. No matter what is on the table or where, there is a surprising universality and commonality to ritual blessings. Typical Pagan blessings acknowledge and give thanks for the earth, wind, rain, sun, and for abundance and fertility of the planet. North American Indigenous people thank the Great Spirit for abundance and for the cycle of life. A Buddhist blessing acknowledges that food is a gift from the universe. In Japan there is a custom before eating of putting one's hands together and saying *Itadakimasu*, which translates to 'I humbly receive'. And a traditional Hindu blessing goes like this, 'This ritual is One. The food is One. We who offer the food are One. The fire of hunger is also One. All action is One. We who understand this are One.'

Toasting, like saying grace, is another universal ritual. Now a predominantly secular ritual, toasting was once based on ancient sacrificial rituals where blood or wine were offered to the gods in exchange for favours. The name is thought to have derived from the 17th century when actual pieces of burnt toast were added to the wine, presumably to reduce the drink's acidity.

A toast is a drink taken as an expression of honour or goodwill, and involves the raising and clinking of glasses prior to sipping the contents. The origin of the ritual clinking of glasses has been the subject of a great deal of speculation. One theory holds that the clinking of tankards would scare away evil spirits. Another theory is that ritual crashing of drinking vessels together would result in a little of each drink being spilled into another – thus ensuring that the drinks were not poisoned. Little concrete proof exists for either argument, but the fact remains that clinking and toasting impacts all five senses – sight, taste, smell, sound and touch – and involves the participation of others in a communal experience, making the toast a highly memorable ritual.

Toasting is common at gatherings big and small, but particularly prevalent at celebratory events such as weddings, retirements and on New Year's Eve. Almost all cultures and faiths around the world have some form of New Year celebrations that mark a fresh start. A New Year is a chance to wipe the slate clean, to begin again and to reinvent oneself. From the Babylonians, to the Ancient Romans, to the Pagans, and the Medieval Knights – essentially for as far back as we can trace – there have always been ceremonies to welcome in the New Year, and all have been connected with making good, atoning wrongs and improving one's self. The Medieval Knights for example, celebrated the New Year feasting on game and bread washed down with ale and mead while reaffirming their commitment to chivalry. Modern-day New Year celebrations in the Western world often mean luxurious food and champagne followed by solemn pledges to reduce our food and alcohol intake in the days to follow.

EMERGING RITUALS

While rituals including the saying of grace before meals and toasting may no longer be a daily event in households around the world, other emerging rituals may be taking their place.

In her book *Drink*, Ann Dowsett Johnston wrote, 'Chopping, dicing, sipping: it's a common modern ritual' (2013, p.159). In fact, there's nothing modern about chopping, dicing or sipping. What is new is the rising importance and emerging ritual of talking about and sharing more of our food and culinary experiences.

Consider the case of photographing food and posting the pictures to various social media sites. This modern ritual could work in similar ways to other pre-dining rituals. The delay required to photograph food before eating may be enough to enhance enjoyment. At the very least, it is a conscious acknowledgment of the food itself, and implies an appreciation of both the aesthetic value and importance of food, as well as sharing that appreciation with others. So before you voice disdain with those disrupting dining procedures to take photographs, take heart – those enthusiastic food photographers may just be on to something, an evolving ritual with the potential for enhanced appreciation of food.

Other emerging food rituals include adapting specialized diets for allergies and food preferences such as vegetarian, vegan, or wheat, dairy and gluten-free diets. The growing number of food allergies has necessitated new food rituals, especially when hosting groups for meals. And with expanding global migration, an increased knowledge of cultural food taboos and food preferences has made food awareness a growing form of cultural diplomacy.

Other modern food rituals include a return to local and shared food resources and food production. Community kitchens and community garden plots are gaining momentum, and cooking is no longer regarded as the exclusive domain of either chefs or women.

MANNERS AND SOCIAL ETIQUETTE

We are not only *what* we eat – we are also *how* we eat. And how we eat matters.

When my eldest daughter, 12 years old at the time, balked about being reminded to use her knife and fork properly at the dinner table one night, she proffered that knives and forks were inefficient, and that a small shovel would be much more expedient, especially when eating peas. It's true, a small shovel might be more efficient, but table manners are rarely about efficiency. Rather, manners are a rigidly held set of rituals – a social contract of sorts, and a potent differentiator of both cultural background and social class. They are among our most revealing social indicators.

How we eat is almost entirely about the set of table manners we were taught in childhood and about how those manners were enforced. About whether we sat at a formal table, complete with linen and multiple pieces of cutlery, or if we rushed into the kitchen and grabbed as much as possible of the good stuff before the others attempted to do the same, eating perched wherever was convenient or in front of the television. The manners we were taught dictate whether we ate slowly and consciously or bolted our food as quickly as possible; whether we smashed our vegetables on the plate; whether we ate with our mouth open or closed; whether we placed the serviette on our lap or ignored its presence entirely; and whether we cut small pieces of food one at a time, or chopped up our entire plate full first before switching the fork from left to right hand before stabbing the morsels and shovelling them into our mouth. Or whether we ate with our hands, from a communal plate, where sharing was paramount. The end result might be the same – we are nourished and satiated, but the delivery is important.

One of the reasons that dating is important in a culture where marriages are not pre-arranged according to appropriate social class is that manners are one of the ways we select for a partner. Dating is a chance for us to showcase our knowledge of manners. We tend to self-select partners and friends whose manners most closely resemble our own. Eating manners are also an indicator of how we will fare in business settings.

Yet, as seriously as we take table manners, they often defy logic, and what may be acceptable and polite in one culture may be deemed absolutely crass in another. Slurping noodles, for example, is considered acceptable and even highly desirable in Japan and Korea, yet quite unacceptable in much of the Western world. Similarly, drinking soup directly from the bowl is acceptable in Japan and distinctly frowned upon elsewhere. In England and most Commonwealth countries, it is considered good manners to eat soup with a spoon and to tip the bowl away from you rather than towards you to spoon up the last remnants (this latter bit being a marker of social class or food manners snobbism).

In Thailand, forks are not to be put into the mouth (only the spoon will do for this purpose) and chopsticks are not commonplace. Asking for chopsticks in anything but a Chinese restaurant in Thailand is considered tacky – an obvious sign of being a tourist. The French would like you to keep your hands visible at the table and not rest them on your lap; in this way they will know that you are not armed. The English would like you to keep your elbows off the table, even if it means placing them on your lap. The Japanese don't want to see your chopsticks stood vertically in a bowl of rice. In Italy, don't chop up your pasta – it should be twirled instead. In Morocco, where the word for bread is the same as the word for life, it is considered by many to be sinful to take a knife to bread (Pollan 2013). And when in China, do not assume that it's a good idea to finish every last morsel of food – to do so could suggest to the host that not enough food was served.

In Ethiopia, food is eaten from a communal plate but one must be careful about reaching all the way across the table – it is considered good manners to take what is closest to you. And in many countries around the world, people eat not with cutlery or chopsticks, but with their right hand. The left hand may be considered unclean, reserved for sanitary purposes.

Table manners are among our most highly ritualized and conspicuous behaviours. And while neither necessarily efficient nor logical, manners are merely conventions, which, if observed, help us to fit in and behave in ways deemed to be socially and culturally appropriate.

WHAT WE EAT AROUND THE WORLD

Though globalization has changed the way we eat and given us virtually unlimited access to foods from around the world, certain foods are eaten ritualistically and remain distinct to particular cultures. Some food rituals are mysterious and prestigious – such as the much-revered Japanese tea ceremony.

Other foreign foods and food rituals may make us feel squeamish and we have a tendency to condemn these food practices, especially those that seem most foreign to us. Some examples of food rituals that remain distinct to particular cultures include a particularly horrendous tasting fermented shark eaten in Iceland; kopi luwak, the world's most expensive coffee, made from coffee berry beans that have been defecated by civets; stinkbugs eaten in Indonesia; mopane, a type of caterpillar eaten in Africa; fried tarantulas eaten in Cambodia; seal blood drunk and raw seal meat eaten by Canadian Inuit; witchetty grubs eaten by Australian Aboriginals; and chapulines, the fried grasshoppers commonly eaten as a snack by Mexicans. And then there are the food competitions – such as eating and drinking competitions, cheese rolling competitions, and record breaking attempts for such things as the world's biggest sandwich or largest pizza.

Some food rituals actually seem to profit from a danger factor. One such example is the Japanese propensity for eating pufferfish, also known as blowfish or *fugu* in Japanese. Pufferfish are the world's most toxic fish. The liver, ovaries, and skin contain a poison called tetrodotoxin that is one hundred times more lethal than cyanide. Though chefs licenced to serve pufferfish undergo rigorous training, the eating of pufferfish is said to account for the majority of Japan's food poisoning deaths.

In South American countries including Peru, Ecuador and Columbia, guinea pigs are not only revered as a food source, but the rodents are also held in high esteem for their supernatural properties including the role they play in the diagnosis of various illnesses and in their ability to heal when rubbed against the body of the ill. Guinea pigs are often given as gifts in South America and used in religious and social ceremonies.

The African Maasai are nomadic people who traditionally depended on the cattle they raised to meet all their needs, living off the meat and also drinking both the milk and the blood of their herds. In recent years, a dwindling cattle population has seen the Maasai turn to other foods such as sorghum, rice, potatoes and cabbage.

Perhaps one of the more unusual and barbaric of all food rituals is the now outlawed French practice of eating ortolans. These tiny rare songbirds weigh in at less than an ounce (approximately 28 grams). Ortolans are captured live while in migratory flight, then force-fed and drowned in brandy before being eaten whole. Considered a rite of passage for French gourmets, the diners cover their heads with a large linen napkin before eating the entire bird in one go, bones and all. The napkin is used to preserve the delicate aromas and is also thought to hide the shame of the eater.

A now past, ancient South American Indigenous cultural tradition of grinding up the bones of the dead and adding them to soup for the relatives to share was believed to have been a mourning ritual – a way of keeping the dead with the living. This practice, known as endocannibalism, though no flesh was consumed, may also have been performed in regions of India as well.

While we need to fill our stomachs, there are times when we would rather go without. Not surprisingly, the foods and food rituals that we are most exposed to are similarly the ones we are usually most comfortable with. Food aversion is often associated with the foods we are least familiar with, or food to which we have had either a negative response, or been taught for religious or cultural reasons to avoid. Food rituals associated with danger or taboo evoke the strongest negative response. Cannibalism remains one of the most widely reviled of all food rituals, followed closely by eating animal totems and pets. Conversely, sharing the foods we were exposed to early in life with those we love the most remains the most desirable of all food rituals.

ALTERNATIVES TO EATING

Those of us fortunate enough to do so eat three meals a day – generally breakfast, lunch and dinner, or some variation on this theme. But with climate change, bee colonies at risk, and a growing global population expected to climb to 9.7 billion by 2050, and 11.2 billion by 2100 (UN 2015), humanity's dramatically increased need for food may drastically change the way we eat.

If we ate only to meet our nutritional requirements, we could satisfy those needs in pill form, or at the very least in some sort of blended drink form. Although a multitude of companies have developed such products for use by specific populations such as the elderly, ill and infirm; dieters; astronauts and submariners; and those stockpiling in case of an apocalyptic disaster – pill form food has not gone mainstream in the population at large. At least, not yet.

Rob Rhinehart, an electrical engineer turned tech entrepreneur in California, hopes to change how we meet our nutritional requirements. Rhinehart considers the human need for food as inefficient and costly to both the planet and the individual. He began to study food as if it were an engineering problem, and compiled a list of the 35 nutrients required for survival, combining them to create Soylent, a chemical powder blended with water.

Rhinehart abandoned eating and existed solely on Soylent for a month and was surprised by how well he felt and looked and how much money and time he saved. Rhinehart and his roommates, who had planned to develop software, began instead to develop a synthetic food business that they felt could help save humanity from what they perceive to be its dual burdens of food and farming (Widdicombe 2014).

Replacing at least some of our meals with synthetic products like Soylent may not be so far off or far out. The US military and space programme have both trialled Soylent. It pays, after all, to be prepared. And with our oceans becoming warmer and more polluted, the melting of the polar ice cap; and the erosion, desertification and urbanization of arable land – combined with a growing population and a warming planet – it is only a matter of time before our need for synthetic food becomes a reality. In the meantime, synthetic food could end global hunger and save lives during humanitarian disasters.

If it seems unthinkable, it's because we haven't yet developed rituals for coping with trading meals for a chalky powder mixed with water. Hominids, though, have a long history of adaption, having survived through ice ages, droughts, floods, famines, wars, plagues, earthquakes and volcanic eruptions. Millions of years of history have proven ritual to be a fundamental tool of adaption.

Humans eat for reasons other than merely meeting their nutritional requirements. In part we eat because we hunger, yearn and desire. We eat to satisfy both our physiological needs and our psychological needs. We eat because it is a return to our earliest memories – memories that we were born with, memories that we developed in infancy. We eat because we must. The rituals we attach to eating are those that make sense of our most fundamental needs – nourishment, love and a sense of community and belonging.

REFERENCES

Albers, S. (2003) *Eating Mindfully: How to End Mindless Eating and Enjoy a Balanced Relationship with Food.* Oakland, CA: New Harbinger Publications.

Brillat-Savarin, J.A. (2011 [1949]) *The Physiology of Taste: Or Meditations on Transcendental Gastronomy.* Trans. M.F.K. Fisher. New York: Vintage Books. [Original published in French 1949.]

Dowsett Johnston, A. (2013) *Drink: The Intimate Relationship Between Women and Alcohol.* New York: HarperCollins.

Pollan, M. (2013) *Cooked: A Natural History of Transformation.* New York: Penguin Group.

Popkin, B.M. (2007) 'The world is fat.' *Scientific American 297*, 88–95.

Salvy, S., Jarrin, D., Paluch, R., Irfan, N. and Pliner, P. (2007) 'Effects of social influence on eating in couples, friends and strangers.' *Appetite 49*, 1, 92–99.

UN (United Nations) (2015) *World Population Prospects: The 2015 Revision.* UN Department of Economic and Social Affairs (DESA), 29 July. Available at www.un.org/en/development/desa/news/population/2015-report.html, accessed on 20 February 2016.

Visser, M. (1991) *The Rituals of Dinner: The Origins, Evolution, Eccentricities and Meaning of Table Manners.* London: Penguin Books.

Vohs, K.D., Wang, Y., Gino, F. and Norton, M.I. (2013) 'Rituals enhance consumption.' *Psychological Science 24*, 9, 1714–1721.

Widdicombe, L. (2014) 'The end of food: Has a tech entrepreneur come up with a product to replace our meals?' *New Yorker*, 12 May.

PART IV

RITUALIZING IN PUBLIC PLACES

12

COMMEMORATIVE RITUAL AND THE POWER OF PLACE

Irene Stengs

Marking the site of a violent death with flowers, candles, hearts, cards or cuddly toys has become a regular practice since the 1990s, at least in the Western world. Murders, traffic or work-related accidents, terrorist attacks, or disasters by human or natural causes often prompt people to bring commemorative objects to the spot where the calamity took place. The death of public figures (celebrities, politicians, royalty) may evoke a similar kind of response. Extraordinary deaths of ordinary people in public spaces and the death of public figures – natural or unnatural – are experienced as public events. This may explain the widely felt need to ritualize grief, empathy and anger in public, irrespective of whether or not the mourner has a formal or personal relationship with the deceased.

This chapter focuses on the importance of place in a 'new public mourning' culture (Walter 2008). Everyone is familiar with the ritualized space occupied by informal roadside memorials, a phenomenon that is gaining in popularity in many Western countries. Typically, such memorials are set up to commemorate the death of the victim(s) of one specific tragedy: a traffic accident, a murder, a suicide or another kind of violent, premature death. Unlike cemeteries, churches and official monuments, these roadside memorials are ambiguous in that they appear in a space that is not intended for public mourning. These kinds of memorials may evoke sympathy, protest or revulsion in passers-by who find themselves unwittingly confronted with the reality of a death.

This ethnographic study examines how this phenomenon, as part of the new repertoire for mourning rituals, is dealt with in the Netherlands. These rituals – whether ephemeral or permanent – commemorate violent, unnatural deaths in public space by marking the very spot where the tragedy happened (Stengs 2012). The two most common kinds of commemorative memorials today are either for people who were killed in traffic or train accidents or for people who died of what the Dutch call an act of 'senseless violence' (*zinloos geweld*). In the Netherlands, as well as in the Flemish-speaking part of Belgium, the expression 'senseless violence' has become a term frequently used for all types of excessive social violence.[1]

The increasing popularity of temporary memorials has prompted local authorities to channel, or even prevent, their appearance in public space. One strategy involves restricting the size, diversity and visibility of wayside memorials. A number of municipalities limit the length of time memorials may be kept up – some tolerate them for only three months, others allow them for up to three years. Some towns only permit memorials that conform to a certain format or are made with specific materials such as a modest flat tile or an ivy plant. In some places, people must apply for a memorial permit and pay a tax, which may be as high as €375. In other places, only first-degree relatives may put up this kind of memorial. Such restrictions are nearly always at odds with the desires

---

[1] The term 'senseless violence' has different meanings in different cultural settings. In the Netherlands, 'senseless violence' evolved into a highly specific concept and societal concern in the 1990s. It does not describe any specific form of violence, but is regarded as a moral category that condemns a whole range of violent acts (including reckless driving). See Anton Blok's approach to violence as a cultural construct that contrasts 'meaningful' and 'senseless' action (2001, p.111). The tendency to qualify [certain forms of] violence as 'senseless' or 'irrational' is neither a typically Dutch attitude towards violence, nor an attitude that is specifically related to our era (Girard 1977). In the US, the expression 'senseless violence' is used in the context of protests against the high death toll from gun violence (approximately 30,000 a year; see Silent March (no date)), owing to widespread gun ownership in the nation. In Germany, the rarely used expression *sinnloses Gewalt* refers to cases of violent death terrorism or vandalism.

of the bereaved for spontaneous, self-styled expressions of their grief. Another way in which local authorities try to control unruly memorials is by erecting collective monuments to commemorate a specific category of victims. Unlike the ephemeral roadside memorials, these monuments are permanent structures, most of which have been designed by artists. The monuments are built to last and to be used by the public.

There are quite a number of these permanent collective monuments in the Netherlands. The majority were erected in the 1980s and 1990s to commemorate victims of the Second World War (van Vree 1995). Recent research by Dutch anthropologist Rob van Ginkel shows that new monuments are still being erected for specific categories of Second World War victims (2011, pp.379-463). This appears to be part of a broader trend that may be described as 'commemorating by category'. Over the last few decades, a number of memorial sites have been created as collective tributes for people who died from cancer, unveiled in 2002 (Tonnaer 2010) and for children in 2004, as well as for police officers in 2006 and fire fighters in 2012 who were killed in the line of duty. Moreover, at least five collective monuments commemorate diverse categories of traffic victims. The fundamental difference between the Second World War monuments and those for more recent victims is that the war monuments honour closed categories of victims while the more recent tributes are explicitly intended as 'open memorials' in the sense that they anticipate future victims and the needs of future mourners.

One may ask whether collective monuments can meet people's needs to publically mourn the loss of their loved ones. In an attempt to formulate an answer to this question, I concentrate on how collective monuments work in ritualizing bereavement caused by traffic deaths. This is a comparative ethnographical study of two contemporary collective monuments for traffic victims in the Netherlands. The first memorial to be considered is the *Maas Tunnel Monument for Traffic Victims* (*Maastunnel Monument Verkeersslachtoffers*), which was put up by the municipality of Rotterdam in 2003. The second marker, the *National Monument for Railway Accident Victims* (*Landelijk Monument Spoorwegongevallen*), was erected about six months later in the city of Utrecht in 2004.

WHOSE MONUMENT IS IT?

While the *National Monument for Railway Accident Victims* is a national tribute to railway victims, the other collective monuments are intended as memorials for regional road traffic victims. Both kinds of monument arose in response to one specific tragic event and were considered only later for collective commemoration. A sculpture in the province of Friesland known as *The Silent Scream* (*de Verstomde Schreeuw*, unveiled in 2000) was erected as a private memorial before being adopted as a collective commemorative symbol of the province's traffic safety policy. In 2003, Wassenaar township unveiled a monument dedicated to people who had died of traffic accidents within the municipality. Another such monument, entitled *Future, Consolation, Tears* (*Toekomst, Troost, Tranen*, unveiled in 2005), is dedicated to young traffic victims from the area around the provincial town of Nuenen (Stengs 2013). The *Maas Tunnel Monument for Traffic Victims* also began with an individual tragedy. Knowing the origins of collective monuments is fundamental for understanding how they work – or do not work – in public space.

Rotterdam's *Maas Tunnel Monument for Traffic Victims* is an example of a memorial that began with one road accident before being turned into a collective commemoration for traffic victims. The monument, unveiled on 28 November 2003, has the status of a municipal memorial. Four years earlier, in the early hours of 27 November 1999, a drunken driver hit a car carrying four young people in a head-on collision in the tunnel. John Goossens was killed instantly and Raymond Stevens died the next day in hospital. The two other passengers sustained critical life-changing injuries. Raymond Stevens' parents request to erect a monument to commemorate their son's death was initially refused by the borough of Charlois and the municipality of Rotterdam, which has a very restrictive policy with regard to roadside memorials.[2] In the end, a memorial was authorized, on the

---

[2] When a request was made (April 2012) for permission to place a monument in commemoration of the death of a seller of homeless magazines, a municipality spokesman summarized the policy as follows: 'The municipality has a general policy with regard to memorials. There are a few places where people may obtain permission for to erect a general monument. There is, for instance, a commemorative wall for traffic victims at the Maas Tunnel.' *Metro* (2012) 'Studente maakt zich hard voor gedenkteken.' 4 April. Available at www.metronieuws.nl/regionaal/studente-maakt-zich-hard-voor-gedenkteken/SrZldd!nu39pQzle3HY, accessed on 24 April 2016.

192　Emerging Ritual in Secular Societies

Figure 12.1. The *Maas Tunnel Monument for Traffic Victims* (Rotterdam)

Figure 12.2. The plateau of the monument frames one-half of the granite memorial stone in remembrance of Raymond Stevens and John Goossens (Rotterdam)

Commemorative Ritual and the Power of Place 193

Figure 12.3. The switchboard box is ornamented with brass plates that are engraved with newspaper articles relating to the accident (Rotterdam)

Figure 12.4. At the tunnel exit below, the other half of the granite stone is inset in the pavement, marking the exact spot of the accident (Rotterdam)

condition that it become a collective monument for all traffic victims in the municipality of Rotterdam and the surrounding areas.³

The *Maas Tunnel Monument* was realized owing to a combination of factors. First and foremost was the parents' determination and perseverance. Raymond's father expressed this in an interview on TV Rijnmond (a local TV channel) on the evening the monument was unveiled. He said that he was proud they had succeeded; it had cost him three-and-a-half years of his life to get to this point. Raymond's brother added that the inauguration represented 'the crowning of my father's work'. Another important factor in the construction of the monument was the substantial media attention generated by the accident itself, which was portrayed by the press as an example of the 'senseless violence of road traffic'.⁴ Social outrage about this particular tragedy, coupled with the emergence of more and more unauthorized roadside memorials for the young people, served to convince municipal authorities to respond favourably to the Stevens family's request. Nonetheless, the authorities insisted on a compromise that turned their memorial into a collective monument intended to forestall future requests for roadside memorials.

The Dutch artist Kamiel Verschuren was commissioned to design the *Maas Tunnel Monument* on the Maastunnelplein, a site just above the tunnel exit where the accident had occurred.⁵,⁶ The monument is an art installation constructed on an existing pedestrian area; it makes use of pre-existing structures and objects. At the left of the site, the artist covered the tiles of the pavement with a 'puddle' of asphalt from which

---

3   *Algemeen Dagblad* (2003) 'Maastunnel Monument komt er voor alle verkeersslachtoffers.' 13 November. Available at www.ad.nl/ad/nl/1401/ad/integration/nmc/frameset/varia/kobala_article.dhtml?artid=rd099986, accessed on 15 May 2016.
4   In an article that appears on the monument, the Rotterdam traffic prosecutor used the words 'senseless violence in traffic' during the court case. One newspaper article is headlined: 'Five years demanded against senseless violence in traffic.'
5   For information about the artist and the monument, see *Beeldende Kunst en Openbare Ruimte*. Available at www.bkor.nl/kunstwerken/maastunnel-monument-voor-verkeersslachtoffers-nl
6   The actual place of the tragedy was deemed unfit, in part for reasons of traffic safety and poor accessibility, and in part because the Maas Tunnel is already registered as a monument.

rises a low plateau. On this plateau he placed one-half of a green-veined granite stone inscribed with the text:

> In remembrance of the lives lost in the early hours of 27 November 1999
>
> and on the following day, November 28…
>
> on account of a serious traffic accident
>
> R.S. & J.G.[7]

The other half of the granite piece was inset into the pavement below on the exact spot of the accident at the tunnel exit. Verschuren also integrated texts onto the pre-existing balustrade and the barrier wall located above the tunnel exit. Large letters on the barrier wall form a text that reads: 'In memory of the random victims of road traffic…that we might all become.' Another line, this one from a poem by the Dutch poet Cees Nooteboom, appears in raised letters on a bronzed portion of the handrail that is just above the exit: 'even if we think of something else, we think of death'.[8] The remainder of the railing is painted bright turquoise, a colour that reappears further along the platform that includes a switchboard box. This box is decorated with four large brass plates. The front plates are engraved with newspaper articles that relate the accident, the subsequent court case and the verdict as well as descriptions of the monument's history and the commemorative ceremony. Empty plates on the rear side are allegedly reserved for reports of any new traffic victims. The switchbox is not only made up of different kinds of messages from various media such as television news, web-based and traditional print articles, but is itself also a medium for transmitting information. As such, the monument demonstrates the interconnectedness, the cross-referencing and the transformation of media.

---

7   Translation from the Dutch by the author.
8   '[S]oms denkend aan de dood maar denken aan iets anders.' Translation from the Dutch by the author. Taken from 'Romantiek' ['Romance'], in *De doden zoeken een huis* [*The dead are searching for a house*], 1956.

On the evening of the unveiling, the authorities closed traffic to the Maas Tunnel and blocked the adjacent Maastunnelplein square during a brief memorial ceremony that gave the bereaved the opportunity to visit the place where their loved ones had been killed. Initially, traffic was supposed to be interrupted every year on this date to commemorate the deaths of all Rotterdam traffic victims. In practice, this aspect of the collective commemoration has not been respected since the second anniversary of the installation.[9]

THE POWER OF PLACE

Memorials like the *Maas Tunnel Monument for Traffic Victims* raise questions about whether collective memorial sites like this one can truly meet the needs of the bereaved. In this particular case, it is significant that the monument has not achieved its intended purpose of uniting people around an annual event that commemorates Rotterdam's traffic victims. This is partly due to the fact that the *place* or public space allotted for the commemoration is ambiguous in the sense that, irrespective of its stated purpose as a collective memorial site, it is first and foremost a memorial for Raymond Stevens and John Goossens. There is no visual evidence that it honours any other road traffic victims from the Rotterdam area.

In order to hone the question about whether collective memorial sites meet public need, we should ask how a collective monument such as the *Maas Tunnel Monument for Traffic Victims* 'works', and what makes 'place' so important for commemoration. It may be helpful to compare the history of this monument with that of the *National Monument for Railway Accident Victims*. The choice of place for the memorial for railway victims contrasts significantly with the place selected for the road traffic victims' monument. The group working on this memorial for railway victims intentionally chose a neutral location in order to commemorate both past and future accident victims.

---

9 When questioned about why the date was not observed, municipal authorities replied that no application for a permit had been requested for some years (a permit is obligatory when traffic is stopped on a public road).

The *National Monument for Railway Accident Victims* was erected in Nieuweroord Park, near Utrecht railway station (2004). It is intended as a commemoration for all those killed on railway tracks in the Netherlands – regardless of the cause of their death – and as a consolation for the bereaved. Dutch artist Anton Broos designed the monument, a three-metre high steel circle that is connected to a 15-metre-long steel strip. The memorial symbolizes 'the dynamics of life, and the stillness of death'.[10] Dutch theologian Anne van der Meiden was inspired by the monument's design to write this poem that was engraved on the strip:

Memories run together

With those who on a railway track

Passed the junction of death

With our feet we measure our sorrow and grief

A loving salute from this silent station

Till we meet again at our next destination.[11]

Work on the monument began following a request from one of the bereaved to erect a memorial for the 95 victims of a railway accident at Harmelen (1962); the writer of that letter's father figured among the victims of the accident[12] which remains, to date, the most deadly rail accident the Netherlands has known. This letter was one of many requests regularly addressed to Dutch Railways (Nederlandse Spoorwegen, NS) and governmental authorities over the years. A growing number of those who lost loved ones to accidents on the railway wanted permission to construct a permanent memorial on the place where tragedy had struck.

---

10   This text is taken from the press information sheet that was distributed at the unveiling ceremony on 16 April 2004.

11   'Herinneringen lopen samen op Met hen die op het spoor De wissel van de dood passeerden Met onze voeten meten wij verdriet en rouw Een lieve groet van dit verstild station Tot weerziens op de volgende bestemming.' Translation from the Dutch by the author.

12   This account of the monument and Dutch Railway's (NS) reasoning are based on information distributed for the press at the unveiling ceremony on 16 April 2004.

Figure 12.5. At the unveiling ceremony of the *National Monument for Railway Accident Victims*, employees of the Dutch Railway honour the victims with roses, 16 April 2004 (Utrecht)

Figure 12.6. Victims of all rail accidents are remembered at the unveiling ceremony, 16 April 2004 (Utrecht)

Figure 12.7. The *National Monument for Railway Accident Victims* (Utrecht)

Furthermore, an increasing number of unofficial memorial sites had sprung up along the railway tracks and on station platforms. In addition to railway passenger victims, there were also railway workers who had died in work-related accidents, and by far the largest category of victims, suicides on the tracks.[13] Putting up temporary memorials along the tracks represents a serious safety issue for the bereaved as well as a hazard for locomotive drivers. Erecting a 'single national monument for all railway accidents in the Netherlands', as the NS put it, could meet 'the need for a place where the bereaved can gather and grieve safely at any time, each in their own way'.[14] The *National Monument for Railway Accident Victims* was erected by NS in cooperation with the bereaved of the Harmelen disaster, and inaugurated on 16 April 2004.

The spot chosen for the monument is symbolic because it is located at the physical and administrative heart of the Dutch rail network (NS and ProRail maintenance). Since it is as close as possible to Point Zero – the place from which all rail distances are measured – the monument occupies a meaningful but neutral public place that is free from any direct association with any one particular tragedy. This monument is not weighed down by the ambiguity that seems to have attached itself to the *Maas Tunnel Monument*. Even so, this has not been reason enough for the railway memorial to become the only place where the bereaved come to mourn the loved ones they have lost to the rail tracks. People continue to put up temporary memorials on or near the spot on the tracks where their loved ones were killed. A concrete example of the ineffectiveness of the *National Monument for Railway Accident Victims* to satisfy the needs of the bereaved was revealed with the commemoration of the 50th anniversary of the 1962 Harmelen train disaster accident. On 8 January 2012 a new monument specifically for the victims of this tragedy was inaugurated near the spot where the accident took place. Clearly, the *National Monument for Railway Accident Victims* does not

---

13   On average, there are 200 suicides every year on railway tracks in the Netherlands (about 11 per cent of the total number of suicides).

14   '[I]n de behoefte aan een plek waar men op elk willekeurig tijdstip en op persoonlijke wijze kan herdenken.' Translation from the Dutch by the author.

satisfy the need on the part of the bereaved for a memorial in proximity to the place of the calamity.

These situations demonstrate how hard it is to channel mourning. Government regulations, policies and initiatives are powerless to lift the emotional charge attached to the place where a disaster struck. The many untold stories of loss and mourning that are tied to such places need to be voiced (de Certeau 1984, p.106). The act of marking such a place transforms it into a ritualized public space, which anyone, even at a glance, can recognize as a spot where someone died a premature and violent death and where others honour the loved ones they have lost. Whether an accident occurs on the railways or in traffic, each event represents an intense personal drama for the people whose world is torn apart by the sudden incursion of death into their lives. Given the number of memorials that arise, it seems clear that many bereaved find it unbearable that a place so heavily charged with meaning for them is not immediately recognizable as such to others.

REFERENCES

Blok, A. (2001) *Honour and Violence*. Cambridge: Polity Press.
de Certeau, M. (1984) *The Practice of Everyday Life*. Trans. S. Rendall. Berkeley, CA: University of California Press.
Girard, R. (1977) *Violence and the Sacred*. Trans. P. Gregory. Baltimore, MD: Johns Hopkins University Press.
Silent March (no date) 'Americans Against Gun Violence.' Available at Silentmarch. org, accessed on 24 April 2016.
Stengs, I. (2012) 'Gedenken op de plek des onheils. Bermmonumenten als materiele uitdrukking van veranderende rouwcultuur'. *Volkskunde 2012 3*, 263-328.
Stengs, I. (2013) 'Giving Public Space a Face. The Agency of Monuments and Portraits Thailand and the Netherlands Compared.' In B. Boute and T. Smålberg (eds) *Devising Order. Performance, Ritual and the Performativity of Practice* (pp.61-80). Leiden: Brill.
Tonnaer, J. (2010) 'Bomen voor het leven. Een studie naar een collectief hedendaags herdenkingsritueel voor overleden kankerpatiënten.' Unpublished PhD thesis, Tilburg/Groningen Universities.
van Ginkel, R. (2011) *Rondom de stilte. Herdenkingscultuur in Nederland*. Amsterdam: Bert Bakker.

van Vree, F. (1995) *In de schaduw van Auschwitz. Herinneringen, beelden, geschiedenis*. Groningen: Historische Uitgeverij.
Walter, T. (2008) 'The New Public Mourning.' In M.S. Stroebe *et al.* (eds) *Handbook of Bereavement Research and Practice. Advances in Theory and Intervention*. Washington, DC: American Psychological Association.

13

NEW RITUAL SOCIETY[1]

CONSUMERIST REVOLUTION AND THE REDISCOVERY OF RITUAL

Gianpiero Vincenzo

The transition from traditional rites to modern ritualizing has meant profound changes in views and perspectives. In the pre-modern age, 'community', with its rites and symbols, took centre stage and played a main role in human life. According to Ferdinand Tönnies (1855–1936), while community is ruled by ties of solidarity, the modern age is marked the decisive feat of 'society', that is to say, a system of social relations ruled by money and focused on trade. As the role of 'community' is minimized in consumer society, market boundaries are obliterated and its influence spreads all over the world.

The emergence of consumer society has led to new coherent systems of meaning that tackle the huge job of redefining unusual behaviours that are now considered ordinary. The ritualistic dimension contributes to our understanding of consumer society: 'Goods…are ritual adjuncts: consumption is a ritual process whose primary function is to make sense of the inchoate flux of events' (Douglas and Isherwood 1979, p.43).

Both in anthropology and sociology, so much has been written about modern symbols and rituals – some of it unrelated to consumerism – that 'the use and abuse of such words are likely to deprive them of their

---

[1] This chapter is an edited extract from *New Ritual Society: Consumerism and Culture in Contemporary Society* which was originally published in Italian in 2014 by Fausto Lupetti in Bologna. An English translation by Enrico Spadaro is available from the same publisher in e-Book format.

semantic efficiency' (Segalen 1998, p.7). However, some of the main features of rituals as well as their structure and function must be addressed. Of course there are fundamental differences, as well as parodic reversals, between traditional and consumer rituals. Nonetheless, the latter's structure is often derived from the former, much as Comte's 'positivist catechism' has its origins in Christian sacraments.

From an etymological point of view, rite contributes to 'order', to harmony between Heaven and Earth. The Latin word *ritus* redirects to the Sanskrit *rita*, which is rendered 'cosmic order' or even 'moving' and 'appropriately'. Every traditional ritual act may be seen as a link between the natural and the supernatural, metaphysically speaking. Durkheim held that, by virtue of this acknowledged feature, rite cannot be separated from beliefs or doctrine. For this reason, rite should not be thought of as a formal practice, but as a practical feature of belief, or as a symbol linked to it. The symbolic aspect is paramount in traditional rites. It may be said that rites are 'working' symbols and every ritual gesture is an 'acted' symbol (Guénon 1946, p.162).

Etymology helps focus on the relationship between rite and symbol. The latter stems from the Greek *symbàllo*, 'put together' and 'complete'. In the Roman world, the *simbolum* was even a sign of *hospitalitatis*. That is to say, families showed their hospitality with a ring or another sign that was both offered and received. It represented a tie that brought their offspring together (Pianigiani 1907).

Shaking hands is a good example of such a ritual. When two people meet, they often shake hands. Millions of people do this every day without thinking much about it. When hands are not shaken, it may be a sign of antagonism; at the very least, it shows a lack of consideration for the other person.

Unintentionally, shaking hands is a legacy from old rituals. Painted hands are seen in the first cave engraving in France, Spain, Africa, Australia and America. In Gargas, near Aventignan in the Pyrenees, there are caves with many painted handprints, 254 in all. More than half of the handprints are black, the rest are red. These handprints date back to the Upper Palaeolithic, some 27,000 years ago. They represent one of the oldest forms of 'art' in human history.

Even today, hand gestures are signs of esteem. The laying on of hands indicates blessing and the transmission of spiritual authority upon the person being consecrated. Hands raised or folded are symbols of prayer. The Greeks shook hands to show they were unarmed. Shaking hands also shows that one is being welcomed into a group. Over the centuries, such gestures could seal a deal, an alliance, as well as armistices and marriages, as in the case of *dextrarum iunctio*, when joining right hands marked a wedding agreement. Touching hands has long been a symbol of harmony.

According to US anthropologist Grant McCracken, consumption rituals transfer cultural meanings from objects to human beings, via four main forms (1986):

1. Exchange ritual. Anthropologists noticed the importance of exchange ritual very early on and this has given birth to a stable tradition of studies on the subject since the beginning of the 20th century (Mauss 1909). However, although gifts once had mainly a symbolic meaning, nowadays these wrapped objects are related to a specific consumptive occasion: Christmas, Valentine's Day, birthdays, etc. In the consumerist context, the exchange of gifts is an important time for comparing the cultural meanings borne by the goods.

2. Possession ritual. Modern consumers spend a lot of their time cleaning, comparing, talking about and showing off their goods. Thus, determining the cultural meanings of consumer goods has become an integral part of life for both individuals and groups. Possession rituals play a significant role in the definition of space and in how people pass their time.

3. Grooming ritual. Since the cultural meanings of consumer goods do not last long, they have to be regularly renewed. This renewal process occurs during the grooming rituals. The possession's body should also be considered part of the consumptive good. It must be prepared and made ready for use, as is the case with automobiles.

4. Changing and divestment rituals. In the first case, the renewal or replacement of an object may imply removing all traces of the former owner, as when a newly purchased home is repainted. Divestment ritual refers to the phase that leads to the sale or destruction of goods.

Individual consumption rituals aim at instilling an almost unnatural serenity, while public consumption rituals tend towards a 'creative effervescence'. The Scottish anthropologist Victor Turner (1920–1983) also supports the creative role of collective rituals. In particular, rites of passage play the role of cyclically deconstructing social organization by reducing the strictness of its inner hierarchies and norms. In a society that would otherwise suppress elasticity and pluralism through its structural patterns, ritual processes help keep them alive within community. Ritual participants cross the borders of the ordinary and enter a sort of 'liminality', by which they deprive themselves of their unique features. Notably, participants experience new and deeper ties of solidarity within the community. Thus, ritual processes also function to fulfil egalitarian ambitions within society.

> It is as though there are two major 'models' for human interrelatedness, juxtaposed and alternating. The first is of society as a structured, differentiated and often hierarchical system of politico-legal-economic positions with many types of evaluation, separating men in terms of 'more' or 'less'. The second, which emerges recognizably in the liminal period, is of society as an unstructured or rudimentarily structured and relatively undifferentiated *comitatus*, community, or even communion of equal individuals who submit together to the general authority of the ritual elders. (Turner 1966, p.113)

New consumption rituals develop and concentrate in the so-called cathedrals of consumption (Ritzer 1999). Shopping malls and theme parks, casinos and cruise liners are built according to consumerist logic, much in the same way contemporary metropolises are shaped. In such a view, even graveyards, such as the nine-story cemetery in Vancouver, resemble theme parks (1999, p.160).

The structure of a supermarket and, on a broader scale that of a shopping mall, shapes public space much in the same way as the cathedral or the town hall did in the pre-modern age. Once people went to church or out of town on Sundays; now families go shopping and have lunch in the 'eternal spring' of shopping malls.

At this point, it is important to underline how consumerism led from an individualistic cult of human beings to a cult of objects. Or, as the American sociologist David Riesman (1909–2002) said, from inner-directed personalities to other-directed personalities. Before the consumerist era, objects were human being's appendices. Consumerism has made the human being an appendix of objects. Purchasing goods keeps alive a relationship to past rituals through evocation and gratification, albeit in a reified world. The consumer's state of trance in a supermarket is a modern substitute for the peace and detachment from the world that one might enjoy in a sanctuary. What the consumer does to get ready for shopping is very similar to priests' preparation for public and private rites.

The mystique of consumption promises enriched individualism, heightened earthly perception, and extraordinary virtuality that exceeds the limits of objective reality. If the mystic aimed at absolute Truth, the consumer is content with a world turned upside down where truth is only one option among many others in the cult of the absolute Relative. Modern gadgets, evocative reproductions of consumption objects and brands, have even been considered by some as an exuberant reproposal of the indulgences distributed in ancient times (Debord 1987).

Consumer society rules body movements, the focus of our mind's attention, and it lays claim to the right to establish new rituals. Without rituals, consumption is likely to be occasional and not compulsive. Yet ceremonies strengthen this activity and settle it into human behaviour. In consumerism, fetishism replaces symbolism, compulsive behaviour marks life's rhythms, and money becomes the protective deity for the creation of new needs.

> People recognize themselves in their commodities; they find their soul in their car, hi-fi set, split-level home, kitchen equipment. The very mechanism that ties the individual to his society has changed, and social control is anchored in the new needs which it has produced. (Marcuse 1964, p.23)

In the cathedrals of consumption, face-to-face interactions are minimized; attention is deflected from human relationships, which are now secondary. They have been replaced by relationships with objects, which constitute an autonomous and self-referential universe of meanings and rituals.

Advertising and objects of consumption tend to occupy our lives. On the one hand, advertising propaganda imposes itself as a communication model. On the other hand, commercial spectacularization is key to the organization of the space where consumer objects circulate as vehicles of cultural meaning.

> Many symbolic and mythical values, which in the past were institutionalized and whose value constituted an irreplaceable heritage for the society of that time, today appear outdated or indecipherable because their symbolic energy has discharged.
>
> We are now witnessing the proliferation of new myths and new rites, based on the weave of new symbolic ties that at first sight appear totally or partially fetishist. (Dorfles 1997, p.30)

Modern shows do not sing of heroes and their deeds anymore, but of consumption and the passions it arouses.

THE SYSTEM OF OBJECTS

According to the French philosopher and sociologist Jean Baudrillard (1929–2007), a true 'system of objects' dominates the contemporary age. It is a system upon which human beings and the related rituals they celebrate depend (1968). The cycle of the death and rebirth of objects plays an important social role in this system. Although this cycle occurs in many traditional rituals, in order to avoid excessive accumulation it is essential to modern consumer rituals. Once consumerism started celebrating trade rather than use, the main act of consumption was completed at the moment of purchase. As in compulsive behaviour, this fleeting fulfilment of desire leads to early dissatisfaction and thus to another purchase. As a result, as Collins (2004) also stated, the constant substitution of ritual objects plays a vital role in modern ritualizing. This is not simply divestment, but in fact a ritual of destruction that starts with objects and eventually includes reified bodies (Baudrillard 1974).

The rhythm of object divestment has become more and more artificial; it is connected now to the relationship between production and consumption cycles. Indeed, planned object obsolescence was first theorized at the dawn of consumerism in 1932 by Bernard London, a New York estate agent who travelled across the country promoting his personal solution for dealing with the Great Depression. He proposed that laws fix an object's life span and that the replacement of old objects should be determined by production needs and the labour market.

> I would have the government assign a lease of life to shoes and homes and machines, to all products of manufacture, mining and agriculture, when they are first created, and they would be sold and used within the term of their existence definitely known by the consumer. After the allotted time had expired, these things would be legally 'dead' and would be controlled by the duly appointed governmental agency and destroyed if there is widespread unemployment. New products would constantly be pouring forth from the factories and marketplaces, to take the place of the obsolete, and the wheels of industry would be kept going and employment regularized and assured for the masses. (London 1932, p.6)

As a matter of fact, the Phoebus cartel had already put into practice a form of built-in obsolescence. Although some of the first lightbulb prototypes lasted up to 30,000 hours, from 1924 onwards, a group of electricity companies – Osram (Germany), Philips (Netherlands), Tungsram (Hungary), Associated Electrical Industries (Great Britain), Compagnie des Lampes (France) and General Electric (USA) – agreed to limit the life span of lightbulbs to 1000 hours of light. This case is very similar to that of the nylon fibre that DuPont began selling in 1939. Nylon tights marked a glamorous commercial success. After the Second World War, however, fibre resistance and duration diminished considerably. Although there is no factual evidence, DuPont's chemical engineers allegedly made the fibre more brittle and thus less resistant (Fox 2002; Slade 2006).

In 1951, in England, the American director Alexander Mackendrick (1912–1993) shot the film *The Man in the White Suit*. The film tells a satirical story of an inventor of a fibre that is made into cloth that neither gets dirty nor wears out. The employers and employees of a failing textile factory chase the inventor out of town. Nowadays, the batteries of music players and smartphones are designed to last a short time and cannot be easily substituted, which leads to the purchase of a new device rather than the repair of the original item (Nocera 2007).

Planned obsolescence may be structural, that is, it may be determined by components that are weaker than potentially achievable, which causes them to break or malfunction prematurely. Functional obsolescence is determined by new models and market standards, which in turn create technological obsolescence for earlier objects. Built-in obsolescence may also be related to style – changes in fashion and object design can render the object obsolete. Since the 1930s, cars and electrical appliances have been intentionally made to last less long so as to avoid saturating the market and to encourage higher consumption. This has led to huge waste disposal problems (Packard 1960).

The aesthetics of object obsolescence appear in cultural representations of consumerism. As a sign of distinction, cars are directly related to accidents that occur in films or TV series; images of car crashes depict a dramatic kind of liturgy.

> Indeed, the car is without doubt one of the main foci of daily and long-term waste, both private and collective. Not only is it so by its systematically reduced use-value, its systematically increased prestige and fashion coefficient, and the outrageous sums invested in it, but – without doubt, much more deeply than this – by the spectacular collective sacrifice of sheet metal, machinery and human lives in the Accident. The Accident: that gigantic 'happening', the

finest offered by consumer society, through which society affords itself in the ritual destruction of materials and life the proof of its excessive affluence. (Baudrillard 1974, p.47)

In the modern imaginary, car accidents have a true cult repertory, as in the frightful plot of *Crash* (1973) by the English writer James G. Ballard (1930–2009). This science fiction novel is about a modern sexual perversion, then known as *symphorophilia*, which is characterized by an erotic excitement that comes from viewing disasters. The protagonists' eroticism occurs in relation to cars and their destruction in crashes, as well as to pictures of wrecks and accidents. The book inspired the homonymous film by the Canadian director David Cronenberg (winner of Jury Prize at the Cannes Film Festival in 1993), which highlights the *danse macabre* between corpses and cars.

With films such as *The Bank Dick* (1940) by Edward F. Cline (1891–1961), American cinema has glorified *car chases*, generally by the police, and made them a main feature of action films in which a huge number of cars are destroyed. Even today, car destruction is connected to a form of exaggerated 'muscular' aggressiveness and eroticism. This is seen in *Fast and Furious*, a seven-film series produced between 2001 and 2015. The need to celebrate the 'death' of a car as a cult object is conveyed in TV news too; car accidents are omnipresent, although they usually only show car wrecks, rather than injured bodies and corpses.

The circle of death and resurrection in consumption rituals has a greater impact when it involves the body, which – once reified – belongs to the universe of objects. If a man wants to be considered successful, he is 'compelled' to possess certain objects as distinctive attributes – car, yacht, private jet – and maybe even male and female bodies in the form of a bodyguard or a beautiful woman.

Divestment and accumulation are interrelated in consumerist rituals. They mark the boundaries of a society of addiction and debt. An addiction to things, habits and people-objects has become one of the main features of modern society. The disease is so widespread that it has developed into conventional drama.

> What is so striking is the massive social pervasiveness of addiction.
>
> This concept, which originally referred almost exclusively to alcohol and drug consumption, has been extended recently to include any area of life. One may be addicted to smoking, food, sex, but also to work, going to the gym, or to love! These areas are interchangeable in the sense that a human being may fight to give up one addiction only to succumb to another. (Perniola 2004, p.15)

'Disposophobia', or compulsive hoarding (or hoarding disorder), is a psychological disorder that prevents one from discarding objects, however useless they may be or seem. It is a dysfunction that is linked to an inability to ritualize divestment.

According to data from the Department of Psychiatry of the University of California at San Diego, at the beginning of this century at least 1.2 million Americans suffered from compulsive hoarding. Most had shown symptoms of the condition since adolescence. The best cure appears to be a pharmacological treatment that increases serotonin levels, combined with a cognitive behaviour therapy. This shows that consumer society has faced psychophysical decompensation since its inception.

Compulsive hoarding became known as 'Collyer Brothers Syndrome' after Homer Lusk Collyer (1881-1947) and Langley Collyer (1885-1947) died in their home under the weight of 140 tons of objects they had collected over several decades. The news spread around the world. Writer Marcia Davenport (1903-1996), wife of the publisher of *Fortune* magazine, dedicated her novel *My Brother's Keeper* (1954) to the story. In the 1960s, a park was opened on the spot where the Collyer brothers had lived.

The system of objects has its victims, but it has its heroes too: robots. Humanoid robots are the first social representations of a system of objects that has acquired full autonomy from human beings.

The author who contributed the most to these ideas is Isaac Asimov (1920-1992), an American biochemist and science fiction writer of Russian origin. Asimov drew upon his Jewish tradition to create a whole universe around robotic artificial intelligence that he defined as a 'positronic brain'. Most of his robots' features came from *golems*, anthropomorphic figures from medieval Jewish mythology. According to these myths, a *golem* is a clay creature that can be brought to life through the use of spells and amulets.

Golem was also the title of a novel published in 1915 by the Austrian Jewish writer Gustav Meyrink (1868-1932). In 1931, the Englishman James Whale (1889-1957) directed the film *Frankenstein*, which was inspired by the homonymous novel by Londoner Mary Shelley (1797-1951). Nonetheless, it was Asimov's universe that conjured up a whole new machine-human reality. In 1942, he wrote the Three Laws of Robotics, a metaphor for the Ten Commandments, which initiated a new alliance between humans and androids (1950 [1977], p.37):

1. 'A robot may not injure a human being nor, through inaction, allow a human being to come to harm.'

2. 'A robot must obey the orders given it by human beings, except where such orders would conflict with the First Law.'

3. 'A robot must protect its own existence as long as such protection does not conflict with the First or Second Law.'

In the novels that followed, especially in *Caves of Steel* (1954), Asimov describes a complex world where the human–android alliance lead to the conquering of the galaxy and the creation of several civilizations that develop human potential under the invisible leadership of a superior robot race. In *Robots and Empire* (1985) R. Daneel Olivaw embodies the perfect android model; over the centuries, he even develops the telepathic ability to read and influence people's thoughts and eventually becomes the fulcrum of the entire galaxy.

The main characters of one of the most famous films of the second half of the 20th century, *Blade Runner* (1982) by Ridley Scott, are particularly evolved humanoids.[2] The protagonist Rick Deckard (Harrison Ford) must kill humanoids who fled from the colonies. They live out the tragedy of being aware that they will die prematurely because their DNA

---

2   Scott's characters are freely inspired by Philip K. Dick's science fiction novel, *Do Androids Dream of Electric Sheep?* (1964).

was programmed to last for only four years. Roy Batty (Rutger Hauer), the humanoids' leader, utters his last words while holding a dove that he releases as he dies. These humanoids are a metaphor for modern humans who now live to a pre-programmed deadline, as do the objects that surround them:

> I've seen things you people wouldn't believe. Attack ships on fire off the shoulder of Orion. I watched C-beams glitter in the dark near the Tannhauser Gate. All those moments will be lost in time, like tears in the rain. Time to die. (Scott 1982)

Comic books also deal with the myths of the integration of human beings with machines. Entire generations of superheroes emerge with powers that are for the most part traceable to contemporary scientific and technological findings: radiation that enhances the senses, genetic mutations that create new races, not to mention the fibres of Spiderman's web and Wolverine's titanium endoskeleton. These robots, androids and superheroes are often portrayed as being more intelligent, sensitive and functional than humans. As a social representation, they render acceptable and familiar a system of objects in which modern people feel progressively more lost, but on which, in spite of themselves, they find they are increasingly dependent.

CONCLUSION

There are many good reasons for the deep rootedness of consumerism in modern society. Consumerism is not only about consumption; it is a steady source of new symbols and rituals. And, if human beings are indeed symbolic (Cassirer 1944) and ritualistic animals (Douglas 1966), then consumerism is one of the many ways we meet our vital human needs. Increasingly in contemporary culture, consumerism is the only way to meet these ritual needs. In recent centuries, an anti-ritual current pervaded much of Western culture; this misled us into thinking we can do without ritual (Douglas 1970). The consumerist revolution of the 20th century arose from a progressive rediscovery of ritual.

This does not mean that rationality is over and done with, or even that it is smouldering under the ashes. Rationality remains the backbone of consumerism, as well as of contemporary society. Yet this internal framework has been enrobed in the objects of consumerism and in the entertainment industry. This occurs much the same way in computers as the cold rationality of the numerical sequences of mathematical processes is concealed by an ever more 'user-friendly' graphic interface. Perhaps we need to invert the hermeneutical process. While it is critical to understand how the world has become consumption-based, it is equally important to discern the processes of symbolic consumption. Comprehension of these processes can lead to healthier human activity, irrespective of consumption. Symbols, rituals and their related narratives (which function as instructions for ritual practice) thus become keys to understanding cultural processes. Elaborating a socio-anthropology of symbolic activity can lead to more responsible and conscious social development.

REFERENCES

Asimov, I. (1950 [1977]) *I, Robot*. New York: Gnome.
Asimov, I. (1954) *The Cave of Steel*. New York: Doubleday.
Asimov, I. (1985) *Robots and Empire*. New York: Doubleday.
Baudrillard, J. (1968) *Le Système des objets*. Paris: Gallimard.
Baudrillard, J. (1974) *La Société de consommation*. Paris: Gallimard.
Cassirer, E. (1944) *An Essay on Man*. New York: Doubleday.
Collins, R. (2004) *Interaction Ritual Chains*. Princeton, NJ: Princeton University Press.
Debord, G. (1987) *La Société du spectacle*. Paris: Buchet/Chastel.
Dorfles, G. (1997) *Fatti e fattoidi. Gli pseudoeventi nell'arte e nella società*. Vicenza: Neri Pozza.
Douglas, M. (1966) *Purity and Danger: An Analysis of Concepts of Pollution and Taboo*. London: Routledge.
Douglas, M. (1970) *Natural Symbols: Explorations in Cosmology*. London: Routledge.
Douglas, M. and Isherwood, B. (1979) *The World of Goods*. London: Routledge.
Fox, N. (2002) *Against the Machine: The Hidden Luddite Tradition in Literature, Art, and Individual Lives*. Washington, DC: Island.
Guénon, R. (1946) *Aperçus sur l'initiation*. Paris: Éditions Traditionnelles.

London, B. (1932) *Ending the Depression Through Planned Obsolescence.* New York [self-published].

Marcuse, H. (1964) *One-Dimensional Man, Studies in the Ideology of Advanced Industrial Society.* Boston, MA: Bacon.

Mauss, M. (1909) *La Prière.* Paris: Alcan.

McCracken, G. (1986) 'Culture and consumption: A theoretical account of the structure and movement of the cultural meaning of consumer goods.' *Journal of Consumer Research*, June, 71–84.

Nocera, J. (2007) 'iPhone spin goes round and round.' *New York Times*, 30 June.

Packard V. (1960) *The Waste Makers.* New York: David MacKay, Co.

Perniola, M. (2004) *Contro la comunicazione.* Torino: Einaudi.

Pianigiani, O. (1907) *Vocabolario etimologico delle lingua italiana.* Rome: Albrighi e Segati.

Ritzer, G. (1999) *Enchanting a Disenchanted World: Revolutionizing the Means of Consumption.* London and Thousand Oaks, CA: Sage.

Segalen, M. (1998) *Rites et rituels contemporains.* Paris: Nathan.

Slade, G. (2006) *Made to Break: Technology and Obsolescence in America.* Cambridge, MA: Harvard University Press.

Turner, V. (1966) *The Ritual Process, Structure and Anti-Structure.* Chicago, IL: Aldine.

14

RITUAL AND CONTEMPORARY ART

Jacqueline Millner

An important site of secular ritual today is contemporary art. If ritualizing is 'a culturally strategic way of acting in the world' (Jonte-Pace 2009, p.vii) that 'takes place in a specific context and involves certain relationships' and effectively coheres 'the occasion, the context and [these] relationships' (Gordon-Lennox 2017, p.72), many contemporary artists engaged in performance and social practice in particular invoke ritual to re-inscribe spaces and activate audiences. Certain forms of contemporary performance and social practice use precisely the same 'materials' as ritualmaking – people, participation and place – and aim, like ritual, to mobilize and harness 'people's bodies, senses, and emotions' (Schirch 2005, p.83) to communicate new ideas and deeper realities in a powerful way (van der Lee 2017). Art and ritual both rely on symbolism to distil meaning into specific marks and gestures, often sharing the underlying aims of transforming or re-integrating participants.[1] Ritual can be a force for bringing people together – to mourn, commemorate or overcome alienation – and many contemporary artists strive for this in their work.

PERFORMANCE AND SOCIAL PRACTICE

Performance and social practice are privileged forms of contemporary art, valorized in major international exhibitions and critical writing.

---

[1] A symbol, Turner continues, is 'the smallest unit of ritual which still retains the specific properties of ritual behaviour...the ultimate unit of specific structure in a ritual context' (Turner 1972, p.1100).

Their currency owes something to the perceived need to differentiate contemporary art from other cultural experiences, such as mass media. The drive to make art participatory assumes that most of the time we consume images passively, unthinkingly absorbing messages that numb our critical faculties. To be forced to act out a different way of being by taking part in a contemporary artwork, by contrast, can potentially shift our habitual patterns and release new ideas. In a similar way, the physical presence of the artist can communicate more forcefully than a mediated representation. We seek in a live performance the promise of authenticity and accountability, the longed-for value of truth in a world where it has proved increasingly elusive. Performance and social practice share embodied presence, participation and transformation with ritual.

While performance art emerged in the 1960s, social practice – also called 'relational aesthetics' and 'participatory art' – is a more recent phenomenon, dating from the 1990s. Social practice is a form of art whose content comprises of the relationships it activates between people and places.[2] In its recent 'return', performance has come to share many qualities with social practice, to the point that there are significant overlaps. These include the underlying rationales, such as the desire for art to be transformative of everyday realities, capable of connecting with audiences beyond traditional aesthetic experiences, and a potential catalyst for collective remembrance and healing. Anthropologist Victor Turner describes ritual as a 'redressive activity that concretizes…opposition to a problematic social structure' (quoted in Alexander 1991, p.83), which aptly summarizes how many contemporary artists would describe their work. Overlaps between performance and social practice also exist in methods, which entail engaging with bodies in real time, public spaces, and big social questions, and actively forging links between the personal

---

2   Renowned examples of social practice, relational aesthetics or participatory art include Rikrit Tiravanija's work that comprised of cooking for the attendees of an exhibition opening, *Pad Thai*, in 1990; Jeremy Deller's 2001 recreation of the Battle of Orgreave, a pivotal event in the UK miners' strike in 1984; and *Gramsci Monument* in 2013 by Thomas Hirschhorn, where the artist coordinated a project in the Bronx over a period of several weeks that entailed all kinds of community activities themed around the ideas of the Italian Marxist thinker.

and the political. Performance is 'an art of actions' (Stiles 1998, p.227), where both performers and viewers are acting subjects who exchange and negotiate meaning in the real social conditions of everyday life. As such, performance from its inception was seen as able to instantiate the possibility for social and political change. It became associated with agency, the power to define oneself, to 'show the show', that is, to self-reflexively stand alongside the ideological apparatus that represents one in culture, and to performatively imagine new realities (Schneider 1997). In its live iteration, performance confronts the viewer with the artist's physical presence in real time, and so makes the viewing experience itself an issue: it renders the spectator less invisible, less distant, and therefore more accountable. In these rationales and methods, we can see how contemporary art can operate as a site for secular ritual. Performance artist Linda Montano observed that, 'One of the wonderful aspects of performance is the permission it gives artists to create initiation rites and ordeals. In our initial innocence, our work often looks like ancient ritual' (Montano 2000, p.366).

EARLY PERFORMANCE ART AND RITUAL

Early performance art explicitly drew on ritual. Japanese/American Yoko Ono's practice (which continues in the contemporary period) is a good example: from the beginning, it blended participation and performance. Her first works date from her association with Fluxus, an international network of artists who, in the 1960s, pioneered new interactions between art and everyday life, including through random public interventions known as 'happenings'. Ono's *Cut Piece*, first staged in Kyoto in 1964, is iconic of her approach and now ranks among her best-known works.[3]

Alone on stage and wearing her best black dress, Ono kneeled in the polite Japanese pose *seiza* assumed in formal environments. She placed a

---

3   Ono re-performed *Cut Piece* in 2003 at the Theatre de Ranelagh in Paris, according to the artist, as her response to 9/11 and as an expression of her hope for world peace. The re-performance of early works of performance is now a widespread tendency that serves to reinscribe these historical works into the contemporary language of performance art.

large pair of scissors in front of her, before inviting the audience to come up, cut off her clothes, and take a piece with them. These were the only words she uttered. Throughout the performance, she sat as impassively as possible while viewers, hesitant at first, but gradually building up momentum, took turns to slice open her dress, leaving her near naked. With its confronting tension between exhibitionism and voyeurism, masochism and sadism, and victim and assailant, *Cut Piece* has been largely interpreted as an enactment of the physical vulnerability of women in a world where they are reduced to objects of male desire. However, the performer in *Cut Piece* is no longer viewed primarily as 'the universal female victim'. Rather, Ono's specific ethnicity and personal history (the artist lived through the atrocities of the Second World War in Japan), and the fact that she invites the audience to act and gives them a token in return (a piece of her dress), move the work into the terrain of war, protest and memorialization. We might see Ono less as a victim than as a witness, one who creates a space of ritual to invite us to remember the consequences of violence, be they historical, cultural or personal, and to be guided by that memory in our everyday thoughts and actions.

Ritual is at the heart of the work of many pioneers of performance art. In her influential practice, Italian Gina Pane constructed rituals that framed her transgression of the line between *Cut Piece*'s implicit violence to actual self-harm. *Sentimental Action* was performed in 1973 in Galleria Diagramma Milan, in front of an invited, exclusively female audience. It consisted of three parts. In the first room, inscribed with the text 'Dedicated to a woman by a woman', three photographs of roses in silver vases surrounded a black velvet square displaying a single white rose. In the second room, a slide projected on the wall depicted Pane cradling a bouquet of white roses. In the third room, Pane, dressed in white, engaged in a ritualistic performance surrounded by a circle of rings drawn in white chalk on the floor. Within each of these rings was written the word 'donna'.

The performance consisted of a series of poses, beginning with embracing and pushing away a bouquet of red roses. She proceeded to remove the rose's thorns and press them into a straight line along the interior of her forearm. She then removed the thorns, allowing her blood to trickle down her arm, and sliced the palm of her hand with a razorblade. She extended her bleeding arm to the audience, offering her blood to the women surrounding her. As Pane cut herself, the voices of two women, one Italian and one French, could be heard reading romantic letters, and recounting the death of one of their mothers and the receipt of a bouquet of roses as solace. Pane repeated these actions with a bouquet of white roses. The white roses, saturated with Pane's blood, eventually turned red. According to curator Connie Butler:

> The transformative power of unrehearsed enactment offered an opportunity to depict the pain of patriarchy and women's agency alongside the shared mortality of the human body, the ability to survive pain, and the persistence of ritual form. (Butler and Mark 2007, p.355)

In this beautiful *mise en scene*, Pane 'dramatizes the pain of patriarchy' but also offers an opening, literally, to the possibility of 'a new social body', as the artist states by reference to the wound. Pane sought for her work to be transformative, for her art to be a catalyst for social and moral change, by acting directly on the viewer. According to art theorist Kristine Stiles, the body of the artist in destruction bears witness to the strategies of survival, especially by those bodies marginalized by the dominant culture. It offers a paradigm for a 'resisting body', 'that private, complex, signifying system of the self, a person who acts both on behalf of the individual and the social body' (Stiles 2016, p.41).[4] The ritual of performance creates a space and time for the audience/participant to consider this transformative potential through embodied interaction with the artist.

CONTEMPORARY ARTISTS AS RITUAL OBJECTS

As performances, *Cut Piece* and *Sentimental Action* rely heavily on the figure of the artist and the frame of the gallery or dedicated performance space

---

4   Gina Pane's performances, like *Cut Piece*, have also been re-performed, most notably by Marina Abramovic in 2005's *Seven Easy Pieces* at New York's Guggenheim Museum.

for their ritualistic power. Pane's work in particular exemplifies a strand of performance where the artwork was seen as a kind of 'altar' (Morgan 2002) and the artist as a spiritual figure or martyr. Such work might be understood as effecting a transformation within the artist through which the audience can vicariously experience catharsis of some kind, a processing of personal or historical trauma through remembrance. A younger generation of artists continues this tradition, although the ritual is now more likely undertaken in public spaces. Regina José Galindo's practice strives to acknowledge over 30 years of civil war endured by her country, Guatemala. In *Who Can Erase the Traces?* (2003), the artist created a ritual action, setting very clear parameters for her performance and using materials and gestures charged with symbolic power: carrying a bowl of blood, she walked barefoot from her home to the steps of the Guatemalan Congress, dipping and re-dipping her feet in the bowl to mark out her journey in blood.

The creation of a framework or strict parameters is central to both ritual and performance: it delineates a 'safe place' that fosters openness to alternate realities and intensifies energy to confront difficult, sometimes traumatic, experiences and memories. This is also evident in American Emma Sulkowicz's *Carry that Weight*,[5] a performance the artist created while a graduate student at Columbia University, New York, after a fellow student raped her on campus and the university failed to act. The clearly defined parameters (or 'rules of engagement') governing the central action of carrying the university dorm standard issue mattress on which she was raped help take this performance into ritual. As publicly asserted by the artist, the rules were: the performance will last until her rapist has left campus; the mattress will only be carried on campus; she cannot ask for help, but can accept it once it is offered; and once a person helps her carry the mattress, they enter into 'the space of performance'. By quite literally bringing the site of the crime (in this case, an ostensibly 'safe' domestic space) into public sight, Sulkowicz's performance relocates its subject in between the shifting grounds of public and private, personal and political.

---

5   Reference to the Beatle's song by the same name, written by John Lennon and Paul McCartney in 1969.

Carry that Weight implies that within the discourse surrounding rape, these categories are inseparable.

EARLY PARTICIPATORY ART AS RITUAL

Another kind of performance approach emerged around the same time in which the artist played less the role of ritual object than conceptual driver and facilitator of a public ritual. This approach proved an important forerunner of contemporary social practice. American Suzanne Lacy was among the pioneers of this way of working. Lacy sought to create ritual actions in public spaces by mobilizing a broad spectrum of lay participants around specific social issues and places, such as rape culture in Los Angeles in *Three Weeks in May* (1977).[6] This was a collaborative work that rather than have the artist at the centre attempted to give the audience equal time and equal space. As Lacy described it, she moved from thinking, 'I want to talk about rape' to 'Who do I want to talk to about rape?' (Lacy 2004, p.111). In particular, Lacy set up the framework for mass consciousness-raising – the distinctive form of second wave feminist activism built around women's disclosure to other women of their gendered experiences, in a safe place.

Lacy brought together a range of artists, feminist organizations, the city council, the police and women in different bureaucracies, who were all working on how to forge a discourse around violence and come up with new strategies, but who had not yet talked to each other. The process created a meta-narrative that entailed a ritual of duration and repetition: public, performative rape reports intended to generate public discourse and gain media attention. Every day at the same time at City Hall, in front of community and press contingents, a giant map of the city would be stamped with the word RAPE in red to signal where the latest sexual assault had occurred. It was a moment to honour the victims, to reflect on the social dimensions of the issue, to build solidarity and to strategize solutions through new conversations. It was Lacy's ritual

---

6   This performance was restaged in 2012 as *Storying Rape in Los Angeles*, and was then adapted for the city of Liverpool in the UK.

framework that allowed these potentially transformative actions to take place, as she steered a move 'from mere chaos and disconnection into significant process' (Turner 1987, p.8), and created an 'indeterminate dimension' where the requirements of existing social structures could be momentarily relaxed to allow 'participants to reconfigure the existing social structure, now experienced as arbitrary, to envision and experiment with alternatives' (Alexander 1991, p.84). And while *Three Weeks in May* is an example of contemporary art as secular ritual, it is relevant to the method and the rationale of this new form of performance that Lacy is a practising Buddhist who directly relates her publicly focused art practice to her spirituality. She explains that 'engaged Buddhists understand service as a practice of mindfulness that leads to an awareness of unity, which in turn generates the desire to serve'. 'The longing to serve', she observes, 'is akin experientially to the yearning to create' (Lacy 2004, p.111).

Lacy's ground-breaking work – she continues making work with similar methods and underpinning rationales today[7] – has recently been acknowledged as anticipating the social practice that emerged in the 1990s.[8] Social practice takes many forms, and not all have a ritual aspect. However, many recent works reflect the integrative structure of Lacy's approach, whereby a public ceremonial activity acts as a focus for a diverse set of engagements with a wide range of participants. The public nature of such work is key: it attempts to expand the field of art practice beyond the gallery and activate more general audiences. Public space is, of course, associated with political agency, and its affiliated aspirations of transformation. While some artists, like Lacy, use performative public rituals as a form of political protest on specific social issues, others take a more poetic approach that is guided by the idea of challenging dominant uses of public space. We could say such approaches are underpinned by a

---

7 A recent collaborative performance was *Between the Door and the Street* in New York, curated by Nato Thompson, sponsored by Creative Time (Lacy 2013). It entailed dozens of activists, whom the artist had brought together in months of preparatory conversations, engaging with the public on issues of gender, race, ethnicity and class on the stoops of a closed-off street in a Brooklyn neighbourhood. See www.suzannelacy.com

8 Helena Reckitt (2013) has convincingly argued the case for the previously unacknowledged links between feminist performance art and social practice.

Situationist understanding of the effect of individual actions intervening in public spaces against the grain to change their dominant meanings.[9]

Australian Bianca Hester's practice exemplifies this 21st-century Situationist take on mobilizing users of public space through ritualmaking.[10]

CONTEMPORARY SOCIAL PRACTICE AS RITUAL

Bianca Hester belongs to a new generation of artists whose practice has developed within the discourse of 'the expanded field',[11] where it is assumed that art exists as much outside conventional exhibition spaces as within galleries and museums. Her practice also reflects contemporary assumptions about the need to democratize the process of making and experiencing art. It is underpinned by a theoretical context where aesthetics are closely tied to politics, in particular as conceived by French philosopher Jacques Rancière, who posited that certain aesthetic practices are capable of redistributing the landscape of the sensible by re-ordering 'the relationship between doing, making, being, seeing and saying' (2004, p.43). Hester aims in her work to re-distribute the material relations between objects, places and bodies to create the conditions for unexpected and newly insightful states and behaviours. She hopes through her particular methods to underline the 'indeterminacy' of matter – the basic building blocks of all phenomena – so as to encourage openness to imagining different ways of being and relating.[12] The 'artist' then is neither so much an individual nor a persona, but 'distributed across a field of relations' where 'they are compelled to grapple with forces and negotiate responsively and dialogically' with 'materials, sites, forces, ideologies, people and politics' (Hester 2014, n.p.). As such, the 'artist' operates in a state of self-reflective uncertainty and risk. However, in order to create

---

9   Two key Situationist strategies were *détournement*, the reuse of existing artistic elements in new ensembles, and *dérive*, a technique of rapid passages through varied ambiances. See www.cddc.vt.edu/sionline/index.html
10 See www.biancahester.net
11 The term 'the expanded field' is taken from a famous essay by American art theorist Rosalind Krauss (1979, pp.30–44).
12 Hester relies on feminist new materialism, in particular the work of Elizabeth Grosz (2010, 2011).

these conditions of potential transformation, Hester designs a framework for participation, that is, she engages in ritualmaking.

One of Hester's early works, presented in 2010, which proved pivotal for future practice is *Please Leave These Windows Open to Enable the Fans to Draw in Cool Air During the Early Hours of the Morning*. This project was hosted by a contemporary art space, the Australian Centre for Contemporary Art in Melbourne. The artist's aim was to create a 'holding environment'[13] where participants could feel safe and stimulated to experiment. Within the gallery, the artist 'marked out an arena for the experience of and negotiation with a range of possibilities' and established a framework aimed at unleashing the unexpected (Hester 2014, n.p.). For example, she instructed certain participants – including peers, students and family members – to perform certain actions in the space, such as clapping hands or blowing a whistle, but to do so randomly and unannounced to create a sense of 'unpredictable liveness'. She also erected a sign that read: '*actions will occur intermittently*', which art theorist Andrew Benjamin argued positioned the exhibition as an enduring activity rather than the presentation of an existing work. In announcing actions to come, this sign granted future actions 'immaterial presence': materially anticipated but not necessarily materially actualized (Benjamin 2010, pp.83–86). But making a space of possibility where a 'rethinking-making of material relations was most active' (Hester 2014, n.p.) required the artist's orchestration of a ritual. She was present throughout so as to underline that the work had limits – rules of engagement, so to speak – but that these were in constant flux depending on the complex interactions of all the different elements – people, places and their interactions. As the artist explains:

> An ethic of negotiation was asserted, in a day-by-day encounter with what arose and with whoever happened to be present... [T]he metaphorical door was left open and a commitment to working with whatever passed across the threshold became paramount. (Hester 2014, n.p.)

---

13   The notion of a 'holding environment' was first conceived of by D.W. Winnicott in the context of object-relations theory, and was recently developed by the feminist political and legal theorist Bonnie Honig (2013).

Hester's ritualmaking has continued in ensuing years in ever expanding sites and with widening public reach. *A World Fully Accessible By No Living Being* (2011) was developed for Melbourne's central plaza, Federation Square. By circulating a set of 'propositions' or ideas for individual interventions, setting up a 'holding environment' by means of a cinder-block wall in the centre of the plaza where the actions could be witnessed, and continually publishing documentation of the actions performed, Hester designed a ritual to stimulate the personal reclamation of public space. In *Fashioning Discontinuities* (2014), presented during the 19th Biennale of Sydney, Hester nominated charged locations around Sydney, certain objects and gestures, and a group of collaborators, and designed a ritual to interpret and experience these sites in multiple ways. In one element of the ritual, *Solar Objects: Various Objects Held toward Evening's Diminishing Westerly Light* (Figure 14.3 and Figure 14.4), objects constructed for the purpose were held towards the setting sun by a group of people, with the aim of 'engaging the sun at a particular moment in its trajectory across the sky, and witnessing the recurring relationship it makes to the materials of the earth that stand in its fleeting pathway' (Hester 2016, n.p.). In another element, *Sonic Alterations of Constructed Space with Metal Objects* (Figure 14.1 and Figure 14.2), a group of people, who then invited members of the public to join in, set large steel rings spinning on their own axes. The spinning rings in their interaction with the ground and bodies created a sonic field that 'seized the space' and 'repositioned these sites from their familiar function to becoming sound-generating surfaces' (Hester 2016, n.p.). Hester's work, then, creates rituals to allow participants to experience and interpret the places they inhabit with openness and creativity, and to reflect on the interconnectedness of their bodies, actions and environments so as to magnify their sense of agency and potential for transformation.

228 Emerging Ritual in Secular Societies

Figure 14.1. *Sonic Alterations of Constructed Space, with Metal Objects* – 1, 2011– Performance at St Mary's Cathedral during the project titled *Fashioning Discontinuities*, for the 19th Biennale of Sydney. Material: mild steel, 1 x 1m, powder-coated 'blaze blue'.

Figure 14.2. *Sonic Alterations of Constructed Space, with Metal Objects* – 2, 2011– Performance on Maungawhau/Mt Eden, July 2015. Material: mild steel, 1 x 1m, powder-coated 'blaze blue'.

Ritual and Contemporary Art 229

Figure 14.3. *Solar Objects: Various Objects Held toward Evening's Diminishing Westerly Light – 1*
Performance in Warrnambool, July 2014 (commissioned by The Cinema's Project, curated by Bridget Crone and NETS Victoria). Material: bronze.

Figure 14.4. *Solar Objects: Various Objects Held toward Evening's Diminishing Westerly Light – 2*
Performance in Warrnambool, July 2014 (commissioned by The Cinema's Project, curated by Bridget Crone and NETS Victoria). Material: bronze.

Contemporary art, in particular certain forms of performance and social practice, is an important site of secular ritual today. Performance and social practice aim to create a 'holding environment' to sow the seeds of alternative ways of thinking, feeling and being. They can be viewed as strategic interventions in existing sets of practices, spaces and relationships that are driven by a desire for transformation, healing or reintegration. Ritual can be a force for bringing people together to dream and embody the world otherwise: this is precisely what many contemporary artists strive for in their work.

REFERENCES

Alexander, B.C. (1991) *Victor Turner Revisited*. Atlanta, GA: Scholars Press.

Behrend, C. (2017) 'Interview with Ritual Artist Ida van der Lee.' In J. Gordon-Lennox (ed) *Emerging Ritual in Secular Societies: A Transdisciplinary Conversation*. London: Jessica Kingsley Publishers.

Benjamin, A. (2010) 'Stalling: Notes on the Work of Bianca Hester.' In *Please Leave These Windows Open Overnight to Enable the Fans to Draw in Cool Air During the Early Hours of the Morning*. Melbourne: Australian Centre for Contemporary Art.

Butler, C. and Mark, L.G. (eds) (2007) *WACK! Art and the Feminist Revolution*. Cambridge, MA: The MIT Press.

Gordon-Lennox, J. (2017) 'The Rhyme and Reason of Ritualmaking.' In J. Gordon-Lennox (ed.) *Emerging Ritual in Secular Societies: A Transdisciplinary Conversation*. London: Jessica Kingsley Publishers.

Grosz, E. (2010) 'Feminism, Materialism, and Freedom.' In D.H. Coole and S. Frost (eds) *New Materialisms: Ontology, Agency and Politics*. Durham NC: Duke University Press.

Grosz, E. (2011) *Becoming Undone: Darwinian Reflections on Life, Politics and Art*. Durham, NC: Duke University Press.

Hester, B. (2014) 'The shaggy edge of open.' Unpublished paper.

Hester, B. (2016) Quotes. Available at www.biancahester.net/?q=node/361417, accessed on 9 August 2016.

Honig, B. (2013) 'Politics of public things: Neoliberalism and the routine of privatisation.' *No Foundations: An Interdisciplinary Journal of Law and Justice 10*, 59–76.

Jonte-Pace, D. (2009) 'Foreword: Notes on a Friendship.' In C. Bell, *Ritual Theory, Ritual Practice*. New York: Oxford University Press. [Originally published in 1992; Foreword appears in OUP 2009 edition.]

Krauss, R. (1979) 'Sculpture in the expanded field.' *October 8*, 30–44.
Lacy, S. (1977) *Three Weeks in May*. Available at www.suzannelacy.com/three-weeks-in-may/, accessed on 9 August 2016.
Lacy, S. (2004) 'Having it Good: Reflections on Engaged Art and Buddhism.' In J. Baas and M.J. Jacob (eds) *Buddha Mind in Contemporary Art*. Berkeley, CA: University of California Press.
Lacy, S. (2013) *Between the Door and the Street*. Available at www.suzannelacy.com/between-the-door-and-the-street/, accessed on 9 August 2016.
Montano, L. (2000) *Performance Artists Talking in the Eighties*. Berkeley, CA: University of California Press.
Morgan, A.B. (2002) 'Revolution is sneakier: Conversation with Vito Acconci.' *Sculpture 21*, 7. Available at www.sculpture.org/documents/scmag02/sept02/acc/acc.shtml, accessed on 9 August 2016.
Rancière, J. (2004) *The Politics of Aesthetics*. Trans. Gabriel Rockhill. London: Continuum.
Reckitt, H. (2013) 'Forgotten Relations: Feminist Artists and Relational Aesthetics.' In A. Dimitrakaki and L. Perry (eds) *Politics in a Glass Case: Feminism, Exhibition Cultures and Curatorial Transgressions*. Liverpool: Liverpool University Press.
Schirch, L. (2005) *Ritual and Symbol in Peacebuilding*. Bloomfield, CT: Kumarian Press.
Schneider, R. (1997) *The Explicit Body in Performance*. London and New York: Routledge.
Stiles, K. (1998) 'Uncorrupted Joy: International Art Actions.' In P. Schimmel, R. Ferguson, K. Stiles and G. Brett (eds) *Out of Actions: Between performance and the object 1949–1979*. London: Thames & Hudson.
Stiles, K. (2016) *Concerning Consequences: Studies in Art, Destruction and Trauma*. Chicago, IL: University of Chicago Press.
Turner, V. (1972) 'Symbols in African ritual.' *Science 179*, 1100–1105.
Turner, V. (1987) *The Anthropology of Performance*. New York: PAJ Publications.
van der Lee, I. (2017) 'Interview by C. Behrend.' In J. Gordon-Lennox (ed.) *Emerging Ritual in Secular Societies: A Transdisciplinary Conversation*. London: Jessica Kingsley Publishers.

15

INTERVIEW WITH RITUAL ARTIST IDA VAN DER LEE

Christine Behrend

Ida van der Lee is a Dutch artist specializing in ritual art. She has designed a broad spectrum of rituals as works of art best known for their social focus. As an artist, Ida considers form and aesthetics to be as important as function. She wants people to experience the rituals she creates as being beautiful and special. The artistic form takes precedence; the content is then injected into the form. The narrative aspect is important too; many of her rituals are designed to evoke 'forgotten' memories or stories.

One of Ida's most successful ventures, called *All Souls' Day Everywhere* (*Allerzielen Alom*), gives fresh impetus to Dutch death culture. It is a modern, secular recreation of the traditional Roman Catholic commemoration of the dead. She has also guided the demolition of buildings and neighbourhoods, treating them as if they were living entities by creating farewell ceremonies for the defunct edifices. Her projects often span several years.

Ida founded Studio Ritual Art in which she works with a network of professional artists and quite a large group of specially trained volunteers. The Studio is a cultural enterprise that produces modern rituals for commemorations, as well as to facilitate communication, storytelling and process empowerment. Organizations and companies use the rituals; among Ida's clients are several Dutch municipalities, the Cultural Heritage Agency of the Netherlands, a refugee organization, several funeral companies, a museum and a company that develops sustainable energy sources.

Ida, why are new rituals needed today?

One reason new rituals are needed is that our modern age – with all its new technology and media, in particular, the internet – has virtualized the human experience. Seeing and hearing is favoured over all the other senses. Ritual experience involves so much more: taste, smell, touch, being in real places... Physically gathering and sharing with others is an important part of ritualizing too.

Another major factor in the need for new ritual is that, as religious institutions decline, traditional rituals have fallen into disuse. Villages may still have a social life, but urban centres no longer function as communities.

Traditional rituals provided us with ways to express forgiveness, thankfulness, cope with death and so on, but that is missing today. In the past, people didn't have to think about what to do; they simply practised these rituals and felt their healing effect. Today, people are at a loss as to how to handle difficult issues in their lives; they know there is a problem but they cannot solve it by themselves so they often turn to therapy.

Designing secular rituals for non-religious people is for me a worthy challenge.

What is ritual art compared with other ritual?

The poetic strength of art imbues ritual with creative power to make it modern and up-to-date. Ritual activity activates the right side of the brain, the part that deals with feelings, creativity, insight, visualization and the senses. These characteristics are also part of art. All of the artistic disciplines – visual arts, dance, theatre and so on – can enhance ritual.

Beauty is a key ingredient in my ritual art. People are touched by the fact that something beautiful has been made just for them. This feeling of specialness allows people to integrate the ritual into their bodies and hearts. When the ritual feels like a gift, people participate, open up, relax, and are trusting.

In masterclasses I train artists, some of whom are or were refugees, how to design a ritual. Sometimes we start with a work of art or one of my ideas. Sometimes the artist will take the first step by bringing in their own ideas, art or a theme, and in this case, the artist works alone to develop the ritual. Most of the time, however, ritual-designing turns into an organic collaborative effort. We all end up working together in a collective creative process.

What is the function of ritual?

All cultures have many types of rituals. At its best, ritual is communication with a deeper reality (Lukken 2005). It is not so much a question of thinking and verbalizing, but more a manner of symbolizing. A symbol points towards a deeper reality. Any object can become a symbol because, at any moment, it may come to represent something in a person's inner world. Since rituals involve symbols, they are powerful tools for commemorating and storytelling.

At Studio Ritual Art we describe ritual as a structured event in which objects, decoration, sound, actions and words all play a role. Participants concentrate on a question or issue and go through a process of visualization in order to reach the authentic heart of the matter.

Ritual is important to human beings in many ways. Through ritual, paradoxes can be resolved and dilemmas accepted. Ritualizing can give structure to people's lives. It can create or restore a balance; it can resolve inner conflict. It allows people to feel something emotionally, in their hearts, instead of reacting on a purely rational level.

In my rituals I focus on tough situations for which there is no easy solution. These situations are often fraught with feelings of anger, impotence, frustration or sorrow. Ritualizing may be the only way to deal with them. It can help us let these feelings exist, give them a shape, and anchor them in the present. Instead of burying the problem, I bring it out into the light, display it for all to see, shift it out of the rational world and let it take effect in the heart.

How do you decide when ritual is needed?

I see the need for ritual when I detect a challenging situation in a community (or in a person, which is more difficult), something hidden underneath that brings tension. Often it has to do with feelings of shame, loneliness, powerlessness, breakdown, anxiety and so on.

Almost every community has situations like that. But when it negatively influences functioning in daily life, then ritual is called for.

How do you go about creating a ritual?

I design rituals with ingredients that are linked to that particular person or community. Their stories and the demolition material from places where they have lived for so many years are ingredients. Their habits or way of life are relevant too. I use all of these elements to transform the situation into something new and meaningful.

Tell me about your childhood and youth.

I was raised in the countryside 20 miles from Amsterdam in a Roman Catholic family. I was the youngest of seven children, five girls and two boys, all born in the space of seven years. My father had a fruit farm. Each one of us children had a job on the farm. There was always work to do on Saturdays and during the summer. Harvest-time was the busiest season; many people came from all around to help. My community art has to do with the way I grew up.

Our family was moderately religious for that period. In the sixties and seventies we went to church once a week, usually on Saturday night. It was not easy for me to be the youngest. My siblings and I had different interests. Since I was a bit more gifted for studies, I went on to higher levels of schooling. Some of my siblings didn't like this and teased me for it. As a result, I tended to go my own way. I found it frustrating that nobody seemed to listen to me, or was even interested in me. My mother had to divide her attention among us all. I am the only one with any artistic talent. In art too I go my own way. Ritual art is really my own invention; it didn't exist before and was not a trend in art.

At the age of 23, I trained as a nurse. Nursing didn't really suit me; teamwork in a hierarchical structure was definitely not for me. However, people's stories always captured my attention. I was also attracted by work in terminal care wards. People tend to let their masks fall when they are facing the end of their lives; I was fascinated to be able to see the essence of their being. My *All Souls' Day Everywhere* ritual is connected to this (van der Lee 2016).

Finally, when I was 27, I went to art school. A new world opened up for me. My way of thinking and observing changed; things were not as clear-cut as I had previously thought. I finished art school in 1995.

What rituals were meaningful during your early years?

When I was a young child, my mother put me to bed. She would make the sign of the cross on my forehead with her finger. If she forgot, I would ask her to do it. I liked praying before going to sleep too.

When something important or difficult was happening – examinations, or illness – my mother burned a candle before the Mother Mary statue. Today I also light candles sometimes. As we speak, a close friend's sister-in-law is at the threshold between life and death, so I am burning a candle for her.

Birthdays were another time for ritual. Where I'm from, people celebrate their birthdays by inviting as many guests as they can fit into their house. I always had mixed feelings about this tradition. On the one hand, it is good to have a party plan you don't really have to think about. On the other hand, even as a child it was hard for me to have so many people around, all talking loudly at the same time. I don't cope with that very well. So I always tried to invent something different and special for my birthday – just a small group of people with whom I could play games, go for a walk, or whatever. This is probably when I started to design my own rituals.

Another childhood ritual was setting a beautiful table and decorating the house at Christmas-time. I loved to lay the table for my mother with fine crockery. My mother loved it as well. My *Dining with the Dead* ritual was inspired by this ritual; it is one of my favourites (van der Lee 2016). The table is beautifully decorated; I collected crystal glasses for this ritual. People use a marker to write about their loved ones on the dishes.

Ritual also came through in some of the household chores: when hanging out the laundry on the washing line, I did my best to organize it by colour and size. This is at the origin of the *Laundry Is Good* ritual I designed (van der Lee 2016).

What was your first public ritual?

The first time I became truly conscious of the power of ritual was during my project *Ontroerend Goed* (literally, *Moving Goods*, 2001–2006, Figure 15.1). In order to accommodate a high-speed train, the railway line was rebuilt through the area of Abcoude and 12 dwellings had to be demolished. It was a nice spot along a small river. Many of the inhabitants had lived there for a long time and were very sad to have to move away. I designed a farewell ritual for the community.

The ritual consisted of uprooting a barn and transporting it over the River Gein to a safe place. People were apprehensive about my farewell ritual. It was such a new idea they didn't know what to expect. Would it feel respectful or would it make things even more painful? One man who had been living there for ages was very cooperative at first, but as the date of the farewell ritual approached he became more and more distant. He finally decided to participate, telling himself, 'I don't want to hear about how it worked out from strangers.' He confided to me later that during the ritual he felt like he was watching his own funeral. But he also observed that the ritual made starting his life in a new place easier and he was ultimately grateful that he had participated (van der Lee 2016).

Have you designed other rituals that commemorate buildings or neighbourhoods?

Yes, the *Zaandam Treasure Box* (2003–2006) ritualized the demolition of a working-class neighbourhood. In 2003, during the first phase of the farewell ritual we crafted a beautiful treasure box out of materials recycled from the homes (Figure 15.2 and Figure 15.3). Occupants deposited their memories and stories in the treasure box, which we then carried in a procession over the Zaan River to the Zaandam Museum (Figure 15.2 and Figure 15.3). In 2004, the houses scheduled for demolition became the setting for an artistic display of these memories in a kind of three-dimensional storybook. Later, one hundred stories were engraved onto as many granite flagstones so that the history of the old neighbourhood was preserved on the streets of the brand-new one (van der Lee 2016).

238   Emerging Ritual in Secular Societies

Figure 15.1. *Moving Goods*
The barn is carried to a spot where it will be safely preserved, in memory of the demolished houses.

Figure 15.2. *Zaandam Treasure Box – 1*
Ida van der Lee prepares an element of the ritual art project in one of the demolished homes.

Interview with Ritual Artist Ida van der Lee   239

Figure 15.3. *Zaandam Treasure Box – 2*
The box containing memories and stories of the demolished homes is about to be carried across the river to Zaandam Museum.

Perhaps your most successful undertaking has been your All Souls' Day Everywhere (Allerzielen Alom) *project?*

Yes, this project has indeed been very popular. *Allerzielen Alom* (Figure 15.4) is a night-time celebration during which visitors have the opportunity to take part in ritual art forms that commemorate their dead. Since 2005, there have been about 100 celebrations at various cemeteries throughout the Netherlands with some 100,000 participants – we've lost count!

Special lighting and decorations are used to make the cemeteries beautiful and create a serene atmosphere. Using the ritual art forms, visitors reminisce about their deceased loved ones and share their stories with others. Narrative is important here. The evening is less about mourning and loss than about celebrating the lives of the deceased and how their legacy inspires the living. The survivor goes from being a victim to being actively responsible for telling a story. This helps with the mourning process (van der Lee 2016).

Figure 15.4. *All Souls' Day Everywhere*
People wander through a maze in the Velsen cemetery (the Netherlands). Lighting is a key element in creating a beautiful, serene atmosphere.

I have seen a video of your Names and Numbers *ritual that commemorates deported Jews.*

One day I consulted a website that lists the names of all the Jewish victims deported from the Netherlands between 1940 and 1945, their addresses and what became of them (Jewish Monument 2016). I discovered that nearly 2500 of the victims lived on my street. This motivated me to design a commemoration ritual in a square in Amsterdam. Participants choose the name of a deported person, make a name plate for them and place it at their last known address on a model of the neighbourhood (van der Lee 2014).

When did it start? How long will you do it? What kinds of reactions have you had?

I started *Names and Numbers* (Figure 15.5) in 2012 and the commemoration takes place every year on May 4th which is our memorial day in the Netherlands. I hope that all the names will have their name plates by 2020!

Interview with Ritual Artist Ida van der Lee   241

Figure 15.5. *Names and Numbers* (Amsterdam)
This May 4th participative commemoration for Jews forcibly expelled from the Netherlands during the Second World War will take place every year until there is a name plate for every deportee.

Reactions are very positive. The total number of Jewish victims of the Holocaust, six million, is so huge that it becomes abstract. With *Names and Numbers*, people feel deeply touched because they can effectively connect to a single, real individual who had a name and an address.

One person said that she had trouble coming to terms with the events of World War II. Accomplishing the ritual was a cleansing and healing process for her. Finally, she could say: 'I exist and that's fine.' People are amazed by the feelings the ritual generates. They are also often impressed by my beautiful decoration, which transforms this ordinary square into a ritual landscape.

Generally speaking, what response do you hope that people will have to your public rituals?

I hope that people feel healing. That something painful is transformed into something meaningful or with a source of strength. That there is a shift in their mindset. That their way of looking at things changes and they can achieve acceptance. Finally, that their suffering is no longer hidden away but brought out into broad daylight where it can been examined and dealt with. I hope that distressing events in society or in our own personal histories can be metamorphosed into significant or even treasured experiences.

I can often tell that something is happening to people by watching their eyes. Sometimes they break down when they make contact with whatever is sitting like a stone inside them. Then they feel better; a disturbed balance has been restored.

I believe you also implement ritual art in businesses and other organizations?

Yes, that is true, although for the time being, it represents a small part of our activity at Studio Ritual Art.

Rituals are already recognized as part of business culture. They play a role in special events such as promotions, New Year receptions, the signing of contracts, employee evaluations, retirement parties and so on. These 'organic' rituals have been studied in order to understand how they work; the principles on which they operate are now being used to develop rituals around the process of change in businesses and other organizations.

After Studio Ritual Art's first experiences with ritual art in this context we cautiously claim that it works. Over the past 50 years, business has been driven by a focus on growth, productivity and efficiency, and decision-making has been based on rationality and logic. The amount of information and data now required to make a logical decision overtaxes rational methods and renders this approach inefficient. Furthermore, digitalization has reduced live communication to a minimum.

What gives a company an edge and sets it apart from the others is decision-making based on gut feeling, conviction, trust and intuition. This frees up time and energy for innovation, communication and creativity. Ritual art activates the right hemisphere of the brain; through the emotional brain (limbic system) the left and right halves of the brain are brought together harmoniously. Participants are aware of the symbolic nature of a ritual but it is effective, leaves a lasting impression and generates insight.

Interview with Ritual Artist Ida van der Lee   243

Figure 15.6. *Irritation Game*
On each crumpled piece of paper is written an irritation that will be transformed into a positive wish.

We used ritual art in a company that works with sustainable energy to help project teams grapple with the abstract theories they were developing. The participants achieved clearer insight into their work when we introduced small objects they could use as metaphors or symbols. Suddenly they had the tools to explain or communicate their ideas. Moreover, as I myself achieved better understanding of the process, I was able to translate their concepts into language that the general public could understand.

Ritual art was used for several start-up projects at the Cultural Heritage Agency of the Netherlands. The project manager was praised for his lively meetings that enabled the groups to transform traditional methods into a new way of working using a different language. An example is our *Irritation Game* (Figure 15.6).

We designed the *Irritation Game* to help business people from different backgrounds open up and work together without their usual prejudices. The game is based on the concept that every irritation is in fact a frustrated wish or desire. Participants write their irritations down on a piece of paper, crumple it up and place it inside a beautiful lotus flower crafted from Venetian blinds. Their irritations can then blossom and flourish, allowing the underlying positive aspirations to break through.

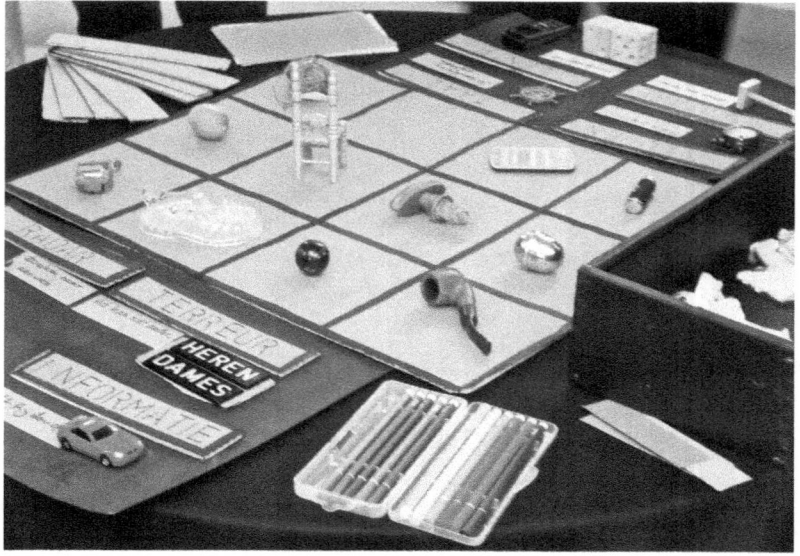

Figure 15.7. *Oracle Game*
The players throw dice to get an object. They then identify a word that comes to mind when they look at the object. With a set of these words they invent an oracle or a mysterious message that is illogical, strange and poetic that encourages them to think about meaning.

What projects are you currently working on?

I am working on a project called *Hidden Legacy*. Through ritual art, elderly people recount their life stories and experiences, talk about people they love and tell their favourite jokes. Once we have collected their narratives we will work them into an artistic will that may take the shape of a poem, a painting, a play or some other art form.

We are conducting a trial version with people suffering from dementia and their families. We call it the *Oracle Game* (Figure 15.7). In the first phase, we work with objects. The person throws a dice and gets a particular object. We start them talking about this object and listen attentively to what kind of stories pop up. At one point, we settle on a certain word that represents the essence of their association with the object. In this manner, ten or more words are collected from each person. In the second phase we ask the person to write an oracle or a mysterious message using these words. Since the oracle is totally illogical, strange and poetic it gets them thinking about meaning.

We hypothesize that this ritual will work because the right side of their brain seems to still function.

I am also learning how to run a good business. At Studio Ritual Art we have many beautiful rituals that I want to benefit as many people as possible. By improving our organizational skills we will be able to make these rituals more widely available.

Thank you Ida.

REFERENCES
Jewish Monument (2016) Available at www.joodsmonument.nl, accessed on 18 July 2016. [Lists the names of all Jews deported from the Netherlands during the Second World War.]

Lukken, G. (2005) *Rituals in Abundance.* Leuven: Peeters.

van der Lee, I. (2014) Video of ritual *Namen and Nummers* [*Names and Numbers*]. 4 May. Available at https://www.youtube.com/watch?v=YnG5vitVfUs&feature=youtu.be, accessed on 18 July 2016.

van der Lee, I. (2016) 'Projects.' Available at http://idavanderlee.nl, accessed on 18 July 2016.

Conclusion

CONVERSATION TO BE CONTINUED

Jeltje Gordon-Lennox

Western secular societies are impressively productive. In the process, they pressurize rich and poor alike into individualism and competition that effectively severs them from the close-knit social and spiritual groups that nourish human life. People may fight their feelings of dislocation with the best adaptive substitutes on offer (shopping, drugs, destructive relationships, power and money), but they often find themselves bereft of happiness. Being happy implies paying attention to our senses, to how we birth, love and die, and to aligning our values and our rituals.

Society's capability of interrupting the process of planetary annihilation without religious belief appears to disturb theorists more than practitioners. Like those who initiated Beat culture, practitioners of secular ritual see that – on both experiential and functional levels – secular means do suffice. The contributors to this collection are concerned about the future of humankind and the Earth. A number of the chapters in this volume demonstrate the power of secular forms of ritual. Though not a goal in itself, ritual can enhance life by making us feel happier, stronger and more connected to each other. It helps transmit meaning from a central source to each person in the assembly by letting them know what other members know. The skills required in ritualizing such as cooperation, support and unity are as important, if not more so, than those of competitiveness and confrontation, to the survival of our species. Superior values such as respect, gratitude, generosity, hospitality and lending a helping hand can guide humanity to turn things around to bring the Earth and society into harmony and stability. Ritual, as an ancient civilizing body-based activity, remains an effective means to make us – individually and collectively – fully human. It is our hope that the transdisciplinary conversation on emergent ritual in secular societies will be continued.

NOTES ON CONTRIBUTORS

Andrés Allemand Smaller is a world news journalist and a secular wedding celebrant who specializes in creating ceremonies for pluricultural couples. Andrés was born in Buenos Aires, Argentina. He grew up in New York, USA and in Geneva, Switzerland, where he now lives with his Australian wife and four children. Andrés regularly writes in French in the international news section for the daily *La Tribune de Genève*.

Christine Behrend is an international qualitative market researcher as well as a secular wedding and funeral celebrant. She was born and studied in the UK before moving to France and then Switzerland. Fully bilingual, she works in both English and French. Christine is based in Lausanne, Switzerland.

Ellen Dissanayake, Hon. PhD, is an independent scholar who writes about the arts from the perspectives of ethology and evolutionary biology. Ellen is a mother of two and has one granddaughter. She has spent significant periods of her life in Sri Lanka, Nigeria, Papua New Guinea and New York City, and now lives permanently in Seattle, USA, where she is an Affiliate Professor in the School of Music at the University of Washington. She is the author of *What is Art for?* (1988), *Homo Aestheticus: Where Art Comes from and Why* (1992), which was translated into Chinese and Korean, *Art and Intimacy: How the Arts Began* (2000) and *L'Infanzia dell'Estetica: L'Origine Evolutiva delle Pratiche Artistiche* (2015), a translation of seven of her published articles. She is now collaborating with Ekkehart Malotki on an ambitious book, *Early Rock Art of the American West: The Geometric Enigma*.

Jeltje Gordon-Lennox, MDiv., is a psychotherapist, a celebrant trainer, and founder of the non-profit Ashoka Association (ashoka.ch). Jeltje lives with her husband and their two children in Geneva, Switzerland. She is the author of three manuals on how to create secular ceremonies of which two are in French, *Mariages* (2008), *Funérailles* (2011), and one is in English, *Crafting Secular Ritual: A Practical Guide* (2017).

Bjarni Jónsson became the General Manager of Siðmennt, the Icelandic Ethical Humanist Association, in 2015 when he was hired on as full-time staff. Bjarni joined the organization in 1990, the year it was founded, and has since served in several capacities such as board member (2000–present) and vice-resident of the association.

Lindy Mechefske is a former scientific copyeditor turned freelance writer. She has lived in England, the USA and Australia, but now resides, along with a big shaggy dog, in beautiful, historic Kingston, Canada. Lindy is the author of *Sir John's Table* (2015) and *A Taste of Wintergreen* (2011). You can find her blogging about her adventures in the kitchen at lindymechefske.com

Jacqueline Millner, PhD, is Associate Dean Research and a lecturer in Critical Studies at Sydney College of the Arts, The University of Sydney, Australia. Jacqueline completed studies in law, political science and visual arts, before consolidating a career as an arts writer and academic specializing in the history and theory of contemporary art. Jacqueline wrote two books on Australian contemporary art, *Conceptual Beauty* (2010) and *Australian Artists in the Contemporary Museum* (2014), which is co-authored with Jennifer Barrett. Her latest book, *Contemporary Art and Feminism* (2017), is co-written with Catriona Moore.

Lene Mürer is Head of Ceremonies at the Norwegian Humanist Association.

Marie Louise Petersen is Vice Chairperson of the Danish Humanist Society (DHS). She also took charge of Ceremonies (2013–2016) and contributed to the development of programmes for funeral and confirmation ceremonies and has practical experience in both fields. She is currently developing a Humanist Chaplaincy programme for the DHS. Marie Louise lives and works as a trained teacher in Copenhagen.

Michael Picucci, PhD, is a psychologist, psychotherapist, Master Addictions Counsellor, Sexologist, Somatic Experiencing Practitioner and Organizational Consultant. Michael lives with his partner in New York City and the Catskill Mountains, USA. He has authored six books on healing; among the latest are *Ritual as Resource: Energy for Vibrant Living* (2005), *Focalizing Source Energy: Going Within to Move Beyond* (2012), and *Focalizing Dynamic Links: A Human Technology for Collectively Engaging Source Energy and Creating a Better Future* (2013). Michael experiences his life and work as dancing on the fulcrum of evolution; the constant emerging newness of this inspires him. See his work at www.michaelpicucci.com

Isabel Russo, BA Hons, is Head of Ceremonies at the British Humanist Association (BHA). Isabel lives with her son and works in London, UK. She worked internationally as an actress in theatre, film and television for 20 years before becoming a humanist celebrant in 2009. Isabel was a funeral, wedding and naming celebrant for four years before becoming Head of Ceremonies at the BHA. The role of ritual and storytelling in shaping and influencing community has been a central thread throughout her working life.

Robert C. Scaer, MD, is a neurologist and psychologist, currently retired from clinical medical practice. Robert is the father of four children and has six grandchildren. He lives in Louisville, USA with his partner. He is the author of a number of books and articles on the effects of trauma, notably *The Body Bears the Burden: Trauma, Dissociation and Disease* (2001); *The Trauma Spectrum: Hidden Wounds and Human Resiliency* (2005); and *8 Keys to Brain-Body Balance* (2012).

Matthieu Smyth, PhD, is a ritual anthropologist, professor at the University of Strasbourg, and a Somatic Experiencing Practitioner. Matthieu lives in Pontarlier, France. He is the father of three children, an avid alpinist and the author of two books *La Liturgie Oubliée* (2003) and *Ante Altaria* (2007).

Irene Stengs, PhD, is a cultural anthropologist and senior research fellow at the Meertens Instituut in the Netherlands. Irene lives in Amsterdam. Her specialty is ritual and popular culture. She is the author of *Worshipping the Great Modernizer. King Chulalongkorn, Patron Saint of the Thai Middle Class* (2009) and *Het fenomeen Hazes: Een venster op Nederland* (transl. *The Hazes Phenomenon: A Window on Dutch Society*) (2015), and editor of *Nieuw in Nederland. Feesten en rituelen in verandering* (2012) (transl. *New in the Netherlands: The Dynamics of Multicultural Ritual*).

Gianpiero Vincenzo, MA, is a sociologist, art critic, novelist and specialist in Islamic studies. After several years at the University of Naples Federico II, in 2010 he was appointed professor of sociology at the Fine Arts Academy of Catania in Sicily, Italy. Gianpiero lives in Sicily with his wife and daughter. He has curated contemporary art exhibitions and published art catalogues, academic essays on Eastern religions and civil ritual and novels. His historical novel *Il Libro Disceso dal Cielo* (2005) was translated into six languages. His recent book, *New Ritual Society: Consumerism and Culture in Contemporary Society* (2015), is available in Italian and English.

Joanna Wojtkowiak, PhD, is a cultural psychologist and assistant professor at the University of Humanistic Studies, Utrecht, the Netherlands, where she initiated one of the first university-level training courses for secular celebrants. Joanna lives with her partner and their two children in Nijmegen. She is the author of *I'm Dead, Therefore I Am – The Postself and Notions of Immortality in Contemporary Dutch Society* (2012).

INDEX

Page numbers followed by lower case *f* indicate figures and illustrations. Footnotes are indicated with n followed by the footnote number.

Abramovic, Marina: *Seven Easy Pieces* 22m4
accompaniment 84
addiction 13, 48, 211–212
adulthood rituals *see* confirmations
advertising propaganda 208
affectation 45, 84
African cultures 51, 183, 204
afterlife beliefs 161–162, 167
Albers, S. 178
Alcoholics Anonymous prayers 152
Alexander, B.C. 218, 224
Alexander, K.B. 13, 48
Allen, D. 83
All Souls' Day 162
All Souls' Day Everywhere (Allerzielen Alom) (van der Lee) 232, 235, 239, 240*f*
Ammerman, N. 160, 162
amplification 143, 144, 146
analgesia 62
androids 212–214
animals 41–42, 48, 184
animism 42–43, 44
anxiety
  humanist ceremonies and relieving guest 129–130
  modern society and increase in 12
  relief of, as ritual function 30, 45, 71, 234–235
  as trauma response 51, 62, 63
art (craft)
  crafts, terminology comparisons 32–33
  elements and qualities of 28, 33–39, 34*f*, 35*f*, 37*f*, 38*f*
  as human requirement 14
  as 'making special' activity 22, 23*f*
  mother-infant relationships as 22–24, 26–29
  performance 19–20, 217–223, 230
  ritualistic process of 24, 26, 31–32

ritualmaking materials for 217
  schools for 25, 38–39
  social practice/ participatory 218–219, 223–227, 228*f*, 229*f*, 230
  see also van der Lee, Ida
Art and Intimacy (Dissanayake) 28
Asad, Talal 71, 71n2
ash objects 159n2, 164
Asimov, Isaac 212–213
Association Against Church Confirmation (renamed Association for Civil Confirmation) 100
attunement
  artistic materiality inducing 36
  definition 59n4
  as group ritual function 43
  mother-infant relationship behaviours of 27, 29, 59
  as trauma therapy neurophysiological feature 59, 66
Augé, M. 46
Aukeman, A. 11
Aung San Suu Kyi 13
Australian Aboriginals 183
authenticity 16, 83–84, 105–106, 108–109
automobiles
  as commodity cult objects 210–211
  traffic accident memorials 188–194, 192*f*, 193*f*, 200–201
autoshaping 45

Baisakhi 174
Ballard, James G. 211
Bank Dick, The (film) 211
Battle of Orgreave recreation (Deller) 218n2
Baudrillard, Jean 208, 209–210, 210–211
Baumeister, R.F. 159
Beat culture 11
beauty 233
Becker, J. 160

beliefs
  mourning rituals and afterlife 161–162
  ritual as expression of 137, 159, 204
  as ritualmaking consideration 99, 115, 136, 162
  spirituality *vs.* religious 106, 160
  see also religion
Bell, Catherine 12, 71–72
Benjamin, Andrew 226
Benore, E.R. 163
Berceli, David 57
Bernts, T. 162
Between the Door and the Street (Lacy) 224n7
BHA (British Humanist Association) 17, 97, 127
bi-hemispheric brain alternating stimulation 59–60, 64
birthdays 100, 161, 174, 175, 205, 236
Biven, Lucy 45, 46
Blade Runner (film) 213–214
blessings 115, 148, 178, 205
Blok, Anton 189n1
Blue Monday 102, 103
boarding schools 51
Bøgh, Annette 100–101
boundary rupture 62
brain anatomy and function *see* neurophysiology
Brainspotting (BSP) 57, 66
bread, as ritual symbol 111
breathing, for source energy 144, 146
Brillat-Savarin, Jean Anthelme 176
Britain
  gay rights and marriage laws 131
  humanist associations in 17, 97, 127
  mourning rituals 160, 162n4
  religious non-affiliation 17–18
  social practice recreations of miner's strikes in 218n2
  table manners 181–182

251

British Humanist
    Association (BHA) 17,
    97, 127
Broos, Anton: *National
    Monument for Railway
    Accident Victims* 190, 191,
    196-201, 198f, 199f
BSP (Brainspotting) 57, 66
Buddhism 104, 105, 117, 178,
    224
Bull, M. 162, 167
business culture 181, 242-
    244, 243f
    see also consumerism
Butler, Connie 221

Caillois, Roger 50
Callahan, Roger 65
Cambodian food rituals 183
Canada 48, 174, 183
cancer victim memorials 190
cannibalism 184
Carry that Weight
    (Sulkowicz) 222-223
casinos 206-207
Cassirer, E. 214
cave paintings 204-205
Caves of Steel (Asimov) 213
celebrants
    funeral ceremonies and
        roles of 121-126
    lifecycle transitions and
        roles of 84
    memorial weddings and
        roles of 129-136
    mourning rituals and roles
        of 76, 77
    multicultural weddings
        and roles of 106,
        107-118
    networking associations
        for 17, 90-91, 97, 100-
        101, 127-128
    smiling, importance of 117
celebrities 160, 188
cemeteries
    cathedrals of consumption
        styles of 207
    personal mourning rituals
        at 161, 162-163
    public mourning rituals at
        162, 232, 235, 239, 240f
    changing rituals 206, 209,
        212
chaos 43, 50, 224
chi (source energy) 140-147,
    141-142, 143f
children
    birthdays 174, 175, 236
    infants and food
        dependency 175

mother-infant relationship
    behaviours 22-24,
    26-29, 30, 43, 59, 64
newborn deaths and
    mourning rituals 83
public commemoration
    monuments for 190
see also confirmations
chimpanzees 29, 42, 48
Chinese rituals 81, 182
Christian III, King 89
Christianity
    afterlife beliefs 162
    cultural influence of 12,
        40-41, 112-113
    Danish education
        requirements 89-90,
        102-103
    food rituals 173-174, 178
    Nordic confirmation
        history 88-89
    prayer rituals 178, 205, 236
Christian VI, King 89
Christmas 174, 205, 236
Cline, Edward F. 211
clothing and costumes
    29-30, 33, 55, 163, 173
Cohen, A. 111n1
coherence 16, 72f, 79f, 81,
    83, 84
Collins, R. 209
Collyer Brothers Syndrome
    212
Colombian food rituals 183
coming-of-age traditions *see*
    confirmations
commemoration *see*
    memorial and
    commemoration
communality
    animal rituals exhibiting
        41-42
    of artistic ritual 37-39, 38f
    collective dynamism
        49-50
    consumerist rituals for 13,
        19, 53, 206-208
    eating as social activity
        173-176
    as ritual component 52
    social bonding 47-49, 59,
        61, 70, 173-176
communication
    consumerist advertising
        propaganda as 208
    kinesic 22, 26-28, 30, 36
    modern styles of 12-13,
        74, 106
    rituals as form of 76
    for social bonding 47-49
    see also gestures;
        interaction
communing rituals 152-153

community
    farewell/divestment
        rituals for demolition
        of 237, 238f, 239f
    modern concepts of 12-13,
        74, 106
    multicultural weddings
        and guests as 114-115
    public consumption
        rituals effects on 13, 51,
        72, 203, 206, 208
    tribal traditions and
        importance of 73
competition 13, 51-52, 72,
    246
confirmations
    Danish secular practices
        99-103
    history of 88-90
    Icelandic civic/secular
        programmes 96-98,
        98f
    Norwegian humanist
        programmes 90-96,
        91f, 92f, 93f, 94f, 95f
    overview and practice
        descriptions 87-88
consumerism
    benefits of 214-215
    consumption rituals of
        205-206
    effects of 13, 51-52, 72, 203,
        206, 207, 208
    expectations of 207-208
    as modern communal
        experience 13, 19, 53,
        206-208
    rituals strengthening 207
    system of objects 208-214
crafts 32-33
    see also art
CRAFTS (Create, Respect,
    Aesthetics, Form, Truth,
    Simplicity) 79f
Craig, Gary 57, 65-66
Crash (book/film) 211
creativity 14, 22-24, 26-29,
    242-243
    see also art (craft)
cremains 159n2, 164
cremation 162, 162n4, 164
Cronenberg, David 211
cruise liners 206-207
Csordas, Thomas 158, 159,
    165, 169
cuddle stones 164
cultural appropriation 80
curious observer self 142,
    143f, 149-150
Cut Piece (Ono) 219-220

Index   253

dance 30, 31, 33, 37, 61
Danish Humanist Society 100–101
dating 175, 181
Davenport, Marcia 212
dead (deceased)
  afterlife beliefs 161–162, 167
  bones of, for food and mourning rituals 184
  cremation practices 162, 162n4, 164
  personal objects of 119–126, 161, 163–164, 166–167, 168
  post-death encounters with 161–162, 164, 167
  symbolic relationship bonding with 160–164
  see also memorial and commemoration; mourning; violent death memorials
de Certeau, M. 201
de Hart, J. 160, 162
de Jong, G. 161n3
Dekker, G. 162
Deller, Jeremy 218n2
dementia patients 224–225, 224f
Denmark 87, 89–90, 99–103
DESNOS (Disorders of Extreme Stress, Not Otherwise Specified) 56–57, 58
dextrarum iunctio 205
Diagnostic and Statistical Manual of Mental Disorders (DSM) 56, 57, 58
Dick, Philip K. 213n1
diets 180
Dining with the Dead (van der Lee) 236
directing source energy 144, 146
dislocation 70, 246
Disorders of Extreme Stress, Not Otherwise Specified (DESNOS) 56–57, 58
disposophobia 212
Dissanayake, Ellen 71
dissociation 50, 51, 52, 61, 62
divestment rituals 206, 209, 212, 237, 238f, 239f
Diwali 174
Do Androids Dream of Electric Sheep? (Dick) 213n2
do-it-yourself (DIY) rituals 81
dolphins 41
Douglas, Mary 71, 203, 214
Dowsett Johnston, Ann 180

Drink (Dowsett Johnston) 180
drumming 55, 61
DSM (*Diagnostic and Statistical Manual of Mental Disorders*) 56, 57, 58
DuPont 210
Durkheim, Emile 40, 204
Dutch Railways monuments 190, 191, 196–201, 198f, 199f
dynamism, collective 49–50

Easter 174
Ecuadorian food rituals 183
elderly life stories 244
embodiment 158–159, 164–167, 168, 169
EMDR (Eye Movement Desensitization and Reprocessing) 57, 64–65
Emotional Freedom Techniques (EFT) 57, 65–66
emotional intersubjectivity 24, 26–27, 37–39
emotions and feelings
  art as expression of 24, 25f
  artistic materiality provoking 36
  expression of, as ritual purpose 30, 33, 234
  intersubjectivity of 24, 26–27, 37–39
  rituals as safety zones for 76
  self-regulation of 15, 28, 43
  symbols inciting 47
  see also attunement
empowerment 61, 65, 66
endocannibalism 184
enemy mentality 13n4
energy
  personal/internal 140–141, 147–149, 153–154
  relationship 154, 157
  source (universal life force) 140–147, 143f
  see also ritual process, energy-based
Energy Therapy 57, 65–66
engrams 75n5
Ernst, L. 51
Ethiopian food rituals 182
ethology 41–42
etiquette, social 43, 173, 180–182
Evans, David 38
everyday rituals 151–153
exchange rituals 205
expanded field art theory 225

Eye Movement Desensitization and Reprocessing (EMDR) 57, 64–65

farewell to neighbourhood rituals 237, 238f, 239f
Fashioning Discontinuities (Hester) 227
Fast and Furious (film) 211
fear conditioning 58, 65, 78
feasts 49–50, 80, 173–174, 179
felt senses
  accessibility methods 146
  curious observer self and suspension of 150
  definitions and descriptions 65n7, 83n12, 142
  as funeral ritual design component 83–84
  negative 148
  source energy connection through 144, 146
  trauma therapeutic uses of 65, 74n4
felt shift 16, 83
female genital mutilation 51
fetishism 207, 208
Finland 87, 87n3, 89
fire fighter monuments 190
First Relationship, The (Stern) 22
Fluxus 219
focusing, for source energy 143, 144, 145
food
  aversions and taboos 184
  eating as social activity 173, 174–176
  global rituals and foreign 180, 182–184
  history and relationship with 14, 172–173, 186
  manners and social etiquette 180–182
  pre-consumption rituals for 178–180
  religious/cultural celebrations with 173–174
  taste influenced by ritual 176–177
  technological alternatives to 184–186
  as wedding ritual symbols 111
food allergies 180
Fox, N. 210
fragmentation 13, 51–53, 70, 75, 246
Frankenstein (film) 213

freeze discharge 52, 61, 62–63, 65
French food rituals 182, 183–184
Freud, Sigmund 45, 160
Frobisher, Martin 174
funeral ceremonies 76, 81, 119–126, 128–136, 159–160, 169
Future, Consolation, Tears (memorial) 191

Gaignebet, C. 50
Galindo, Regina José: *Who Can Erase the Traces?* 222
Garces-Foley, K. 160
Gendlin, E. 83
Gergen, K.J. 166
Germany 89, 176, 189n1, 209
gestures
  of artistic ritual 36, 37, 217
  hand 204–206, 205, 236
  as magic/sorcery ritual component 46
  mother-infant relationship behaviours 22, 26–28, 30
  ritual development and use of 46–47
  ritual planning and meaningfulness using 82
  as source energy concluding action 146–147
Gibson, M. 161, 163, 167, 168
gift giving 205
Girard, R. 189n1
glass clinking 179
globalization 72–73, 106–108, 118, 182–184
global street 14n5
Godelier, M. 51
Golem (Meyrink) 213
golems 212–213
Goossens, John 191, 192f, 194
Gordon-Lennox, J. 217
Gramsci Monument (Hirschhorn) 218n2
Grand, David 57, 66
gratitude
  food-centered celebrations expressing 174
  mourning rituals effect 129
  for ritual closure 143, 144, 147, 150
  taste impacted by 178
graveyards *see* cemeteries
greetings 42, 43, 204
grief *see* memorial and commemoration; mourning

grief work hypothesis 160
Grimes, Ronald L.
  do-it-yourself (DIY) rituals and risks 81
  embodiment 159
  material objects and meaningfulness 167
  ritualmaking process 84n13
  ritual terminology usage and definitions 158, 158n1
grooming rituals 205
grounding 143, 144, 145
group (collective) ritualization
  of animals 41–42
  benefits and effects of 42, 43, 47–50, 70, 151
  for mourning 161, 190
  public consumption as 13, 19, 53, 206–208
  traditional purpose 45
  see also public space rituals
Groz, Elizabeth 225n12
Guénon, R. 204
guild traditions 38–39
guinea pigs 183
gun violence 189n1

habits 12
hands 34–36, 182, 204–205, 236
happiness 13–14, 127, 246
Harmelen rail disaster 197, 200
Hayden, B. 46
healing
  bio-energy unblocking for 140–141
  memorial weddings for 136
  as ritual function 33, 63, 233
  rituals for trauma 78, 153–154
  somatic psychotherapies for trauma 57–58, 57–66
  trance states for 55, 61
  tribal traditions for 55, 56
Heessels, M. 163, 164
Heinskou, Marie Bruvik 77
Hell, B. 50
Herman, Judith 56–57
Hermans, H.J.M. 166
Hester, Bianca
  art theories and philosophies 225–226
  Fashioning Discontinuities 227

  Please Leave These Windows Open to Enable the Fans to Draw in Cool Air During the Early Morning Hours 226
  Solar Objects: Various Objects Held toward Evening's Diminishing Westerly Light 227, 229f
  Sonic Alterations of Constructed Space with Metal Objects 227, 228f
  World Fully Accessible By No Living Being, A 227
Hidden Legacy (van der Lee) 244
Hinduism 108, 112, 178
hippy movement 11
Hirschhorn, Thomas:
  Gramsci Monument 218n2
hoarding disorders 212
Holcomb, J.S. 160
holding environments 226–227
holidays 162, 174, 205, 236
Holloway, Margaret 83, 84, 167
Holocaust victims 240–241, 241f
homeostasis
  disruption of 45, 51–52, 56, 142, 148–149
  optimal states of 63
  as ritual benefit 43
  trauma healing rituals for 63–64
Honig, Bonnie 226n13
hospitality 204, 246
human body 158–159, 164–167, 168, 169, 207, 211
humanist ceremonies
  association networks for 17, 90–91, 97, 100–101, 127–128
  in Britain, statistics 17–18
  history of 127–128
  popularity growth of 128
  see also specific types of rituals
Humanist Ceremonies™ 17, 127–128
Humanistisk Samfund 100–101
humming therapies 60, 66
hunter-gatherer societies 43, 47, 73

Iceland
  confirmations 89–90, 96–98, 98f
  food rituals 183

political history and education requirements 89–90
Icelandic Ethical Humanist Association (IEHA) 96
I Ching 75
identity 12, 47–49, 176–177, 208, 211
indigenous tribal traditions
 cultural appropriation of rituals from 80
 empowerment as ritual feature 61
 food rituals 178, 183, 184
 handprint cave paintings 204–205
 modern cultural evolution impacting 73
 ritual purpose in 55–56, 59, 60–61
 social bonding practices 47, 48–49
 trauma-inducing rituals of 51
 world consciousness and ritual narratives 43
individualism 72, 207, 208, 246
individual rituals 151–153
Indonesian food rituals 183
infants
 food and dependency of 175
 hand gestures 36
 mother-child relationship behaviours 22–24, 26–29, 30, 43, 59, 64
 rituals for impending death of 83
integrating, for source energy 143, 144, 145–146
intention 141, 142, 143*f*, 146–147
interaction
 communal shopping as 13, 19
 consumerism impact on 203, 208
 eating as social activity 173–176
 as framework for multicultural rituals 80n10
 in modern culture 12–13, 74, 106
 of mother-infant relationship 22–24, 26–29, 30, 43, 59, 64
 of performance art 220, 222
 as ritual function 55
 self-regulation rituals of 42, 43, 204

of social practice/participatory art 226–227
for trauma therapy effectiveness 63–64
see also attunement
Inuit food rituals 183
Irritation Game (van der Lee) 243–244, 243*f*
Isherwood, B. 203
Itadakimasu 178
Italian food rituals 182

James, William 165
Japan
 food rituals 176, 178, 181, 182, 183
 war commemoration performance art 219–220
jewellery, as mourning objects 161, 163, 164
Jewish victim memorials 240–241, 241*f*
job raise rituals 150–151
Jonte-Pace, Diane 71–72, 217
Judaism 111, 114, 116–117
Jung, Carl 153

Kaiser, B. 100
Kalishuk, R.G. 161
kindling 58
kinesic communication 30
see also gestures
Klass, D. 163
Kloosterboer, M. 162n4
Klugman, C.M. 161, 167
kopi luwak 183
Kopytoff, I. 166
Korean food rituals 181
Krauss, Rosalind 225n11
Kreting, J. 161n3
Kronjee, G. 160
Kühl, H.S. 42
Kwanzaa 174

Lacy, Suzanne
 Between the Door and the Street 224n7
 Three Weeks in May (or, *Storying Rape*) 223–225
Lampert, M. 160
Landelijk Monument Spoorwegongevallen (National Monument for Railway Accident Victims) (Broos) 190, 191, 196–201, 198*f*, 199*f*
Laundry Is Good (van der Lee) 236
Lebow, Victor 13n1
LeDoux, Joseph E. 78

Lenoir, Frédéric 73, 74
Levine, Peter A.
 memory impermanence 78
 ritual benefits 77, 80
 safety zones for stress/trauma management 74–75
 somatic psychotherapies of 57, 62n6, 65
 trauma and emotional pendulation 74n4, 77n7
 trauma and memory imprints 75n5
 trauma diagnostic definitions 56n1
Lewis, M. 49
LGBT (lesbian, gay, bisexual and transgender) 128, 130–131, 160
 see also memorial weddings
Liebst, Lasse Suonperä 77
lightbulb obsolescence 209
Liu Xiaobo 13
London, Bernard 209
Lukken, G. 158, 234
Luther, M. 89n14
Lutheranism 89, 91

Maasai food rituals 183
Maas Tunnel Monument for Traffic Victims (Verschuren) 191–196, 192*f*, 193*f*, 200
Mackendrick, Alexander 210
madness 34–36, 35*f*, 37*f*
magic 46, 142, 144–145, 157
'making special' activities 22, 23*f*, 30, 33, 37, 71
Mandela, Nelson 13
Man in the White Suit, The (film) 210
manners 43, 173, 180–182
Marcuse, H. 208
Mark, L.G. 221
marriage 105
 see also memorial weddings; multicultural weddings; weddings
materiality 34–36, 35*f*, 37*f*
maturity rites *see* confirmations
Maurois, André 135
Mauss, M. 205
McCracken, Grant 205–206
McLeod, J. 160
meaningfulness
 art symbolism for 217
 for do-it-yourself (DIY) rituals 81
 embodiment for 165–166

meaningfulness *cont.*
  as individual endeavour 18
  for memorial weddings
    134–136
  mourning rituals and
    material objects for
    166–167
  mourning ritual timing
    and 169
  for multicultural weddings
    105
  ritual adaptations for 80
  ritualmaking for 82–84
meditation 61, 145, 178
Memoirs (Maurois) 135n1
memorial and
  commemoration
  at cemeteries 161, 162–163,
    232, 235, 239, 240f
  collective monuments,
    types of 190
  Dutch practices, statistics
    161n3
  funeral ceremonies 76,
    81, 119–126, 128–136,
    159–160, 169
  holidays for 162
  for Jewish deportations
    and Holocaust victims
    240–241, 241f
  multicultural 81
  municipal restrictions on
    public 189–190
  for railway victims 188–
    189, 190, 191, 196–201,
    198f, 199f
  symbolic relationships
    with dead for 160–164
  for traffic accident victims
    188–194, 192f, 193f,
    200–201
  see also memorial
    weddings; mourning
memorial weddings
  benefits and effects of 136
  deceased's inclusion and
    role at 133–134
  design requirements
    131–132
  guests' roles at 129–131,
    132–133
  marriage symbolism
    134–136
  overview 128–129
  ritual success markers 129
memories
  food evoking 172, 173
  impermanence of 77–78
  as personal resource
    148–149
  ritualization effect on
    77–78, 232

trauma affecting 56, 57, 62,
  74n4, 75
trauma therapies and
  features impacting 58,
  61, 65
Metcalf, Bruce 32–33
Mexican food rituals 183
Meyrink, Gustav 213
Mitchell, J.P. 162, 167
modern culture
  effects of 13, 51–53, 70, 75,
    246
  need for ritual in 45, 80,
    233
  religious views and
    influences on 12, 40–41,
    112–113
  social relation styles in
    12–13, 74, 106, 203
  survival requirements for
    74–75
  see also consumerism
Molendijk, A.L. 160
Montano, Linda 219
Moore, Sally F. 11, 164
Morgan, A.B. 222
Morgan, Lucy 25
Moroccan food rituals 182
Morrison, Bryce 128–136, 137
mother-infant relationship
  behaviours 22–24, 26–29,
  30, 43, 59, 64
mourning
  afterlife beliefs 161–162
  of animals 41
  embodiment for
    sensemaking in
    165–166
  embodiment importance
    of 164–166, 168, 169
  emotional states and
    descriptions of 76
  endocannibalistic
    practices 184
  objects of deceased
    119–126, 161, 163–164,
    166–167, 168
  overview and history of
    159–160
  post-death encounters
    with deceased 161–162,
    164, 167
  psychotherapeutic
    theories on 160–161
  see also memorial and
    commemoration;
    memorial weddings
Moving Goods (van der Lee)
  237, 238f
multicultural rituals 80–81,
  80n10, 83
  see also multicultural
    weddings

multicultural weddings
  creation and planning
    108–109
  design challenges 104–105
  guidelines for 108–117
  modern culture and need
    for 106–108
  reasons for 105–106
murder victims 188
music 28, 33, 84, 119–126
My Brother's Keeper
  (Davenport) 212
Myerhoff, Barbara G. 11, 164

Nader, Karim 77–78
Names and Numbers (van der
  Lee) 240–241, 241f
*National Monument for
  Railway Accident Victims*
  (Broos) 190, 191, 196–201,
  198f, 199f
*Nature of Craft and the
  Penland Experience, The*
  (Books) 22n1
Nederlandse Spoorwegen
  monuments 190, 191,
  196–201, 198f, 199f
Netherlands
  afterlife beliefs in 162
  commemoration practices
    161n3
  cremation practices 162n4,
    164
  personal/public memorials
    189–190, 191, 191n2, 194
  pluralism and memorial
    practices 162–163
  railway suicides in,
    statistics 200n13
  railway victim monuments
    194–201, 198f, 199f
  ritual innovation in 160
  senseless violence,
    definition 189
  traffic victims monuments
    190–194, 192f, 193f, 198f,
    199f, 200–201
neurophysiology
  brain diagrams 60f
  consumerist competition
    effects on 52
  emotion and memory
    triggers 78
  grounding exercises and
    chatter 145
  memory impermanence 78
  mother-infant relationship
    behaviours and
    development of 29, 64
  ritual emotional
    expression and
    homeostasis regulation
    77n6

ritual experiences and 167
ritualistic therapies for healing 63
ritual process and hemisphere activity 140, 233, 242, 245
trauma effects on 56-57, 59-60, 62-63, 75, 153
trauma-inducing rituals affecting 52
trauma therapies and features impacting 57-64, 62n6, 64-66
New School for Social Research 22
New Year's Eve 174, 179
Nickman, S.L. 163
Nocera, J. 210
Nooteboom, Cees 195
Norway
  confirmation ceremonies in, statistics 87
  confirmation traditions in history 89-90
  humanist associations in 90-91, 97, 100
  humanist confirmations in 90-96, 91f, 92f, 93f, 94f, 95f
  political history and education requirements 89-90
Norwegian Humanist Association (NHA) 90-91, 97, 100
Nowatzki, N.R. 161
nylon tights, and obsolescence 210

objects, material
  consumerism and cult of 207, 208
  consumerism and system of 208-214
  for funeral symbolism and meaningfulness 119
  meanings and biographical changes of 168
  for mourning ritualization 119-126, 161 163-164, 166-167, 168
  multicultural wedding symbolism 111
obsolescence of objects 209-210
olfaction 58n3, 76, 78, 163, 168
Ono, Yoko: *Cut Piece* 219-220
Ontroerend Goed (*Moving Goods*) (van der Lee) 237, 238f

Orecle Game (van der Lee) 244-245, 244f
ortolans 183-184

Packard, V. 210
Pad Thai (exhibition) 218n2
Pane, Gina: *Sentimental Action* 220-221, 222
Panksepp, Jaak 45, 46
Papuasian Baruyas tribe 51
Park, C.L. 159, 163
participatory art (social practice) 218-219, 223-227, 228f, 229f, 230
  see also van der Lee, Ida
Passover 174
patriarchy, as performance art theme 221
Pavolian conditioning 58
pendulation 74n4, 77n7
Penland School of Crafts
  anniversary publications of 22n1
  communality of 38-39
  founding and history 25
  studio views 25f, 34f, 35f, 37f, 38f
perceptual surround 61
performance art 19-20, 217-223, 230
Perniola, M. 212
personal rituals 151-153
Peruvian food rituals 183
pets, as food taboo 184
photographs 161, 163, 180
Pianigiani, O. 204
Pietism 89
play 22-24, 26-29, 30
Please Leave These Windows Open to Enable the Fans to Draw in Cool Air During the Early Morning Hours (Hester) 226
pluralism 160, 162-163
police officer memorials 190
politicians 81, 188
Pollan, M. 182
polyvagal theory 43, 77n6
Popkin, B.M. 177
Porges, Stephen 43, 52n4, 63-64, 76, 77n6
possession rituals 205
Post-traumatic Stress Disorder (PTSD) 56, 56n1
Power of Two Ritual 154-157
Prado, Pedro 83
prayer 152-153, 178, 205, 236
primate studies 29, 42, 48
procedural memory 56, 57, 58, 62
PTSD (Post-traumatic Stress Disorder) 56, 56n1

public space rituals
  cemetery visits for mourning 161, 162-163, 232, 235, 239, 240f
  commemoration memorials overview 188-190
  consumerism and communal shopping 13, 19, 206-207
  neighbourhood demolition and farewell ritual art 237, 238f, 239f
  performance art 19-20, 217-223, 230
  railway victim memorials 189, 190, 191, 196-201, 198f, 199f
  social practice/participatory art 218-219, 223-227, 228f, 229f, 230
  traffic accident victim memorials 188-196, 192f, 193f. 200-201
pufferfish 183

ragging rituals 51
railway victim memorials 188-189, 190, 191, 196-201, 198f, 199f
Ramadan 174
Rancière, Jacques 225
rape 51, 222-223, 223-225
reception, as framework for multicultural rituals 80n10
Reckitt, Helena 224n8
relational aesthetics (social practice) 218-219, 223-227, 228f, 229f, 230
  see also van der Lee, Ida
relationships
  couple 154-157, 175-176, 181
  mother-infant bonding behaviours 22-24, 26-29, 30, 43, 59, 64
  mourning deceased and symbolic 160-164
  see also communality; interaction
religion
  British religiously unaffiliated, statistics 17-18
  celebrations and food 173-174
  communality as component of 52
  cultural influence of 12, 40-41, 112-113

religion *cont.*
  development of 46
  diversity and
    intermarriage 106–107, 108
  driving force of 45
  Dutch affiliation statistics 160
  French philosophical views of 40
  institutional ritualization development 73
  mourning rituals and afterlife beliefs 161–162
  Nordic history of 88–89
  prayer rituals 178, 205, 236
  ritual as experience of reality 44
  social practice art and 224
  spirituality *versus* 106, 160
  wedding ceremonies and dependency on 117–118
  see also Christianity; multicultural weddings
Religion in Essence and Manifestation (van der Leeuw) 47
resources 142, 143f, 147–149
retirement 179
Rhinehart, Rob 185
Ricci, Matteo 81
Riesman, David 207
rites of initiation 51, 55, 59, 63, 175
  see also confirmations
'Ritual, Play, and Art' class (New School for Social Research) 22
ritualmaking
  components of 158
  design process 79f, 233–234, 235
  guidelines for 84
  requirements of 82–84, 136, 162
ritual process, energy-based
  everyday uses of 151–153
  examples of 150–151
  for relationships 154–157
  steps of 143–150, 143f
  for trauma healing 153–154
rituals, overview
  behaviours associated with 55
  benefits of 12, 47–49, 70, 71, 76–77, 78, 151
  contexts for 72f
  definitions 29–30, 60, 141, 158, 158n1, 218, 234
  effectiveness requirements 16, 82–84
  effects of 43, 47–49, 70

elements of 141–143, 143f
ethological studies 41–42
etymology 204
functions of 30, 55, 78, 80, 129, 140–141, 204, 234
goals of 167, 168
habits enhanced by 12
human need for 45
materials for 217
in modern culture 11, 55–56, 72–73, 80
origins of 30–31, 45
purposes of 55, 72
scholarship on 11–12
skill requirements for 246
tribal traditions 43–44, 46, 55
see also ritualmaking; ritual process, energy-based
Ritzer, G. 206–207
roadside memorials 188–189, 194
robots 212–214
Robots and Empire (Asimov) 213
Roman Catholic Church 88–89
Romanoff, B.D. 159, 168
Rutanen, Tuomas 87n3

sacraments 88, 147
safety 63, 74–77, 78, 222
Salvy, S. 176
same-sex marriage 128, 130–131
Sassen, Saskia 14n5
Satin, Jill 128–136, 137
Scaer, Robert C.
  kindling and neurosensitization 58n3
  ritual and emotional safety 76
  trauma diagnostic definitions 56n1, 58n2
  trauma effects 52n4, 75
  trauma-inducing rituals 51
Schirch, Lisa 76, 217
Schneider, R. 219
sciences 43, 44
Scott, Ridley 213–214
SE (Somatic Experiencing) 57, 62n6, 65, 74n4
Second World War 190, 220, 240–241, 241f
secularism 71
  see also humanist ceremonies; *specific types of secular rituals*
Secular Ritual (Moore and Myerhoff) 11
Segalen, M. 204

self
  curious observer 142, 149–150
  identity 12, 47–49, 176–177, 208, 211
  shadow- 153–154
self-compassion 151
self-mutilation 61
self-regulation
  emotional 15, 28, 43, 73
  manners and social etiquette 43, 173, 180–182
sensemaking
  definition and description 82n11
  do-it-yourself (DIY) rituals and requirements of 81
  embodiment for 165–166
  for ritual effectiveness 16, 82–84
  see also meaningfulness
sensory perceptions
  of artistic materiality 34–36
  as emotional triggers 78n8
  food rituals influencing 173, 176–179
  in modern society 12–13
  for mourning rituals 76, 78n8, 83, 161, 163, 164–165, 166, 168
  multimodal vitality affects compared to 28
  neurosensitization and susceptible 58n3
  perceptual surround awareness 61–62
  as trauma triggers 75n5
  see also felt senses
Sensory Processing Disorder (SPD) 58n3
Sentimental Action (Pane) 220–221, 222
'Serenity prayer' 152
Seven Easy Pieces (Abramovic) 221n4
shadow-self 153–154
shamanism 55–56
shame 184, 234
Shapiro, Francine 57, 64–65
Shelley, Mary 213
shopping malls 13, 19, 206–207
Sidmennt 96
sign of the cross 236
Silent March 189n1
Silent Scream, The (memorial) 191
Silverman, P.S. 163
Situationalism 225
Slade, G. 210
'slow is fast' philosophy 149

smell (sense) 58n3, 76, 78, 163, 168
smiling 26, 27, 117
Smyth, Matthieu 78
social bonding 47–49, 59, 61, 70, 173–176
social etiquette 43, 173, 180–182
social gatherings 49–50, 80, 173–174, 179
social practice 218–219, 223–227, 228f, 229f, 230
see also van der Lee, Ida
Solar Objects: Various Objects Held toward Evening's Diminishing Westerly Light (Hester) 227, 229f
Solstice 174
Somatic Experiencing (SE) 57, 62n6, 65, 74n4
somatic psychotherapies
  benefits of 57–58
  effectiveness requirements 63–64
  neurophysiological features for trauma healing 58–64
  treatment techniques 57–58, 62n6, 64–66, 74
Somatization Disorders 57
song 30, 37, 61, 66
Sonic Alterations of Constructed Space with Metal Objects (Hester) 227, 228f
sorcery 46
sound 27, 75n5, 78n8, 169, 179
South American food rituals 183, 184
South Korean food rituals 176
Soylent (meal replacement) 185–186
SPD (Sensory Processing Disorder) 58n3
spirituality 106, 160
sports 52, 53
Standaert, Nicolas 80–81
Stern, Daniel 22, 28
Stevens, Raymond 191, 192f, 194, 196
Stiles, Kristine 219, 221
Storying Rape (formerly titled *Three Weeks in May*) (Lacy) 223–225
stress dyshomeostasis
  consumerist competition contributing to 51–52
  ritual as resource practices alleviating 142, 148–149
  ritual origins as response to 45

as trauma-inducing ritual effect 51
Studio Ritual Art 232, 234, 242, 245
suicides 48–49, 188, 200
Sulkowicz, Emma: *Carry that Weight* 222–223
superheroes 214
supermarkets 19, 207
surfing 111
survival
  animal ritualistic practices for 42
  food for 172
  infants and eating dependency 175
  mother-infant relationship behaviours adapted for 15, 28–29, 33
  performance art themes of 221
  trauma responses of 52n4, 62
  trauma therapies related to 58
Swedish confirmation traditions 89
symbols and symbolism
  art reliance on 217
  consumerism and advertising effects on 208
  of consumption rituals 205–206
  definitions 217n1
  for do-it-yourself rituals for meaningfulness 81
  etymology of 204
  food as 175
  funerals and material objects as 119–120
  for meaningfulness 84
  memorial/mourning and material objects as 162
  for multicultural wedding planning 110–113
  rituals as working 47, 204–205, 234
symphorophila 211

table manners 180–181
taste 75n5, 80, 173, 176–179
tattoos 112, 164
Terenzio, M. 159, 168
terrorism 188, 189n1
Thai food rituals 176, 182
Thandeka 45
Thanksgiving 174
theme parks 206–207
Think About It! (NHA) 93–94
Thought Field Therapy 65

Three Laws of Robotics (Asimov) 213
Three Weeks in May (Lacy) 223–225
time 44–45, 76, 169
Tiravanija, Rikrit 218n2
titration 6, 62n6
toasting 178–179
Toekomst, Troost, Tranen (memorial) 191
Tonnaer, J. 130
Tönnies, Ferdinand 203
touch (sense)
  art and sensory experience of 28
  artistic materiality and 34–36
  as attunement source 59
  grounding process and 145
  hands and 36, 205
  modern misinterpretations of 13
  mourning and sensitivity to 76, 78n8, 83, 163
  relationship rituals using 155
  as ritual behaviour 55
traffic accident memorials 188–194, 192f, 193f, 200–201
train victim memorials 189, 190, 191, 196–201, 198f, 199f
trance states 50, 55, 61, 207
transcendence 44, 77, 161–162, 164, 167
trauma
  Chinese philosophy on 75
  diagnoses for 56–57
  neurophysiological effects of 52, 57, 61, 62–63, 75
  neurophysiological processes for resolution for 77, 77n7
  relationships and past 154–155
  ritual as healing component for 78, 153–154
  rituals creating 51
  somatic psychotherapies for 57–58, 62n6, 64–66, 74n4
  somatic psychotherapy features for healing of 58–64
Trauma Releasing Exercises (TRE) 57
tribal traditions *see* indigenous tribal traditions

TRIPODS (Titrating, Resourcing, Integrating, Pendulating, Organizing, Discharging, Stabilizing) 77n7
tuning in, for source energy 143, 144, 145
Turner, Victor 206, 217n1, 218, 224

Ullmann, Liv 13n4
United Kingdom (UK)
  gay rights and marriage laws 131
  humanist associations in 17, 97, 127–128
  mourning rituals of 160, 162n4
  religious non-affiliation statistics 17–18
  social practice recreations of miner's strikes in 218n2
  table manners 181–182
United Nations 184
universal life source (source energy) 140–147, 143f
Unruh, D.R. 163

vajra 142
van der Kolk, Bessel 56–57, 56n1, 58n2, 75, 77.6
van der Lee, Ida
  artist networks founded by 232
  businesses and ritual purpose 242–244
  childhood descriptions 235–236
  participant response and effect 241–242
  ritual art descriptions 232, 233–234
  ritual functions 217, 234
  ritualmaking process 233–234, 235
  ritual need recognition signs 234–235
  ritual needs in modern culture 233
  All Souls' Day Everywhere (Allerzielen Alom) 232, 235, 239, 240of

Dining with the Dead 236
Hidden Legacy 244
Irritation Game 243–244, 243f
Laundry Is Good 236
Moving Goods (Ontroerend Goed) 237, 238f
Names and Numbers 240–241, 241f
Oracle Game 244–245, 244f
Zaandam Treasure Box 237, 238f, 239f
van der Leeuw, Gerard 47
van der Meiden, Anne 197
van Gelder, Sarah 13–14
van Ginkel, Rob 190
van Keulen, M. 162n4
van Vree, F. 190
Venbrux, E. 160, 161, 163
Verschuren, Kamiel: *Maas Tunnel Monument for Traffic Victims* 191–196, 192f, 193f, 200
Verstomde Schreeuw, de (memorial) 191
violent death memorials
  Jewish deportations and Holocaust victims 240–241, 241f
  municipal restrictions on memorials for 189–190
  public mourning rituals for, overview 188–189
  railway victims 189, 190, 191, 196–201, 198f, 199f
  senseless violence, term definitions 189
  traffic accident victims 190–196, 192f, 193f, 200–201
violinists' funerals 119–126
vision statements (intention) 141, 142, 143f, 146–147, 147
Visser, M. 175
visualization 141, 146, 234
vitality affects 28, 34–36
Vohs, Kathleen 177, 178
vows, wedding 109

Waard, J. 51
Walter, T. 160, 161, 168, 188
Warburg, M. 12

warrior initiations 51
Watts, Alan 11n1
weddings
  in British churches, statistics 18
  civil ceremonies for 105
  civil requirements of 105
  emotional quality of 76
  food rituals at 179
  meaningfulness requirements 82
  see also memorial weddings; multicultural weddings
Whale, James 213
White, Amanda 78n8
Who Can Erase the Traces? (Galindo) 222
Widdicombe, L. 185
widows 51, 161
Winnicott, D.W. 226n13
Wolfall, Robert 174
wolves 41–42
woodwoses 50
words 46–47, 82, 109
world consciousness
  embodiment and 158–159, 164–167, 168, 169
  group ritualization effects on 43
  modified states of consciousness impacting 50
  ritual development and 42–43, 46–47, 47
  ritual timelessness and 44–45
  tribal traditions and relationship to 43–44
World Fully Accessible By No Living Being, A (Hester) 227
World War II 190, 220, 240–241, 241f

Yalom, I.D. 159

Zaandam Treasure Box (van der Lee) 237, 238f, 239f